LIBERAL EDUCATION AND DEMOCRACY

LIBERAL
EDUCATION
AND
DEMOCRACY

—— BOB PEPPERMAN TAYLOR

University of Notre Dame Press
Notre Dame, Indiana

Library of Congress Control Number: 2024947148

ISBN: 978-0-268-20955-1 (Hardback)
ISBN: 978-0-268-20951-3 (WebPDF)
ISBN: 978-0-268-20952-0 (Epub3)

GPSR Compliance Inquiries:
Lightning Source France, 1 Av. Johannes Gutenberg, 78310 Maurepas, France
compliance@lightningsource.fr | Phone: +33 1 30 49 23 42

She proposed that education would no longer be centered on theological instruction, no longer placed exclusively in the hands of Brahmin priests trained at the sprawling Mandana *mutt*, the complex of temples and seminaries where the influence of Vidyasagar and his Sixteen Systems was still inescapable. Instead, she set out to create a new professional class of people who would be called, simply, "teachers," who might be members of any caste, and who would possess and seek to impart the best available knowledge in a wide variety of fields—history, law, geography, health, civics, medicine, astronomy. These so-called "subjects" would be taught without any religious slant or emphasis, with a view to producing new kinds of people, broad in knowledge and mind, still well-versed in matters of faith but with a deep additional understanding of the beauty of knowledge itself, and of the responsibility of citizens to coexist with one another, and with a commitment to advancing the well-being of all.

—Salman Rushdie, *Victory City*

Read not the Times. Read the Eternities.

—Henry David Thoreau, "Life without Principle"

CONTENTS

■ ACKNOWLEDGMENTS

I have been fortunate in the support I received while writing this book. The University of Vermont generously provided me with a sabbatical leave for the 2023/2024 academic year. My dean, Bill Falls, and my department chair, Peter VonDoepp, offered much appreciated encouragement. I received remarkably thorough, insightful, helpful, and generous reviews from three anonymous readers for University of Notre Dame Press (UNDP). Megan Levine and all the other support staff at UNDP have been a pleasure to work with.

Special thanks are due to Ben Minteer and Alex Zakaras, exemplary friends and colleagues, readers of an early draft of the manuscript who helped me think more soberly about a number of my concerns, claims, commitments, and intentions; Stephen Wrinn, director of UNDP, who was instrumental in guiding me to this project and supporting me throughout the writing and publication process; Fran Pepperman Taylor, who, after all these years, continues to be my most reliable and loyal reader; and Patrick Neal, who, since the late 1980s, has engaged me in a more or less continuous conversation about the theory and practice of liberal education. Pat obviously can't be held accountable for my opinions and arguments, but it is also true that this book would have taken a very different form, or perhaps would never have been written, were it not for our ongoing discussions about teaching and education.

A number of paragraphs in chapter 1 first appeared in Bob Pepperman Taylor, "But Could Your Persuade Us, If We Won't Listen?," *Soundings: An Interdisciplinary Journal* 104, no. 2–3 (2021): 252–58, https://doi.org/10.5325/soundings.104.2-3.0252. Used with permission from Pennsylvania State University Press.

Introduction

My intention in this small book is to look closely at three common arguments made in support of what has come to be known as liberal education. One of these arguments stresses vocational rewards, a second focuses on civic benefits, and a third makes claims about intrinsically valuable philosophical, aesthetic, or even "cultural" goods. My view is that there are merits and weaknesses to each of these arguments, but the merits and weaknesses are neither equivalent nor symmetrical. I will suggest that the arguments for liberal learning become more robust and persuasive as we move from the vocational to the civic to the philosophical. In doing so, I am arguing somewhat against the grain of the positions most often defended in higher education by, for example, university administrators (frequent and vocal advocates for vocational payoffs) and politically engaged faculty (champions of the civic benefits of "politically aware" and "socially engaged" graduates). Although I don't want to minimize the value of vocational skills or responsible democratic citizenship, I do intend to say a good word for the pleasures of thinking, understanding, and reflecting as the crowning achievements of a liberal education.

I also hope to show that the relationship between liberal education and democracy is essential, intimate, complex, and fraught. Democracies will probably always find themselves provoked and irritated by liberal learning. Democracies cease to be democracies, however, when they attack, harass, or abolish this form of education. Liberal learning frequently and inevitably finds itself in tension with the common sense of democracy, but just as democracies, sometimes to their chagrin, incubate liberal thinking, liberal thinking requires democracies to survive even as it often finds itself in tension with the institutions and values from which it springs. There is an essential, but sometimes difficult, relationship between these two worlds. Friction in this relationship is not surprising, since liberal learning promotes individual freedom but democracy promotes the will and interests of majorities. Certainly, we cannot expect free individuals to always agree with or conform to the opinion of the many, or majorities to always be happy with the eccentricities or demands of free individuals. Tension is baked directly into this relationship, even as free individuals are found among both majorities and minorities. One of our oldest political stories suggests the truth of this: the first great democracy both produced and murdered Socrates, the man Jonathan Marks refers to, correctly in my view, as the "patron saint of liberal education."[1] Democracy both needs and is occasionally frustrated by liberal learning; liberal learning both needs and is occasionally frustrated by democracy. I write at a moment in which this mutual frustration is particularly pronounced.

It is not news that the liberal arts and sciences are currently on the defensive. Students are increasingly flocking to vocational and applied programs in STEM (science, technology, engineering, mathematics) fields and avoiding more conventional programs in the "arts and sciences." The cost of higher education is growing ever higher, and this burden has been significantly privatized over the course of my lifetime, as witnessed by the student debt crisis. Students and parents rightly worry about the vocational payoff of pursuing a liberal education, especially considering the life-constraining financial burden so many will be forced to assume to receive one. In addition, one might think, the practical problems we face are so immediate and severe that an education promoting reflection on, say, literature, philosophy, history, and art looks more like an expensive and time-consuming indulgence than a necessity or even a priority. Perhaps we should just focus on training the engineers, chemists, medical technologists, architects, and other specialists we so desperately need. The more quickly we can put these cadres of well-prepared experts and technocrats to work, the quicker we can find solutions to the problems threatening our health, environment, and social order. There appear to be both private economic incentives and public emergencies encouraging us to focus more on applied than liberal knowledge.

Liberal education requires at least a partial remove from practical problems and applied learning; such a remove can seem an insult or an elitist rebuke to the crying needs of both individuals and society at large.

For both political and economic reasons, then, liberal education in general, and the humanities in particular, have drawn a great deal of criticism in recent years. My hope is to say something meaningful in their defense. In so doing, I also hope to avoid both exaggeration and polemic, which are vices common, even ubiquitous, in so many discussions of education today. Those searching for ammunition with which to engage the contemporary culture wars will likely find what follows disappointing. My intention is to take at least half a step back from these conflicts and reflect on what I take to be the fundamental commitments of liberal learning. Such reflection, I believe, is essential if liberal learning is to survive the political turmoil of our times.

What follows is an attempt to develop honest answers to questions about what we mean by, and might hope for from, a liberal education—both as individuals and as a society. That's it. I don't intend to argue about how we can afford liberal education, how to promote or market it, how to administratively organize higher education to do more of it, or any of these or related practical matters. There are excellent books (from which I have greatly benefited) on such problems, and on many more of the array of issues facing higher education, such as the corporatization of the academy and the growth of nonacademic elements in universities. It will come as no surprise that I have opinions about these matters, and I will occasionally allow these opinions to be obvious to the reader (yes, I do believe a strong liberal education is both a public good and a private right deserved by every citizen; no, I do not think it is honest or even necessary to emphasize only or even primarily the vocational payoffs of such an education when promoting it). Most importantly, however, my concern is prior to the practical; it is to understand the normative claims of liberal education as best I can. If I am right about the value of this form of education, and the benefits of its complex, difficult, and necessary relationship to liberal democracy, then working out the practical matters (such as making it available to all students, and not only the sons and daughters of the affluent) becomes much more compelling and worthwhile. Until we are confident about the experiences and values promoted by liberal learning, we will be equivocal in answering the attacks liberal colleges and universities are currently enduring. Until we are honest about what it is we are promoting, we will not be clear about how to practically achieve our goals.

Liberal education is currently under pressure in part because democracy is under pressure. Although liberal education and democratic politics are different activities that require a level of separation to maintain the integrity of each, the battle for one is nonetheless related to the battle for the other. Neither can survive alone.

The question haunting this book is a simple one: Is there any reason to maintain faith in liberal education? Is this an enterprise that can continue to command our democratic support, or is it now clear that it represents a set of failed and bygone dreams, or perhaps a practice too weak to meet the challenges of our time? Is it worthwhile to continue to teach the arts and humanities in our present climate, or are such topics mere indulgences, the playthings of elites and aesthetes who set themselves apart from and beyond the real work of our society? Many people have come to think this way about the project of liberal education. Conservative politicians attack liberal education as a political foe, as the source of a form of liberal intolerance toward their own political values, as a threat to what they view as traditional (and appropriate) political and religious values. Even liberal politicians, however, such as former president Barack Obama (himself, it should be noted, the beneficiary of an excellent liberal education) have implied that studying such humane topics as art history increasingly looks like a waste of time and resources compared to focused vocational training.[2] Students, sadly, appear to agree more and more with those who question the utility of liberal studies, as they increasingly choose college programs to prepare themselves for careers in business, education, technology, and health care. This boon to professional preparation, pushed in large part by the growing private cost of higher education, has come at a significant cost to liberal studies, especially in the arts and humanities, and colleges and universities across the country find themselves frantically adjusting their offerings accordingly.[3] What can we say to students and their families, to our colleges and universities, and to our fellow citizens about the value of liberal education and the need to preserve and even extend our commitment to it?

In the chapters that follow I will focus primarily on college and university education, as higher education has provided my professional home for almost four decades and has therefore attracted my greatest personal attention over the years. I will be asking the question I raised at the outset: What are the arguments that have been offered to defend and promote liberal education? In chapter 1, I briefly discuss what I take to be some of the essential historical sources of our concern for and understanding(s) of liberal education, from ancient Athens to Victorian Great Britain to the American colonies and U.S. national history. In the following three chapters, I divide the arguments that have been given in favor of liberal education, as I have found them in the contemporary literature, into three general categories: chapter 2 will address claims that liberal education prepares students for active, engaged, and practically effective lives; chapter 3 will examine arguments that liberal education promotes a kind of moral virtue required within free societies; chapter 4 will look at the ancient and perhaps surprisingly resonant claim that liberal education stimulates the sheer pleasure of "vision," or understanding, to the young adult. All three of these arguments can sometimes be found together in the same texts or promoted by the same advocate, and sometimes they appear singularly. I will argue, however, that as we move from the first to the third of these ideas, from chapters 2 to 4, the questions left unanswered, or unsatisfactorily answered, or incompletely answered, by the more "practical" arguments generate an interest in the arguments that follow; the utilitarian arguments will leave us looking toward the civic, which will in turn suggest the need for and value of philosophical vision. What looks to many at the outset like the least promising arguments for liberal education may, at the end of the day, become the most persuasive.

The purpose of this investigation is to discover if a convincing argument can be made, in the context of a democratic society, that we should commit valuable attention and resources to the promotion of liberal education and that this education should be offered as widely as possible to those coming of age in that society. Are there persuasive arguments to be given to a skeptical, practically minded democratic citizenry?

I hope so.

Liberal Education and the American Tradition

What we think of today as liberal education has deep roots in the Greek philosophical tradition. Consider the opening passage of Plato's *Republic*, which finds Socrates walking with a young friend and student, Glaucon, in Piraeus, the port of Athens, where they had come to observe a religious festival. They are spotted by another young man, Polemarchus, who sends his slave ahead to ask Socrates to wait for him. What follows is a comic parody of Socrates's arrest, with Polemarchus pointing out that he has several friends with him (including Adeimantus, Glaucon's brother), and he would like Socrates to stay in Piraeus and accompany him and his group to his family's home. Socrates appears to be preparing to return to Athens, and Polemarchus says to him, "Well, you must either prove stronger than we are, or you will have to stay here." Socrates responds, "Isn't there another alternative, namely, that we persuade you to let us go?" Polemarchus's reply to this is certainly a conversation stopper: "But could you persuade us, if we won't listen?" Socrates has to admit that this is impossible, and he submits to the "arrest" and joins the group in visiting Polemarchus's home, where the conversation constituting the rest of the dialogue takes place.[1]

"But could you persuade us, if we won't listen?" A powerful point. Conversation is only possible among those who listen and consider the positions of those who speak. Without that kind of sympathetic listening, debate is just a surrogate for force—it isn't the words that matter; what is decisive, in that case, is the relative strength, measured in terms of votes, guns, wealth, or some other standard unrelated to the reasonableness of the words, of the person or people uttering them. Philosophy, really any form of reasonable discussion, is certainly not possible when we measure one another only by the physical force we wield. This represents the world of necessity, rather than the world of ideas and free choice.

The story of Socrates's trial and execution is a foundational story for our Western philosophical and democratic traditions. In the opening passage of the *Republic*, Plato is poetically re-creating Socrates's arrest, trial, and imprisonment by citizens of Athens. He was viewed by many democrats as a critic of all they were committed to, perhaps even constituting a threat to democratic stability. He was famously accused of both impiety and corrupting the young, then convicted and executed. That the world's first great democracy murdered one of the world's first great philosophers suggests that philosophical reflection and democratically dispersed political power are tragically, even "naturally," in opposition to one another. Philosophy, of course, often implies expertise, uncommon insight, and perhaps even the quest for singular answers to difficult normative questions about which many of us disagree (and will be annoyed by the claim that any position, and certainly one that is not ours, is the clearly "right" one). Democracy, on the other hand, is committed to recognizing the legitimacy of a wide range of views and finding ways to compromise or institute fair processes for selecting among them. Philosophy can seem judgmental, democracy suggests respect for common sense; philosophy inspects and criticizes popular opinion, democracy celebrates it. In the person of Socrates, Athens found a critic who called all its assumptions into question, appearing to mock and subvert the equality and common sense of Athenian citizens. What more pessimistic and terrible story about the incompatibility of philosophical reflection with democratic politics could be found than the trial and execution of Socrates? What greater symbol is to be found in the Western tradition of this tragedy than this story growing from the foundations both of democracy and philosophy?

Yet, the *Republic* hints at a more optimistic possibility. In the *Apology*, Plato's account of Socrates's trial, Socrates notes that the vote to convict him was quite close—a change of just 30 votes out of (probably) 501 cast would have led to an acquittal (large juries such as this were chosen in Athens by lottery from citizen volunteers).[2] He even suggests that he believes he could have won over these additional thirty votes if he had more time to speak to the charges against him. In the *Apology*, of course, Socrates is constrained by the procedures and norms of a trial, and so he runs out of time. After his execution, however, Plato could give his teacher the literary gift of the *Republic*, an imagined dialogue in which Socrates is offered the opportunity to try to persuade those who "arrested" him to choose to listen and argue rather than rely only on force and power to win their way. The first book (of ten) in the *Republic* includes an abortive attempt to develop a successful dialogue between Socrates and an able and arrogant young man named Thrasymachus, which fails at least in part because Thrasymachus is unable to put aside the idea that the conversation is a test of power rather than a mutual seeking for the truth. After this failure, however, others catch the spirit of dialogue and engage in a good-faith philosophical exploration with Socrates. There are two important points here. The first is that words rather than weapons and muscle might, at least under some circumstances, resolve differences. The second is that, once we sincerely turn to words, we follow the logic of reason rather than the logic of power. The *Republic* becomes an extended conversation about the meaning of justice, and the interlocutors are swept into a conversation leading in directions they could not have predicted at the outset.

In the brief opening passage of Plato's dialogue we are presented with intimations of paramount importance for two prominent and interrelated contemporary concerns: the dramatic contrast between democratic and undemocratic institutions and practices, and the valuable role an education in "dialogue" (conversation and discussion) can play in turning democratic politics into something reasonable and away from the mere assertion of oppositional forces. We might even say that we find here in the golden age of Athens the tap root of not only democracy and philosophy but also of liberal education. By this we mean the use of language and the arts of persuasion with the aim of transforming political life from a realm of brute force into a practice of speech and a search for agreement. At its best, this is the goal of democracy and the resolution of its historical conflict with philosophy. Such an education will become central to the maintenance and health of a democratic politics and society.

Democracy in Athens was, of course, significant and pathbreaking, but it was also significantly limited in reach. Only a small minority of men were thought to constitute the *demos*, the democratic citizenry. In fact, Aristotle believed politics, and the education required for it, was best limited to those who could engage in what he called "leisured activity." By this he meant those who were not constrained by economic necessities. Citizens are contrasted with craftsmen, farmers, and workers (and slaves) of all kinds. For Aristotle, they should be those released from the demands of labor to a degree that allowed them to participate in the culture and politics of public life. Two points are important to attend to here: first, liberal education aimed at the cultivation of an elite with special abilities of leadership and judgment, even as it assumed that such leadership and judgment were incompatible with lives revolving around the necessities of work and the demands of nature; second, these skills focused on speech and rhetoric, the arts of argument and what we might think of as public reason (that is, reasons given to others to persuade and mobilize them). Looking ahead more than two thousand years, much of the educational practice in the American colonies and the young U.S. republic, as in ancient Greece, still placed a strong emphasis on the cultivation of a governing elite, even if the shape and character of this elite differed significantly from that found during the age of Pericles. Later, the expectations for liberal education would become much more democratic, aiming (at least ideally) for a universal citizenry of free individuals. But in both less and more democratic contexts, the emphasis on liberal education would be on the education for a politics in which words rather than military force or threats of violence would rule.

A critical point that grows from these observations is that liberal education originated as the idea of education for political freedom, and this freedom is contrasted both with a politics of brute force and with the practical demands on those without the resources required for "leisure." "It is evident, then, that there is a certain kind of education that children must be given not because it is useful or necessary but because it is noble and suitable for a free person," Aristotle states. Indeed, it is "completely inappropriate for magnanimous and free people to be always asking what use something is."[3] An education for freedom, in Aristotle's view, must be separated from the utilitarian concerns about practical application, especially economic or material concerns. Free citizens are free precisely because they have been liberated from such concerns and can take a more expansive view of human possibilities. Those trained in trades and crafts, or engaged in manual labor, are controlled by the demands of their work. Leisured citizens are those who seek higher and freer forms of education, including learning the art of "enjoying, loving, and hating in the right way."[4] This suggests that an education in freedom in these early formulations has what we might think of as philosophical content.[5] It is aimed at questions addressing the best and most worthwhile human lives, which are assumed to be options only for leisured citizens simply as a matter of fact. The crucial contrast was with an education in vocational skills and the utilitarian demands of material life.

These hopeful yet restricted ancient formulations of liberal education give us some sense of the stakes involved. When we fast-forward more than two thousand years to two of the most influential modern English-language statements about liberal education, those by two great nineteenth-century men, Cardinal John Henry Newman and John Stuart Mill, we find significant continuity with the ancient roots of these ideals and practices.

Newman, in *The Idea of a University* (1852), provides perhaps the most famous defense of what we might think of in our own era as conventional liberal education.[6] A Catholic priest (he converted from Anglicanism in 1845) writing to a primarily Catholic audience, Newman assumes that "all knowledge forms one whole, because its subject matter is one; for the universe in its length and breadth is so intimately knit together, that we cannot separate off portion from portion, and operation from operation, except by mental abstraction."[7] The created universe has a singular coherence, even if our imperfect human minds need to break the totality of knowledge into different subject matters for the sake of our imperfect yet careful and systematic understanding. Universities should be places that expose undergraduates to as many of these disciplines as possible: "It is a great point then to enlarge the range of studies which a University professes, even for the sake of the students; and, though they cannot pursue every subject which is open to them, they will be the gainers by living among those and under those who represent the whole circle."[8] So the first point to note about Newman's claims is that liberal learning is concerned not with any one specific or a narrow set of disciplines, but rather with the complete universe of knowledge, the full range of what we might refer to today as the "arts and sciences" (his phrase for this is "universal knowledge").[9]

Newman's Victorian language on this point can be confusing today, because he refers to this "universal" knowledge as "Philosophy or, in an extended sense of the word, Science."[10] Our convention today is to distinguish between "philosophical" and "scientific" knowledge in our everyday language in order to explain the difference between, say, rational argument about moral ideas, on the one hand, and the empirical study and description of the material (natural and social) world on the other. Newman, however, is referring to any knowledge that "stands on its own pretensions, which is independent of sequel, expects no complement, and refuses to be *informed* (as it is called) by any end, or absorbed into any art, in order duly to present itself to our contemplation."[11] What he means is that philosophical/scientific knowledge, in his sense, does not gain its importance either from its use or practical application or from its importance in serving some other field of knowledge. It stands on its own, is important in its own right. This range of liberal knowledge constitutes the appropriate subject matter of university education and requires no justification in relationship to any goal outside of itself: "Such is the constitution of the human mind, that any kind of knowledge, if it be really such, is its own reward."[12] Newman's university curriculum aims not at any practical or vocational application, but rather at the sheer pleasure and satisfaction of understanding. Liberal education, as opposed to technical or vocational instruction, aims at producing a sense of awe and appreciation of the beauty of reality: "This process of training, by which the intellect, instead of being formed or sacrificed to some particular or accidental purpose, some specific trade or profession, or study or science, is disciplined for its own sake, for the perception of its own proper object, and for its own highest culture, is called Liberal Education."[13]

It is clear enough that Newman thinks of university education as something quite different from vocational preparation or technical training. Liberal learning cannot be "utilitarian" in any narrow sense. On the contrary, it must aim, we might say, at knowledge as its own reward. But this doesn't mean that for Newman there are no worldly consequences for pursuing this kind of knowledge. In fact, there are, he hopes, very practical consequences even if they aren't utilitarian in our conventional or economic sense. Newman argues that the education offered by an ideal university "implies action upon our mental nature, and the formation of a character; it is something individual and permanent, and is commonly spoken of in connexion with religion and virtue."[14] The idea seems to be that exposure to "universal" or "philosophical" knowledge, by bringing students into contact with a reality beyond their mundane experience, will train the individual character to aspire to the loftiest things. Newman, a Catholic priest, suggests that "liberal education makes not the Christian, not the Catholic, but the gentleman."[15] It cultivates the intellect and aims at "nothing more or less than intellectual excellence."[16] This excellence, for Newman, is indistinguishable from shaping the human character to care for the greatest human goods: "But a University training is the great ordinary means to a great but ordinary end; it aims at raising the intellectual tone of society, at cultivating the public mind, at purifying the national taste, at supplying true principles to popular enthusiasm and fixed aims to popular aspiration, at giving enlargement and sobriety to the ideas of the age, at facilitating the exercise of political power, and refining the intercourse of private life."[17]

Far from a self-contained good, liberal education for Newman will have the effect of producing social elites committed to the highest conceptions of the public good. His vision is that such leadership will inspire and raise the moral character of society. Liberal education, in his view, shapes both the moral character of individual students and, through them, the society at large. Although the student must grow to love learning for its intrinsic beauty and pleasure, Newman assumes that those who develop such a perspective will in fact be a blessing to the world when they eventually enter professional and civic life.

John Stuart Mill, in a lecture delivered as rector of the University of St. Andrews in the decade following the publication of *The Idea of a University*, elaborates on themes we find in Newman's book. He agrees that university education "is not a place for professional education."[18] It is not that he opposes schools for the professions; in fact, he suggests that Great Britain could use more of these. University education, however—what we would today call undergraduate education—should aim to cultivate the intellectual experiences and sensibilities that will later be brought to one's professional training and career: "What professional men should carry away with them from an University, is not professional knowledge, but that which should direct the use of their professional knowledge, and bring the light of general culture to illuminate the technicalities of a special pursuit."[19]

Liberal education, then, provides the student with "a general knowledge of a subject," which only includes the subject's "leading truths." Advanced knowledge requires specialist training, but the college student can be expected to understand the basics "not superficially but thoroughly."[20] In addition, the university is an environment that encourages students to develop a sense of intellectual unity from the array of fields they are exposed to. Teaching the disciplines and their (inter)relationships, Mill suggests, "comprises the whole of a liberal education, from the foundations upwards."[21]

In addition, liberal education requires that for fields where controversies exist, such as moral philosophy, the aim is for the student to understand these controversies and, "in a general way, what has been said on both sides of them."[22] Education must not be polemical or dogmatic. It is not the university's responsibility to make sure that students become advocates for a particular side in such controversies: "It is not the teacher's business to impose his own judgment, but to inform and discipline that of his pupil."[23] In fact, it is well beyond the university's power to "educate morally or religiously" in any doctrinaire sense: "The moral or religious influence which an university can exercise, consists less in any express teaching, than in the pervading tone of the place."[24] The experience of liberal education can promote the development of moral character—through commitment to reason, to curiosity, to intellectual toleration and fairness, to truth—but it does this mainly by providing the example of practicing and promoting these intellectual virtues.

Mill's concluding comments speak directly to our purposes in understanding the goals of liberal education. One might expect, given Mill's utilitarianism, a strongly consequentialist conclusion about the importance of bringing a liberal education to university students. What he says, however, warns us of the dangers of thinking too narrowly along these lines.

> I do not attempt to instigate you by the prospect of direct rewards, either earthly or heavenly; the less we think about being rewarded in either way, the better for us. But there is one reward which will not fail you, and which may be called disinterested because it is not a consequence, but is inherent in the very fact of deserving it, the deeper and more varied interest you will feel in life, which will give it tenfold its value, and a value which will last to the end. All merely personal objects grow less valuable as we advance in life; this not only endures but increases.[25]

As Newman does, Mill expects liberally educated students to become responsible adults in their social and civic lives. The "chief of all ends of intellectual education to qualify us for," he tells us, includes "the exercise of thought on the great interest of mankind as moral and social beings—ethics and politics, in the largest sense."[26] He does not, however, develop this claim about civic consequences to the same degree that Newman does. Instead, he emphasizes that the humane aspirations encouraged by a liberal education include a kind of overcoming or forgetting of oneself. In the final analysis, such an education draws us out of our own narrow concerns and into the world at large. An admirable life loses its preoccupation with or focus on its personal rewards, yet this paradoxically becomes, in fact, the most rewarding life available to us. One is reminded of David Foster Wallace's comment in his 2005 Kenyon College commencement speech: "And I submit that this is what the real, no-shit value of your liberal arts education is supposed to be about: how to keep from going through your comfortable, prosperous, respectable adult life dead, unconscious, a slave to your head and to your natural default setting of being uniquely, completely, imperially alone, day in and day out."[27] Liberal education, for both Mill and Wallace, takes us out of our solitary individualized world and brings us into contact with possibilities much greater than our narrow interests can provide. Mill had earlier written, in his famous *Utilitarianism*, that "next to selfishness, the principal cause which makes life unsatisfactory is want of mental cultivation."[28] Such cultivation does not require that we become professional philosophers, but it does expose us to the "fountains of knowledge" and exposes us to the "inexhaustible interest" in the "objects of nature, the achievements of art, the imaginations of poetry, the incidents of history, the ways of mankind, past and present, and their prospects in the future."[29] Liberal education must enrich the lives of the students, make them more valuable and more satisfying, and prepare students to live responsibly as professionals and citizens. As with the ancients, so with these modern defenders of liberal education: properly understood, liberal learning promotes a freedom that benefits both the individual and the society within which they live.

▬▬▬▬ A central theme of U.S. history is a preoccupation with the importance and value of education. When the Boston Public Library opened in 1895, the north façade was inscribed with the words, "THE COMMONWEALTH REQUIRES THE EDUCATION OF THE PEOPLE AS THE SAFEGUARD OF ORDER AND LIBERTY." The trustees of the library certainly captured a belief that was pervasive in the United States not only at

the end of the nineteenth century but throughout our colonial and early national history, continuing as a common faith throughout much of our own
time. Puritans in New England promoted what was at the time the widest
literacy in the world so that individuals in every generation would be competent to read, interpret and be instructed by the Bible.[30] In the new nation,
although there was disagreement about who should control the education
of children, there was near universal agreement on the importance of primary education for all children. Democrats feared that the Whig promotion
of common, that is, public, schools was a plot to promote their own religious and political ideologies against democratic majorities, an idea alive
and well in our own culture wars today.[31] Despite such disputes, historian
Carl Kaestel points out that in England in the nineteenth century there was
an "extended, passionate debate over the wisdom of educating the poor," but
in the United States "there was virtually no debate."[32] What looked like im-
prudent provocation of the working class to the English looked to the
Americans like a requirement for republican citizenship (which, of course,
is why our history is full of examples of restrictions on teaching literacy to
enslaved African Americans). In 1845, Silas Wright, governor of New York,
declared that "the only salvation for the republic is to be sought for in our
schools."[33] Well into the twentieth century, the belief in the value and importance of universal public education reflected not so much a sense of what is
owed to children as a matter of right, but rather a belief in the power of education to promote the public good and protect democratic government.

Historian after historian comes to similar conclusions about the
uniquely American commitment to public education. Maris Vinovskis sees
the nineteenth-century promotion of mass education as a secular extension
of the Puritan preoccupation with literacy,[34] and Merle Curti writes, "Public
schools were to give every son of toil a chance to better himself, to withstand
the temptation of the dram shop, the lure of the brothel, the binding grip
of the slum. Public schools were to realize the dream of the Revolutionary
fathers. The direct action and militancy they had appealed to was now to give
way to the method of the schoolroom."[35] Ira Katznelson and Margaret Weir
conclude that the "commitment to educate all children in primary schools
paid for by the government was the most distinctive American public policy
of the early nineteenth century."[36] Diane Ravitch surveys our national history and suggests that "probably no other idea has seemed more typically
American than the belief that schooling could cure society's ills."[37] Political

theorist Rush Welter reaches a similar conclusion: "In order to understand the American people one must understand their belief in education." Indeed, in the United States, "democratic theory has often been identical with a theory of education" (as perhaps most importantly found in the intimate relationship between the educational and democratic philosophies of John Dewey).[38] In this, as in so many things, W. E. B. DuBois captures the point as well as anyone: "The one panacea of Education leaps to the lips of all."[39]

This preoccupation with education has not been confined to the primary level of instruction. Harvard College was founded in 1636, only six years after Jonathan Winthrop landed in Massachusetts Bay. By the time of the American Revolution, the colonies supported nine colleges. Perhaps as many as 700 colleges were founded between the Revolution and the Civil War, with approximately 200 of these surviving into the twentieth century.[40] Historian Frederick Rudolph notes that during the nineteenth century, England had four universities to serve a population of 23 million, but the state of Ohio had thirty-seven colleges to serve 3 million citizens.[41] The Morrill Act, passed during the Civil War, invented the agricultural college system. Reconstruction witnessed the building of the immensely important (and shamefully underfunded) network of Historically Black Colleges and Universities.[42] The establishment of Johns Hopkins University in 1876 brought the first research university to the United States. During the twentieth century, the state university systems grew, prospered, and served larger and increasingly democratic constituencies, opening to large numbers of women (who, by 1980, constituted the majority of college students,[43] and by 2010 constituted 57 percent of college graduates[44]) and then, increasingly in the second half of the twentieth century, underrepresented ethnic and racial groups. Enrollment has grown in recent years to more than 18 million undergraduates,[45] more or less doubling the number from a half century earlier.[46] Colleges and universities in the United States today employ more than 830,000 full-time faculty.[47] For all the troubles facing U.S. higher education today, and they are considerable, the broad narrative of higher education in the United States is one of unprecedented historical growth and prosperity, of a system that blossomed into the greatest university system in the world after World War II. For all the manifold tensions between our institutions of higher education and the broader U.S. society, the modern university system has been prosperous, powerful, and, at least initially, popular. Just as the U.S. commitment to primary education constitutes a significant element of our national development, so does our historic commitment to higher education. Thomas Jefferson is perhaps our most representative founder on this score: he devised a plan for public primary education in Virginia[48] and became the architect (in multiple senses) of the University of Virginia. Our commitment to primary, secondary, and higher education in the United States has historically deep roots.

The ancient concern with liberal learning was, of course, fundamentally aristocratic, and even nineteenth-century theorists of this tradition, such as Newman and Mill, were concerned with the production of a responsible social and political elite. In the United States we find pressures for a much broader "republican" learning. It is true that the college system in the colonies and the first hundred years of the republic was focused on the cultivation of elites in the clergy, law, and commerce,[49] but there have been powerful forces encouraging a much more democratic primary, secondary, and eventually higher education. We are, or at least have been in the past, a nation defined to a large degree by our faith in schools and schooling, and this faith grew with the evolution of popular and republican government. This belief in the need for and power of education was nicely captured in the nineteenth century by Catharine Beecher (Harriet Beecher Stowe's sister) in a book promoting the responsibility of women as educators: "The grand point . . . is that a people without education have not intelligence enough to know what measures will secure safety and prosperity, nor virtue enough to pursue even what they know to be right, so that, when possessed of power, they will adopt ruinous measures, be excited by base passions, and be governed by wicked and cruel men."[50] Her view is that our commitment to education has saved and will continue to save the United States from the calamitous mob violence witnessed in the French Revolution: "Nothing can preserve this nation from such scenes but perpetuating this preponderance of intelligence and virtue."[51] If the people, or at least some significant element of the people, would rule in the United States, the ancient concern for preparing citizens for freedom would have to be expanded to include a larger civic cohort. Schooling and liberal learning would have to become popular.

████████ In the early 2000s, Derek Bok observed that "it is . . . difficult to find any period during the past century and a half when educators were united around a common unifying vision of liberal education."[52] My guess is that this difficulty extends even further back than this. Untangling the history of liberal education in U.S. higher education is not a straightforward task, in part because of the flexibility and ambiguity with which the term has been used over time. One of our most distinguished historians of U.S. higher education has remarked that early in the twentieth century, for example, particularly between the world wars, the idea of liberal learning became so expansive as to lose any coherent meaning.[53] Be that as it may, a central contrast in the history of higher education in the United States is between the system of colleges that established themselves very early in our national and even colonial history and the university system that began to emerge in the post–Civil War period and flourished in the twentieth century to become what was widely recognized as the greatest system of higher education in the world. Overall, the purposes and ideals of these two institutions stand in some tension with one another: the colleges, emphasizing studies in the humanities and languages and the education of undergraduates; universities growing as scientific research institutes, emphasizing the development of applied knowledge and the training of graduate students. This tension would produce significantly variable and hybrid institutions over the course of the twentieth century. To understand this tension, it is important to take a quick survey of the history of U.S. higher education.

The original college system, growing in large part from the British "Oxbridge" system, was established when the Puritans built Harvard College in 1636; eight more institutions of higher education were chartered in the American colonies before the American Revolution. There was an explosion of college building between the Revolution and the Civil War. Historian John Thelin reports that by 1800 there were twenty-five degree-granting colleges in the new United States, that this number doubled by 1820, and then by the time of the Civil War there were 241 such colleges in the country.[54] One Absalom Peters suggested in 1851 that "our country is to be a land of colleges,"[55] and that seems to have become very much the case. It is true that most of these institutions were much closer to secondary schools than what we would think of as institutions of higher education today. Nevertheless, colonial and early U.S. history is rich with an unprecedented burst of college building.

The curriculum in these colleges was "liberal" in the sense that it generally was built around classical learning and ancient languages. Even early in the nineteenth century, however, there were pressures from the young and practical U.S. society to reform this educational model. The faculty of Yale

College felt this pressure: "From different quarters, we have heard the suggestion, that our colleges must be new-modelled; that they are not adapted to
the spirit and wants of the age; that they will soon be deserted, unless they are
better accommodated to the business character of the nation."[56] In response,
in 1828 they issued what would become a famous report defending the classical curriculum: "Our object is not to teach that which is peculiar to any one
of the professions, but to lay the foundation which is common to them all."[57]
This requires what the Yale faculty referred to as "general knowledge" of the
sort that can lead to the "elevation and dignity of character" and a "com-
manding influence in society and a widely extended sphere of usefulness."[58]
The education in classical culture will help the graduate "to diffuse the light
of science among all classes of the community,"[59] that is, it will produce social
elites with both the background knowledge and quality of character required
for virtuous and effective leadership: "Familiarity with the Greek and Roman
writers is especially adapted to form the taste, and to discipline the mind,
both in thought and diction, to relish of what is elevated, chaste, and simple."[60]
Indeed, the study of the classics, they claim, provides the "most effectual discipline of the mental faculties,"[61] and "can hardly fail to imbue" the student's
"mind with the principles of liberty, to inspire the liveliest patriotism, and to
excite to noble and generous action."[62] The goal is to produce gentlemen who
will fill the professions and the "public councils."[63] They admit that the
branches of knowledge change and evolve over time, and that liberal education must reflect these changes. They deny, however, that classical languages and literature are no longer of the greatest importance. On the contrary, these languages continue to provide the foundations for both European
and American literature, and the ancient authors continue to be the "surest
interpreters of nature itself" available to us.[64] Liberal education requires providing the first lessons in our cultural inheritance, and to skip this foundation would be to build our knowledge on inferior modern literature (they
specifically name Voltaire as an illustration of such inferiority).[65] The beauty
and moral content of the classics disciplines the mind and spirit of students
better than any other available resources. This discipline must come first, before modern and practical topics, if the students are to have the intellectual
resources that allow them to be free in their later lives.

The Yale Report provided a detailed explanation of what, for example,
the founders of the College of Rhode Island (later Brown University) meant

when they declared, in the college charter of 1764, that "institutions for liberal Education are highly beneficial to Society, by forming the rising Generation to Virtue, Knowledge & useful Literature & thus preserving in the Community a Succession of Men duly qualify'd for discharging the Offices of Life with usefulness & reputation."[66] In the words of the Yale Report, "A liberal, is obviously distinct from a professional, education. The former is conversant with those topics, an acquaintance with which is necessary or convenient, in any station of life, the latter, with those which qualify the individual for a particular station, business or employment. The former is antecedent in time, the latter rests upon the former as its most appropriate foundation. A liberal education is fitted to occupy the mind, while its powers are opening and enlarging."[67]

The "Knowledge & useful Literature" referred to by the College of Rhode Island founders captured the general commitments of the classical college curriculum: an education that would be useful not because of an immediate vocational application, but because it will expose the student to the deepest truths about human nature and human excellence. South Carolina College (founded in 1801, later the University of South Carolina) went so far as to claim, in its motto (here translated from the Latin, *Emollit mores nec sinit esse feros*), "(Learning) humanizes character and does not permit it to be cruel."[68]

The self-understanding of nineteenth-century college faculties insisted on distancing the education they provided from practical or vocational training, but we should also note that this is a little misleading: the classical education promoted in the colleges had its roots in the training of clergy, for whom knowledge of ancient languages was directly relevant to their vocation. For nineteenth-century college students *not* entering the clergy, the argument about the liberal virtues of a classical education appears to have been developed to suggest that access to ancient literatures and wisdom would morally prepare them for a wider range of vocations. The point to note here is simply that the development of the classical curriculum was not as innocent of vocational concerns as was and is often suggested.[69]

The conventional contrast in the history of U.S. higher education, nevertheless, is between the college system coming to a crescendo in the nineteenth century and the university system emerging from the Morrill Act and the influence of German research universities among American scholars in the late nineteenth and early twentieth centuries. This provides largely a contrast in understandings of the proper role of higher education in U.S. society. Although Thelin suggests that the liberal arts colleges "displayed considerable resilience in the post–Civil War decades,"[70] the research university was being born in the period following the Civil War. Within half a century, the classical curriculum and small college were more or less replaced by the modern university. These new universities were open to significantly more students, guided by the scientific ideal of research, and committed to serving the needs and development of a modernizing economy. Like the colleges, universities also aimed to cultivate the leadership for society. What this was understood to mean, however, was transformed from the cultivation of the clerics, merchants, and professional classes of preindustrial society to a focus on the scientists, administrators, entrepreneurs, and modern professionals demanded by Progressive Era society and beyond.[71] "The professional-managerial class is without doubt the majority clientele of the twentieth- and twenty-first-century university,"[72] says John Guillory, and the university was adjusting to serve this group. On balance, applied science, rather than liberal education, thus became the ideological commitment of the new university system. A focus on faculty research replaced attention to the undergraduate curriculum (it is noteworthy that it is during this period that the "extra-curriculum" of student life—athletics and student organizations— began to flower) and the undergraduate curriculum evolved from a set curriculum to an electives system (developed early by President Eliot at Harvard and adopted quickly throughout the new university system, emphasizing the appeal to students' personal interests and career intentions).

There was pushback against the triumph of the science-driven university, primarily by conservative professors of an older sensibility. In fact, in intellectual historian Bruce Kuklick's analysis, the "humanities, as they came into existence from 1890 to 1920, composed the least worldly leavings in the university, after hiving off of the social sciences."[73] Because these topics had little practical utility, they would have to be valued "for themselves alone." Thus, the humanities as they first were defended against the enterprise of the modern research university grew more from conservative orthodoxy than the radicalism we associate, for example, with Renaissance humanism.[74] At least in the first third or more of the twentieth century, the humanities fought a rearguard cultural action against the progressive social engagement of the research university.

Most representative of this reaction, perhaps, was Irving Babbitt at Harvard, who argued in his 1908 *Literature and the American College* that the "humanities need to be defended to-day against the encroachments of physical science, as they once needed to be against the encroachments of theology."[75] Criticizing the emphasis on applied knowledge, Babbitt revived the ideal of shaping individual character: "What is important in man in the eyes of the humanist is not his power to act on the world, but his power to act upon himself."[76] The goal of higher education should not be for "service and training of power, but training for wisdom and training for character."[77] If the ideal of the modern university in the United States was service to industrial society, the first pushback of liberal education was to revive the older notion of developing the moral sensibilities of unformed students. To the degree that the new university took the developing industrial and administrative goals of modern society for granted, the outlook of someone such as Babbitt represented an attack on such assumptions: the function of higher education "is not, as is so often assumed, merely to help its students to self-expression, but even more to help them to become humane."[78] The idea of "repose" is foreign to the modern university, as busy as it is with supporting and improving society, but it is precisely this more aristocratic notion of leisure that Babbitt contends is required for the kind of humane education we hope higher education can provide.[79] Only this could provide students with the intellectual tools for imagining their actual moral obligations rather than simply assuming them and concentrating on the skills required for success in contemporary society.

Liberal education and the undergraduate study of the humanities would receive new defenses in the 1920s and 30s, in the attempt to revive and protect undergraduate exposure to and study of literature, philosophy, history, and the humanities in general. Notable here were the works and writings of Alexander Meiklejohn, then at Amherst College, and Robert Hutchins at the University of Chicago. We will return to these two influential educators in chapter 3, but for now it is sufficient to note that they thought of undergraduate education as requiring a broad exposure to our cultural inheritance rather than merely a utilitarian or practical education. They also defended this project on more democratic grounds than did the conservative Babbitt. Meiklejohn writes, in explaining and defending "the liberal college," that the heart of his educational mission is to make clear "the value of knowledge: not the specialized knowledge which contributes to immediate practical aims, but the unified understanding which is Insight."[80] The college teacher, far from being deeply involved in practical affairs, should "remain apart from the machinery of life" and refuse "to be busy with it."[81] Instead, the liberal college aims to "learn and teach what can be known about a man's moral experience, our common speech, our social relations, our political institutions, our religious aspirations and beliefs, and the world of nature which surrounds us and molds us, our intellectual and aesthetic striving and yearnings."[82] As Newman was in the previous century, Meiklejohn was persuaded that all these topics could be understood as expressions of a single normative unity, and that exposure to this cultural inheritance would prepare students to become thoughtful social leaders; indeed, he suggests that liberal education produces "men of power" who "could lead and dominate the men about them."[83]

Robert Hutchins is associated even more closely with the promotion of a "great books" approach to liberal education. Writing during the height of the Depression in 1936, he complains that in the modern university, "the pursuit of knowledge for its own sake is rapidly obscured in universities and may soon be extinguished." He fears, in fact, that "soon everybody in a university will be there for the purpose of being trained for something."[84] As does Meiklejohn, Hutchins believes the deepest human questions are being ignored, mainly for the purpose of promoting immediate social goods: "The justification for the privileges of universities is not to be found in their capacity to take the sons of the rich and render them harmless to society or to take the sons of the poor and teach them how to make money. It is to be found in the enduring value of having constantly before our eyes institutions that represent an abiding faith in the highest powers of mankind."[85] An unthinking commitment to the ideal of progress has given the modern university an attitude of contempt toward our cultural inheritance, leaving faculty and students alike less able to thoughtfully evaluate our true condition and options: "Our erroneous notion of progress has thrown the classics and the liberal arts out of the curriculum, overemphasized the empirical sciences, and made education the servant of any contemporary movement in society, no matter how superficial."[86] The complaint we find in writers such as Meiklejohn and Hutchins is that the scientific and practical orientation of the modern university is threatening to subvert the intellectual traditions that could allow us to reflect on our condition more thoughtfully.[87] The tradition of resisting vocational and applied programs of study is revived and given twentieth-century form by these thinkers. It is not the classical program of the nineteenth-century college that they are attempting to resurrect, so much as a new emphasis on a broader conception of intellectual cultural heritage.

World War II transformed this new understanding of the liberal arts once again, as it strained against the agenda of the modern research university. In 1945, a faculty committee at Harvard published the influential report *General Education in a Free Society*. Modern education, it declared, must "preserve the ancient ideal of liberal education" and "extend it as far as possible to all the members of the community."[88] Whereas Hutchins and Meiklejohn both connect their defenses to democratic culture, the Harvard Committee authors were even more explicit in tying their understanding of liberal learning to democratic education. In the past, vocational and liberal learning may have been restricted to an elite and privileged few, but in a democratic society, they contend, students from all walks of life must have experiences with both forms of education: "Thus the two kinds of education once given separately to different social classes must be given together to all alike."[89] Liberal and vocational education are still distinct projects, but a democratic society, without a leisured and aristocratic class, requires both for all citizens.

The case for liberal learning is that it aims to "break the stranglehold of the present on the mind."[90] By teaching "effective thinking" it will also help shape character, presumably by allowing the student to judge the elements of what will constitute a good life for themselves as both individuals and citizens.[91] This general or liberal education will promote not just professional competence but "responsible private judgement."[92] Perhaps most importantly, by exposing students to the ideas and ideals that have informed modern, and presumably free, civilization, liberal education will address the "supreme need of American education" in supplying "a unifying purpose and idea."[93] Louis Menand has pointed out that *General Education in a Free Society* is a "Cold War document,"[94] and he's certainly correct to suggest that it aims to promote ideals and values that are truly liberal and free, as opposed to those promoted by the Soviet Union. The authors of the report made it clear at the outset that general education aims at promoting "common standards and common purposes."[95] It is true that democracy ensures the "right to differ," and thereby encourages a pluralist society, but it "yet depends equally on the binding ties of common standards."[96] Liberal education will expose students to a wealth of different views and perspectives, but the intention and hope is that beneath these differences a consensus about the values of liberal democratic society will emerge. Promoting such consensus became a project of liberal education in the wake of World War II and the onset of the Cold War.

Two years after the publication of *General Education in a Free Society*, the Truman administration released *Higher Education for American Democracy: A Report of the President's Commission on Higher Education* (1947). This was the first major report on higher education commissioned by the federal government, and it is a remarkable document to the degree to which it amplified and extended the ideas in the Harvard Committee's report. It promoted not only a familiarity with U.S. and Western culture, but with histories and cultures from around the world. Given the recent world war, it is perhaps not surprising that the conception of citizenship defended in this report is cosmopolitan: "In the new world it is not enough to know and understand our own heritage. Modern man needs to sense the sweep of world history in order to see his own civilization in the context of other cultures."[97] No longer is it possible to study our own culture apart from others: "East and West are coming together in one world order. We could not stem this development if we wanted."[98] The liberal education envisioned by the Truman Commission would not only promote democratic norms, values, and processes, but must promote these even against social practices of the present. Education's "role in a democratic society is that of critic and leader as well as servant; its task is not merely to meet the demands of the present but to alter those demands if necessary, so as to keep them always suited to democratic ideals."[99] True to this promise, the commission insists that higher education be made available equitably not just to white men from different social classes, but also to women and people of color: "Colleges should become laboratories of inter-race and interfaith fellowship."[100] Our colleges and universities must "become the means by which every citizen, youth, and adult is enabled and encouraged to carry his education, formal and informal, as far as his native capacities permit."[101] Higher education must become an engine of equity and meritocracy, and a school of democratic ideas and practices: "To teach the meaning and the processes of democracy, the college campus itself should be employed as a laboratory of the democratic way of life."[102] The democratic idealism of this remarkable document, like that of the Harvard Committee's report, must be viewed in the context of the recent war and the challenges of Cold War competition between the United States and the Soviet Union.

In this renewed and modern version of liberal education promoted in our colleges and universities in the postwar period, exposure to a canon of philosophical and literary texts replaced the nineteenth-century understanding of classical studies as the core of a liberal education, and it is assumed that properly pursued, liberal education will generate a broad and stable moral consensus. Victor Butterfield, for example, president of Wesleyan University in Connecticut, presented a sketch of his vision of liberal education in his 1955 Annual Report to the university's Board of Trustees. He suggests that liberal arts colleges such as Wesleyan are responsible for helping to produce the "wise and courageous leadership" that society was "desperately in need of."[103] Such leaders must be "free men," and it is the "purpose of liberal education to produce" such men who are "free not only through release from ignorance, prejudice, and provincialism, but free also in the sense of knowing and therefore of being better able to choose and accomplish what is best for man and society."[104] Butterfield appeals to Plato's notion of education as "fundamentally learning to like the right things," and William James's idea that "in the last analysis the purpose of education is to recognize and work for excellence in all areas of human endeavor." Lest we not fully appreciate his ambition, he follows this comment by suggesting that it "is the vivid appreciation of the Good and the Beautiful, as well as the True, that fulfills our education."[105] Butterfield's conception of liberal education focused on the liberation of the individual by exposing him (Wesleyan was not yet a coeducational institution in 1955) to the arts and sciences that would expand and shape his conception of human goods and possibilities. Such an education aimed at producing the *right kind* of leaders for the professions and society, people who would share commitments to the right, the true, and the beautiful. As the president of a small liberal arts college, Butterfield's emphasis on the education of a virtuous elite is narrower than the ambitions found in the Truman Commission's report, which promotes the education of the democratic citizenry more broadly. The goal of both perspectives, however, is to generate a set of shared moral understandings and commitments among students of the liberal arts and sciences.

Historian Julie Reuben stresses this point, that in the early and mid-twentieth century, U.S. educators looked to liberal or general education to teach the "unity and the values in the college curriculum."[106] The idea was to cultivate a core of civic education that had been provided in an earlier era by classical and theological curricula. The aim was to ensure "that students appreciated democracy and its superiority over other political systems and would be disposed to be engaged citizens."[107] We might think of the 1960s and 70s as the final years of the golden age of this postwar project. The turmoil of the last third or more of the century would make clear that such a consensus about moral values or the nature of good citizenship was far from an inevitable consequence of liberal learning.

In the last decades of the twentieth century, then, two developments led to a strain on liberal studies as they were understood in the middle years of the century. The first looks like a perverse outcome of the very success of postwar liberal education. Indeed, the lesson may be, at least for conservatives, to be careful what you wish for. By the early 1960s, students involved in the civil rights and antiwar movements were less inclined to reject liberal education than to take it seriously and demand its expansion. The very democratic ideals that were promoted by the Truman Commission became the ideals used by students to criticize the hypocrisy within society and injustices in U.S. dealings with other nations. Journalist Will Bunch comments: "The kids, it turned out, were executing the blueprint of the Truman Commission and the post-war idealists. It was the grown-ups that were screwing it up."[108] It appeared that liberal education could be extremely powerful and effective. It also became clear that such an education could be very disruptive to the status quo and a strong force for dissensus rather than consensus.[109] Reuben points out that this generated a shift in the understanding of "neutrality" in liberal education, from the promotion of a shared set of uncontested (and in this sense "neutral") commitments, to, instead, the exposure of students to widely diverging and competing perspectives and viewpoints.[110] This expansion of viewpoints, of course, included previously underrepresented voices within Western culture, but also a growing interest in colonized societies and non-European cultures. This second understanding of "neutrality" encouraged, unsurprisingly, relativistic perspectives and increasingly cosmopolitan and inclusive understandings of the appropriate terrain of study in the humanities. Both of these developments would drive conservative counterattacks, from Allan Bloom's *Closing of the American Mind* to John Agresto's *The Death of Learning*.[111]

The second development is that the radicalism of the student movements and the campus disruptions of the 1960s and 70s would lead to a conservative backlash against public support for higher education as a public good to be supported by public expenditure. Economist James Buchanan and Nicos Devletoglou, in *Academia in Anarchy* (1970), suggest that student unrest was traceable to three facts: students aren't paying for the cost of their education, faculty doesn't have to sell its products on a market, and taxpayers own public universities but don't control them.[112] The solution? To privatize the universities to the degree possible so that the market would discipline the key actors and put an end to public subsidies for what the authors viewed as destructive and subversive behavior. This was precisely the strategy Ronald Reagan pursued when he became governor of California in 1967 when he declared that college should be about workforce development and that "taxpayers shouldn't subsidize intellectual curiosity."[113] Will Bunch notes, "Reagan's election in many ways ended the post–World War consensus that higher education should be liberal in outlook and accessible to everyone."[114] The conservative program would be to privatize higher education (and not only higher education), which forces the educational costs back on to individual students and their families.[115] This is the origin of our current student debt crisis with its subsequent significant incentives for students to concentrate on vocational rather than liberal education, given the extraordinary cost they must shoulder alone to pursue higher education in any form. This would make the pursuit of liberal studies more of a personal choice, and an expensive one at that, than a public program in the promotion of broadly civic purposes.

The attack on higher education as a public good would quickly fan the flames of conservative attacks on primarily the humanities and social sciences as bastions of elitist, undemocratic, and un-American thinking, so that in recent years, for example, we can hear Donald Trump Jr. criticize universities as places that teach students to "hate their country" and "hate their religion."[116] Liberal education has thus become a focal point in the culture wars growing out of the conflicts of the 1960s and 70s and continuing, even accelerating, today.[117] The meaning and status of liberal learning has been deeply influenced by these political fights.

■■■■■ This very brief walk through some of the historic roots of liberal education suggests that such an education has consistently been thought to be committed to goods other than vocational preparation and training. Andrew Delbanco has objected to such a distinction between vocational and liberal studies, suggesting that this is a false opposition.[118] He is certainly right, at least in principle. It is true that many of the roots of what we think of as liberal education run deep into the historical roots of vocational education of, primarily, the clergy. It is also true that the skills, habits, and capabilities cultivated in rigorous liberal studies are by no means irrelevant to career success: clear thinking, communication skills, problem-solving, and a wide understanding of the (both natural and social) world around us are all likely to be assets in the practice of a range of careers and professions. Nonetheless, it is important to recognize that much of the focus of historical liberal education has been self-consciously removed from vocational concerns, primarily because it was thought to be addressing civic and philosophical issues above and beyond the vocational. An implication is that a focus on vocational preparation may distract us from this other essential educational work. Delbanco's objection, for all its truth, shouldn't prevent us from appreciating the importance of this concern.

The reason for the broad perspective of liberal education, beyond career training, is simple: the content of a free human life is much greater than one's vocation, and a liberal education is concerned with matters not only related to career but at least equally to civic and personal development. In fact, if we return to concerns raised about the possibilities of cultivating reason and the willingness to settle matters with discussion and debate rather than brute force or power, we can see some of the deepest roots of liberal learning in our earlier observations about the opening of Plato's *Republic*. The appeal to discussion, to a conversation where each side listens to and considers the views of the other, is increasingly drowned out today by hateful online political screeds and tweets. Such anger and hatred overwhelm and threaten to destroy the communal life and commitment required by democratic debate. Much of our current political "intelligence" is unapologetically committed to insult, put-down, dehumanization, and inflammatory assertion. A significant number of U.S. citizens are today unable or unwilling to distinguish between real information and even the most outrageous of conspiracy theories (including the revival, within the odious

QAnon world, of blood libel). Indeed, we live at a moment in which the very idea of a shared reality, of a truth that transcends party and interest, has come under attack at the highest levels of political leadership. This is a world in which Polemarchus's challenge to Socrates—"But could you persuade us, if we won't listen?"—is all too real, all too serious and present as a working political strategy. Clearly, vocational preparation is not the only, or even the primary, challenge facing our educational institutions.

A world of brute power makes a mockery of both democracy (by caring nothing for deliberation or just process) and liberal education (by insulting the commitment to reason), two of the most deep-seated values professed by society throughout much of our history. The project for Socrates in the *Republic* was to somehow transform his relationship of submission into a conversation, a dialogue, in which the participants would listen to one another, discuss, argue, and find common knowledge. Socrates's early exchange with Thrasymachus takes on more of the character of verbal warfare than of conversation. After Socrates leads Thrasymachus into contradiction, however, and in this way embarrasses and silences him, Socrates settles in and succeeds in transforming the evening from a contest of clashing wills and opinions into a shared effort to understand the nature of justice. Regardless of our opinion about the substantive views Socrates develops with his interlocutors in the remainder of the dialogue, one of the deeply optimistic messages of Plato's dialogue is simply that Socrates was able to transform a situation in which relative power determined the course of events into one in which reason and conversation ruled, if only for an evening.

This optimism is a key source for hope about the possibility of actually engaging in what Socrates calls philosophy, but which we may think of (so as to avoid an overly technical or specialized understanding of what philosophy might mean) simply as the commitment to reasoned investigation of important matters, or better yet, "education." Plato would have us believe that such investigation requires a community of participants and a willingness to suspend conventional sources of authority ("forces," that is) for the free and full play of reason and conversation. The optimism built into the structure of the *Republic* is chastened by our knowledge of the broader story of Socrates: he was executed by Athenian democracy for teachings that appeared to a majority of citizen jurors to subvert the substantive commitments of Athenian society and, to add insult to injury, corrupted the young who witnessed and shared in Socrates's philosophical investigations. Despite (and perhaps partly because of) this tragedy, Socrates's martyrdom inspires the entire Western philosophical project and the best of its educational commitments. Philosophical inquiry obviously gets off to a rough start, but it nonetheless raises the possibility of learning to become free in an essential sense: learning, that is, to think about what is right and true, and not merely reacting to the forces—natural, political, social—acting (or attempting to act) upon us. This is another way of suggesting that there is hope for the possibility of what we might think of as liberal education.

In its most general sense, it is hard to improve on John Stuart Mill's suggestion that liberal learning requires a "general" yet "thorough" understanding of the "leading truths" of the various disciplines in the arts and sciences. Free and responsible individuals need to understand basic realities, as best they can be understood, of the natural, social, and cultural worlds in which they live. Only this will allow them to gain a responsible grasp on the constraints, wonders, and possibilities of their world. Liberal learning also requires, Mill says, that students study the disciplines and topics that generate controversies, including moral controversies, become familiar with "what has been said" on contending sides of these, and be aided in developing their own informed and responsible views of these matters. This is why the humanities and arts, which address many such controversies directly, play such an outsize (and frequently contentious) role in contemporary discussions of liberal education (including my own in the chapters that follow). These are, not surprisingly, the elements of liberal education most frequently questioned if not under assault.

To thrive, liberal education requires a political context in which "philosophical" investigation (that is, honest consideration of important matters, from scientific to normative and humanist concerns) is tolerated, even encouraged, even though it will inevitably generate dissent and disagreement. By far the friendliest political environments in our world for such investigations are liberal democracies, in which there is a wide tolerance for alternative and conflicting views, relatively wide and democratic access to the conversations themselves, and a significant commitment to educating the young to develop the skills and commitments for participating in this philosophical project. In fact, we might think that such an education is not only tolerated and encouraged in modern liberal democracies, but required by them because democracy, self-rule, promises a high level of choice for all citizens.[119] Political freedom assumes such choice. Choice requires deliberation, debate, the consideration of alternative views, the ability to form a view about what might be *good*, and not merely what looks *necessary* or inevitable. Democracy promises, or at least aspires to, a certain level of self-rule for all citizens. This means, in turn, widespread participation in public choices about leadership and policy. Considering this, we can see why liberal democracy is historically so intimately tied to liberal education: this education seeks to promote precisely the skills and commitments to deliberation, reasoned debate, and free choice that are the cornerstones of democracy, and it seeks to promote them for all citizens even though they have historically been reserved, in less democratic and undemocratic regimes, for the privileged and powerful few. Democratic citizens are asked for their views and their choices. Such a request assumes that these choices are not simply inevitable reflections of power and interest; it assumes at least a modicum of rationality and autonomy. It assumes, that is, that the citizens are free. And this freedom assumes that the skills of freedom—most essentially, the rational capacity for deliberation, evaluation, discussion, and debate—have been either allowed to flourish spontaneously or have been cultivated among the citizens. Assuming that we cannot rely entirely on the spontaneous appearance of such skills (and I would submit that we cannot), freedom requires a philosophical or liberal education.

The commitment to liberal education for the sake of encouraging the cultivation of free, democratic citizens has, as I have suggested, a deep (if complex and not yet fully realized or equitable) history in our society. One of the greatest ironies of this history, as many have noted, is that although we are a substantially schooled people, we are also famously anti-intellectual and practically minded. Alexis de Tocqueville observed that democracy assumes a learned, civilized society,[120] but he also noted that citizens of the United States are "less occupied with philosophy" than citizens of any other "civilized" country.[121] We have vigorously developed educational institutions at an unprecedented rate but have often asked that they serve less to cultivate the life of the mind than to stimulate the economy. We can find oceans of rhetoric supporting the value of intellectual independence and reflection, but our schools of both primary and higher education have consistently aimed much more commonly at doctrinal orthodoxy and (economically) useful skills. Horace Mann hoped to promote the public schools in Massachusetts as institutions for cultivating thoughtful citizens immune from the plagues of passion and party. He found instead, however, that he needed to sell his project on the grounds of economic development.[122] The explosion of college building in the nineteenth century grew primary from the impulse to promote sectarian religious agendas. The building of the massive state university systems in the twentieth century was tied primarily to the growth of agriculture and professional schools, and to the stimulation of economic prosperity in general. The moralized program of the nineteenth-century college and the technological and economic development promoted by twentieth-century universities are certainly as central (and, in honesty, probably more central) to the evolution of our higher education than is a commitment to intellectual excellence, independence, and exploration. In developing the greatest popular educational system in the world, Americans have succeeded also in developing a deep skepticism toward intellectual projects more conventionally associated with scholarly life. We have a well-schooled democratic citizenry deeply distrustful of the inequalities and privileges so often promoted by the academic world.[123] Pragmatic skills and what Beecher calls "moral virtue" may produce sober citizens, or at least we can hope so, but not necessarily intellectually curious or adventurous ones. It is such curious and intellectually independent citizens, however, that we hope liberal education will produce.

Historian Jill Lepore, in her sweeping history of the United States, asks: "Can a political society really be governed by reflection and election, by reason and truth, rather than by accident and violence, by prejudice and deceit? . . . This question in every kind of weather is the question of American history."[124] The degree to which our politics is reduced to force and fraud is the degree to which we must clearly and frankly recognize this development for what it is: an assault upon the promise of our democracy, and on the intellectual virtues and practices upon which democracy must rest.

Action

In book 7 of the *Republic*, Socrates discusses the kind of education to be provided for the philosophically inclined citizens of Kallipolis, his imagined "beautiful city." He suggests that mathematics, geometry specifically, will play a special role in helping guide the young to an appreciation of pure knowledge, that is, truths not contingent on the continually changing conditions of the world of experience. The point is to "draw the soul towards truth," to train the student to focus her or his capacities, which are so naturally distracted by the ever-changing earthbound drama, on the eternal. Socrates admits that the mathematical arts have practical applications in the earthy domains society's leaders are responsible for, such as the art of war. But for him, the value of philosophical studies is the degree to which they draw the intellect away from the ephemeral to the unchangeable, for "the sake of knowing what always is, not what comes into being and passes away."[1] This is a step toward helping the student take the journey away from opinion and toward knowledge, in drawing her toward the art of "dialectic" and pure abstraction—from the shadowy truths of "the cave" to the universal sunlight of the unchanging forms found outside and beyond the boundaries of our dim and confining world.

Glaucon, Socrates's student and interlocutor, agrees about the value of geometry. Socrates then suggests that astronomy should probably be included in this ideal philosophical education. Glaucon responds, "That's fine with me, for a better awareness of the season, months, and years is no less appropriate for a general than for a farmer or navigator." Socrates is amused.

He tells Glaucon he is "like someone who's afraid that the majority will think he is prescribing useless subjects."[2] Glaucon, in short, is having difficulty with the idea that practicality isn't a primary educational concern.

So do most of us. We will return to Socrates's argument in chapter 4, but it is sufficient for the moment to have some sympathy for Glaucon. Even if we believe that there may be truths beyond the mundane world of experience, it is the everyday world, the world of "the cave," within which we live and that consumes the bulk of our attention. And, truth be told, many of us don't believe in a reality beyond the contingent, beyond what John Dewey referred to as "the problems of men," and many of us therefore find the world of experience to be the only world deserving of our love and commitment. At the very least, Glaucon's preoccupation with the practical is perfectly understandable to most of us, regardless of how amusing it seems to Socrates. The world we experience draws us back to itself over and over again, regardless of any interest we may have (and many of us, today, don't have any at all) in contemplating an unchanging realm beyond.

Henry Adams, in his famous autobiography, laments the irrelevance of the education he received in the nineteenth century for the world as he found it at the turn of the twentieth: "The American boy of 1854 stood nearer the year 1 than the year 1900. The education he had received bore little relation to the education he needed. Speaking as an American of 1900, he had as yet no education at all."[3] Although Adams's concerns were larger than Glaucon's desire to apply astronomy to farming and navigation, he insists that education must be relevant to the times and conditions under which people live. In our own day, more than 100 years after Adams expressed his frustration with trying to adjust to the new world produced by coal and machines, sympathy with Glaucon's perspective can help us understand the popularity and influence, for example, of Cathy Davidson's *The New Education*. The fundamental premise of her critique of contemporary higher education is that "college is no longer good at equipping graduates to succeed in an ever more complex and bewildering world."[4] Her claim resembles that made by Dewey, in the same period during which Adams was writing his *Education*, when he argued that we were trying to educate our students with methods and institutions developed in and for a fundamentally different time and place. I argued in the introduction that the practice of liberal education has generally been more committed to a temporary remove from, rather than an engagement with, career preparation and practical affairs, but we can also see a nontrivial countercurrent defending liberal education precisely on the grounds that it prepares the student to engage in such worldly action.

Davidson is not alone in capturing this particular *Zeitgeist* in contemporary higher education. Mark Taylor, in *Crisis on Campus*, made a similar point a few years earlier by claiming a "widening chasm between the ivory tower and the world at large," suggesting that "just as the modern university was created at the moment of transition from an agricultural to an industrial economy, so what might be called the postmodern university must be created to negotiate the shift from industrial and consumer capitalism to financial capitalism and a network-driven world."[5] Jason Wingard, too, claims that "higher education is losing its value," and suggests that the "existing model of learning for our time, the one leading to a college degree, needs to be revised if the skill needs of the future are to be met."[6] When we scan the intellectual horizon for recent attempts to defend and rejuvenate liberal education, it is not at all unusual to find arguments about how to make such an education increasingly relevant, up-to-date, and useful. Corinne Ruff recommends Stanford University's "blended programs," which bring computer science into conversation with more conventional humanities.[7] Jeffrey Selingo sings a popular tune in suggesting that we need to move beyond conventional discipline-based education to give students' studies relevance in solving today's problems.[8] The use of internships is increasingly popular to help students prepare for the working world. Problem-centered learning is promoted to generate interdisciplinary or multidisciplinary or, perhaps, transdisciplinary studies (whatever these all may mean) to complement demands for relevance and practicality. The Education Advisory Board (EAB), a division of the Advisory Board Company—an education consultant—admits that liberal arts majors often make less income right after college than students with vocationally oriented majors, but suggests that students and universities aggressively publicize the fact that over time they often outearn their peers; the skills developed in liberal studies must be marketed for their usefulness to potential employers.[9] In a similar vein, marketing and branding firm SimpsonScarborough promotes "selling the value."[10] The editors of *Scientific American* praise Steve Jobs for understanding that "technology alone is not enough—that it's technology married with liberal arts, married with the humanities, that yields us the result that makes our hearts sing."[11]

Demands are heard that we become more aggressive in promoting the use of technology in the liberal arts classroom, as a way to both reach and responsibly train our students. (Davidson, for example, assures us that "technophobia hamstrings our youth instead of preparing them.")[12] Scott Jaschik reports on a recent study suggesting that "attending a liberal arts college for most students leads to meaningful economic mobility."[13] Randall Stross concludes his widely read book, *A Practical Education: Why Liberal Arts Majors Make Great Employees*, by suggesting that "nothing yet discovered is more practical for preparing for the unpredictable future."[14] The dean of the faculty at Trinity College in Hartford, Connecticut, praises the wedding of liberal education to work experience,[15] echoing Matthew Hora and others who call for a "new vocationalism," or "a program based on the liberal arts traditions of cultivating well-rounded students via a multidisciplinary education, but with careful attention to students' career prospects and needs."[16] William G. Durden, former president of Dickinson College, recommends that "liberal arts colleges initiate a suite of trade-like programs that lead to various forms of certification that parallel the liberal arts curriculum"—by which he means, quite literally, training programs in trades such as electronics, coding, farming, auto repair, and culinary arts.[17] There seems to be no end to demands to remake, reform, or market liberal education so as to assure students, parents, and employers that such an education will create productive, capable, useful, and perhaps most importantly, affluent workers.

Socrates's comment to Glaucon certainly appears relevant for us: defenders of liberal arts education today, as Glaucon, act as if we are "afraid that the majority will think" we are "prescribing useless subjects." It is true that many of the more thoughtful commentators and advocates for liberal education will offer several arguments in its favor, the vocational being just one among others. The American Association of Colleges and Universities (AAC&U), for example, claims a "truly liberal education" prepares us "to live responsible, productive, and creative lives," suggesting that vocational productivity must share the stage with other civic and aesthetic values.[18] Likewise, Danielle Allen identifies four primary goals of education, of which "breadwinning" is only one,[19] and similar sensibilities are found in Fareed Zakaria's recent book on liberal education[20] and in Mortimer Adler's older *Paideia Proposal*.[21] Even so, it is striking to see the degree to which vocational anxiety is driving current conversations about liberal education. Recall Barack Obama's 2014 comments, mentioned in the introduction, that skilled manufacturing and the trades may be much more lucrative than an art history degree from a liberal arts college.[22] Even noting his apology a few days later, and that he never suggested in the first place that the only values of an art history degree are economic, what is striking in our times is the sense of anxiety about the practicality of conventional liberal studies.[23]

We saw in chapter 1 that as early as 1828, Yale was feeling pressure to incorporate more science and practical learning into its curriculum. The demand for relevance in higher education is obviously not a uniquely contemporary matter. It is not until the Progressive Era, however, that we see the successful replacement of the older college by the modern university with its modern sensibilities. Woodrow Wilson, writing as president of Princeton in 1909, captures the new way of understanding this mission. Students will prepare in college, he suggests, to "be a master adventurer in the field of modern opportunity."[24] The college graduate must become "in some degree a master among men," and his higher education "is for the training of the men who are to rise above the ranks." In fact, if they do not rise to such a level, "college was not worth his while."[25] Wilson does say that "the object of college is intellectual discipline and moral enlightenment,"[26] but this sounds more like a platitudinous afterthought in contrast to his earlier emphasis on masterful action. Even his attack on what he takes as flippant and trivial extracurriculars reflects his insistence on preparation for vigorous, active social leadership in the modern world: "The side shows . . . must be subordinated" to the primary academic training, since that alone will prepare young men to be leaders in "modern life."[27] Bringing an old college into the modern age required transforming the pedagogic emphasis from reflection to the requirements of successful mastery of the emerging modern world.

For many, it will not be at all surprising to see language like this emerging within the modern university in the United States. From the outset these universities have been committed more to the project of modern science than the humanist investigation of purpose and meaning. The great Progressive Era historian Carl Becker borrowed from Aristophanes and declared that in our world, "Whirl is king, having deposed Zeus." We live, that is, in a world of facts (Whirl) without a coherent or persuasive sense of meaning or intention (Zeus).[28] A few years earlier, Max Weber had made a similar point, that as our abilities to control the natural world increase, our philosophical sense of understanding of, and even comfort within, the world deteriorates.[29] The story gets even worse: the growth of science not only challenges the metaphysics and sense of belonging found in the prescientific world; it also generates culturally relativist (or at least morally neutral) social sciences aimed at description and control more than normative analysis. Contemporary Israeli historian Yuval Harari echoes Weber's observation that the modern social compact includes an agreement to give up meaning in exchange for power: "On the practical level modern life consists of a constant pursuit of power within a universe devoid of meaning."[30] This doesn't mean we don't know what we want: comfort, pleasure, safety, longevity, convenience. We might expect that such a sensibility will generate demands for higher education to be more engaged with the utilities of action than with providing a space for reflection and normative evaluation; at the very least, we won't be surprised to find this to be a trend in the modern university. Consider, for example, just this fact: 31 percent of federally funded research in universities is funneled into medical fields, and when we include biomedical research within this calculation, these fields together account for more than half of all such sponsored research.[31] The real money in higher education is aimed, in short, at the "relief of man's estate," to use Francis Bacon's memorable phrase. With the university so obviously committed to applied and practical knowledge, it is not surprising that demands are made for the education provided by these institutions to have a strongly utilitarian component. If Socrates taught that the unexamined life is not worth living, Bacon taught that the only knowledge that mattered was knowledge that produced power over our natural and material world. The Socratic project may not be fully defeated, but it is certainly on its heels in the contemporary world. The Baconian sensibility has become our "common sense" more than an argument to be engaged. Baconian utilitarianism seems, at times, to be so ascendant as to be almost as invisible as the air we breathe. Even in a world without significant cost pressures on students, there would still be a clear bias in modern universities toward stimulating and guiding action—this from an institution we might naïvely have expected to be committed to more reserved "ivory tower" reflection.

■■■■ When we hear demands today that we reform our educational practices to make them more relevant, more practical, more oriented toward helping students become successful participants in the economic world, we are hearing echoes of arguments that were prominent a century ago, during the first generation of the modern university system. Just as to-day's educational reformers attack what they consider to be stultifying educational conventions and intellectual attitudes, so did the educators of the Progressive Era hope to pioneer educational understandings and practices to prepare students for the emerging industrial society.

The all-out assault on the conventions of pre-twentieth-century humanist education would find its strongest voice in the greatest of Progressive philosophers, John Dewey. Much of what Dewey said in the course of his educational crusade has become a kind of conventional wisdom among reformers today, as can be seen by the ease with which we promote pedagogies of "problem-solving," of "active learning," of group projects, and of direct engagement with what we take to be the primary interests and concerns of students. Dewey developed the intellectual infrastructure, we might say, of a reformed educational system, and this infrastructure is more often assumed than reflected on by those who once again aim to make higher education vital to the economic life of our society.

Dewey's position wasn't simply that earlier educational systems and values, with their humanist emphasis on literary culture and classical language study, were wrongheaded, or ineffective, or intellectually deadening—although they were, in his view, all these things.[32] Even worse, they represent a political assault upon the democratic ethos and values of our times: "For wherever you find a social reactionary there you will find an enthusiast for either classical learning on the one hand or technical or specialized training on the other."[33] The very separation of liberal and technical learning, he argues, represents the needs of a powerful ruling class and the consequent subordination of a laboring class. It is a sign of currently unjustifiable inequality and a longing to retain undemocratic forms of social organization in the emerging democratic age. Dewey suggests that the "old distinction between the vocational and the liberal, the professional and cultural has lost somewhat of its force as the distinction between slave, the bond-serf and the free citizen has disappeared."[34] Dewey's view is that the cultural inheritance promoted by many proponents of liberal education offers little, or even negative, value to contemporary students. That older conception of culture grew from and reflected the needs of a different world, and it was a world with profoundly undemocratic institutions and values. The liberal college "has undertaken to maintain the continuity of culture," but the "sole reason for maintaining the continuity of culture is to make that culture operative in the conditions of modern life, of daily life, of political and industrial life, if you will."[35] Classical liberal culture, that is, fails to speak authentically to the conditions of modern life. At best, it will fail as irrelevant (driving students away from the classroom and scholarship and into extracurriculars). At its worst, it distorts our understanding of and commitment to contemporary possibilities. Such a vision is politically reactionary, as Dewey made clear in his exchanges with advocates of more conventional liberal learning.[36]

Dewey claims, then, that "so-called cultural education has always been reserved for a small limited class as a luxury."[37] We might think that the task of democratization would simply require making what had been confined to a "small limited class as a luxury" available to the democratic public as a whole. Such a project, however, misunderstands what democratized education requires. Dewey's contention is that conditions for a democratic culture have already emerged, in part and in potential, in the world of science, technology and industry, and that our understanding of education must adopt to and reflect this reality. The project isn't to simply bring high culture to the democratic many, but to develop an entirely new democratic culture to convey to our students. In *The School and Society*, Dewey writes that "the merely intellectual life, the life of scholarship and of learning . . . gets a very altered value" in contemporary society. "Academic and scholastic, instead of being titles of honor, are becoming terms of reproach."[38] He approves of this development, since it recognizes the need for a new understanding of intellectual life and the educational project. He suggests that conventional "academic and scholastic" values are necessarily aristocratic, since the "simple facts of the case are that in the great majority of human beings the distinctively intellectual interest is not dominant."[39] The distinction between knowing and doing grows from social class distinctions and privileges; no such distinctions may be admitted in a democratic society. We must argue, instead, that by rejecting this distinction, democracy reunites knowing with its proper object: the solving of practical problems. By discarding the ancient notion of knowing as a kind of detached observation or contemplation, democracy enthrones knowing to its proper, even natural (for Dewey), role of wrestling directly with the practical affairs faced by common people in everyday life.

So, what would a democratic educational culture look like?

First and foremost, it would have to be tied to elements of students' lives about which they have a normal, natural, and intrinsic interest. The "most promising approach lies in a consideration of the future of professional rather than in the past of liberal education."[40] That is, Dewey assumes that students will have a natural curiosity about their future work. Indeed, his assumption, found throughout his educational writings, is that economic life represents the overwhelming bulk of our natural concern and interest. Because of this, any educational program that separates vocational from intellectual life is alienated from the concerns and problems that stimulate thought, and students, in a democratic society in the first place. If we begin from this observation, we recognize that the most basic achievements of modern life grow from the remarkable success of science, technology, and industry in addressing the difficulties presented by the demands of material life. Any culture we develop to replace the aristocratic cultures of the past must "be consonant with realistic science and with machine industry, instead of a refuge from them."[41] Aristocratic culture embraced the leisure of the powerful and held the labor of the many in contempt. Modern democratic society rejects this dualism between leisure and work, freedom and necessity, and insists on a culture of labor and industry, in which our intelligence works to humanize economic life rather than withdrawing from it.

In his greatest educational work, *Democracy and Education*, Dewey refers to science as "the agency of progress in action."[42] For Dewey, the successes of science in mastering the natural world spring from its virtues as a social activity. This remarkably effective method of problem-solving has grown, first, from the insistence that we focus experimentally on the particular problems before us rather than on general or abstract problems imagined by philosophers: "The ages when scientific progress was slow were the ages when learned men had contempt for the material and processes of everyday life."[43] Once modern thinkers, inspired by Francis Bacon, looked to solving the practical matters found in our material daily life, they discovered that experimentation and cooperation were essential to understanding, and that understanding grew from practical successes in solving clearly defined problems through experimental processes. The profound success of modern science and technology, Dewey believes, illustrates an equally profound breakthrough in the understanding of thought itself: "Science is a name for knowledge in its most characteristic form. It represents in its degree, the perfected outcome of learning,—its consummation."[44] This leads to the second essential insight captured within the scientific method: thinking and knowing are cooperative social activities in which a community of inquirers work together to address their common concerns. For Dewey, the very notion of intelligence and intellect as something individualized and apart from these social activities is a mistake. Instead, intelligence is tied to becoming properly socialized to the methods and activities of a successful community of inquirers. Intelligence is social and active.

Dewey believes that science provides, therefore, a rough template for democracy itself. Those who appeal to premodern cultures as the stuff of a proper humanist education miss the essential opportunities of our time. Education "must accept wholeheartedly the scientific way, not merely of technology, but of life in order to achieve the promise of democratic ideals."[45] The scientific community discovered the power of shared problem-solving. Without this cooperative element, the scientific community could never have achieved the successes that it has. In this way, science has opened the door to democratic practices more generally: "The very heart of political democracy is adjudication of social differences by discussion and exchange of views. This method provides a rough approximation of the method of effecting change by means of experimental inquiry and test: the scientific method."[46] Science is less a challenge to democracy than a model for it. The conventional humanists, as Dewey understands them, have been distrustful of the world brought into existence by the forces of modern science and technology, and of these forces themselves, and therefore stand in opposition to the basic liberatory potential of contemporary society.

From Dewey's perspective, then, what conservative humanists hail as our cultural inheritance is, in fact, no relevant culture for us at all. In *Democracy and Education*, he declares that "the past just as past is no longer our affair," and that the "true starting point of history is always some present situation with its problems."[47] Any cultural inheritance separated from the present demands for immediate and thoughtful action acts as nothing more than a "dead, mind-crushing load."[48] The reason students are so bored with conventional humanist education is precisely because of its separation from the real problems and demands of the current society. Our true culture, Dewey suggests, is "something to achieve, to create."[49] To emphasize culture as an inheritance to be preserved is to miss the point: all human inheritance is relevant only to the degree to which it speaks to the particular needs of the present, and that the vast bulk of prior human culture simply does not speak to the age of science, the machine, and democracy. The culture that will be useful in this new social milieu has yet to be created.[50]

We know several elements of what such a culture requires, however. Most importantly, it must reflect the lesson of science that we become free and powerful individuals only to the degree to which we learn to self-consciously participate in and contribute to a community of shared problems, concerns, and intentions. Individualist egoism is a vestige of an undemocratic society in which a few were released from responsibility to others by virtue of their social power and standing. The promise of a modern democratic society is the promise of the intelligent participation of individuals from every walk of life in the common project of democratic society. It is true that "our economic conditions still relegate many men to a servile status,"[51] but the potential of modern society is for "every individual" to "have opportunities to employ his own powers in activities that have meaning."[52] Instead of literary training, the demand of democratic culture is that all individuals understand their role in the processes and techniques of the modern economy and be given the tools in their education that they would need to become intelligent contributors to the further development and refinement of these processes for the good of all: "We must surrender that superstitious tradition which identifies humanism with the interest of literary training, and which in our country, whatever it may have accomplished elsewhere, produces only a feebly pretentious snobbishness of culture."[53] "But," he says in *Democracy and Education*, "the essence of the demand for freedom is the need of conditions which will enable an individual to make his own special contribution to a group interest, and to partake of its activities in such ways that social guidance shall be a matter of his own mental attitude, and not a mere authoritative diction of his acts."[54] The educational task, then, is the cultivation of what Dewey refers to as a "socialized disposition,"[55] through which we come to embody the habits and skills, the modes of action, required for our effective participation in democratic life. Put more plainly, it requires that we understand our own needs and successes as being intimately tied to the needs and successes of the broader community. To be a free contributor to this community requires that we be fully and equitably integrated into it insofar as every member is self-consciously involved in defining and solving the problems facing the whole. "All education," Dewey declares, "which develops power to share effectively in social life is moral."[56] "Some are managers and others are subordinates," he says in *School and Society*. The goal of successful education is not to abolish differential authority or a hierarchy of roles in economic and social life, but rather that "each shall have had the education which enables him to see within his daily work all there is in it of large and human significance."[57]

Such is what Dewey means when he speaks of education as producing in students a "socialized disposition." The culture we need to convey through our education is primarily the culture growing from our shared contribution to the modern industrial economy. The problem for the liberal arts college in a (potentially) democratic society is not to reproduce the distinctions between liberal and vocational learning, so central to earlier understandings, but rather "*seeing to it that the technical subjects which are now socially necessary acquire a humane direction.*"[58] Students should learn not just the mechanics and functions of the modern economy, trades and professions, but also how they can contribute to these processes self-consciously and creatively. These are the crucially humanizing contributions to modern material life, in which the satisfaction of human wants and needs transcends the ancient "realm of necessity," and becomes, instead, the realm of freedom, creativity, and humane community. Only an education designed to achieve this new democratic disposition can be liberal, or liberating, for Dewey.[59]

■■■■■■ Friedrich Nietzsche, in his 1872 lectures titled "On the Future of Our Educational Institutions," complains bitterly about the democratization of what we might think of as cultural or liberal education: "The rights of genius are being democratized in order that the people may be relieved of the labor of acquiring culture, and their need of it."[60] Michael Oakeshott, in the next century, echoes Nietzsche's complaint, but with less explicit hostility toward democracy, suggesting that education has been replaced in contemporary society with socialization, and that schooling has been replaced by apprenticeship to "domestic, industrial and commercial life."[61] Democratic educators might very well agree with the substance of these complaints but object to the view that this is an unhappy development. On the contrary, Dewey claims, an undemocratic form of socialization is being replaced by a democratic form, and that requires a transformation of our very conception of culture. Yes, it is desirable that we learn to adjust to and cultivate the democratic potential of our industrial and technological society.

Dewey presents us with a general philosophy of education, but his influence has been most direct and obvious in shaping the progressive education movement aimed at children in public schools. Nevertheless, he is also clearly articulating and representing the perspective of the university system as it emerged in the twentieth century. Recall his contempt for the colleges of the previous centuries. These comments from Christopher Jencks and David Riesman capture a similar condescension toward the earlier college system: "The nineteenth-century liberal arts college had almost no connection with the main intellectual currents of its time, and its curriculum was by no stretch of the imagination responsive to the kind of questions that troubled its more curious students. It was rather a degenerate survival from an earlier era, whose program reflected partly the professional needs of aspiring clergymen and partly the culture of eighteenth-century gentlemen."[62]

Only with the rise of the university, Jencks and Riesman suggest, has "higher education . . . ceased to be a marginal, backward-looking enterprise shunned by the bulk of the citizenry."[63] Or consider this, from economist Harry Gideonse, writing from the University of Chicago in 1937 against the views of his president, Robert Hutchins: "Other things being equal, the test for deciding the inclusion or exclusion of a given subject matter in the curriculum must be its significance for living the life of our society. Nothing, however, should be included in such a curriculum merely because it has the prestige that comes with antiquity or because it is called a classic."[64] Dewey was representative of those who embraced the modern university because of its commitment to science, to relevance, and to service to the contemporary society. Dewey, that is, was not alone in emphasizing that the older cultural perspective must be replaced by an emphasis on engagement and action. The shift in emphasis from letters to science, from the development of character to the cultivation of leadership and management skills, from a temporary retreat from society to a full engagement with political and economic institutions, all reflect a significant shift for the academy in the twentieth century.

Even many of the most vocal critics of higher education today are critical not because of the turn toward utility and vocation, but because of the failure of our colleges and universities to achieve these goals to a satisfactory degree. Debunkers of the modern university suggest not that the emphasis on vocation is a mistake, but rather that it is a failure. Jason Brennan and Phillip Magness, for example, suggest that "given the incentives and trade-offs they face, what's most important to students is that college opens doors for them. Learning can't be the point."[65] Given that higher education is fundamentally about vocational training and professional advancement, the remarkable fact about universities is that their claims concerning their effectiveness on this score are almost entirely without merit; the vocational preparation of college students through the experience of a liberal education is, they argue, almost entirely a "failed mission."[66]

Egalitarians, on the other hand, suggest that the vocational elements of the contemporary academy are all too successful in assuring graduates' success in the economic sphere. One hundred years ago, Upton Sinclair complained that "the universities are on the side of special privilege."[67] Today, Michael Sandel makes similar claims: "Once widely seen as an engine of opportunity, the university has become, at least for some, a symbol of credentialist privilege and meritocratic hubris." "In practice, most colleges and universities do less to expand opportunity than to consolidate privilege."[68] For the debunkers, claims about the value of liberal education for vocational preparation lack persuasive evidence. For egalitarians, the institutions of higher education are too efficient in reproducing social class standing and advantage from generation to generation through the meritocratic credentialing process. The point here is that even many critics of the contemporary academy assume that a properly functioning system of higher education would give more successful, and just, access to the professed economic benefits of university education.

In comparison to today's focus on utility and social action, however, Dewey's ambition one hundred years ago is breathtaking. Today's educators offer liberal education as a source of vocational capacities simply in the hope that graduates will be able to successfully earn their living. Dewey had faith that we were on the precipice of building not just a democratic government but also an economy and society saturated with democratic commitment and practice. The educational project was to socialize students to a new democratic sensibility, to make them co-adventurers in the development of increasingly humane control of our growing industrial and technological capacities. This is obviously a far cry from the blunt utilitarianism of many of today's defenses of liberal education. And this contrast is not surprising. It is difficult, to say the least, to share Dewey's democratic optimism under the conditions we find ourselves facing in the twenty-first-century economy. Nonetheless, Dewey's legacy, diminished as it may be, remains strong among educators emphasizing the usefulness of liberal learning. We can see this when we consider the ubiquity of projects for "problem-based learning," or the common promotion of group-based learning as a requirement for learning to work under contemporary conditions, or the insistence that we adjust our educational practices to reflect the demands of our evolving economy. All these elements of contemporary liberal pedagogy clearly have deep roots in Deweyan soil, even as their aims are significantly more modest than Dewey's democratic hopes. Most importantly, so much contemporary commentary about liberal learning reflects Dewey's insistence that education must be understood, fundamentally, as preparation for action in the world. Liberal arts, in this understanding, is less a preparation for understanding—let alone, contemplation— than it is for doing. Understanding is subordinate to or justified entirely by successful action. Or, perhaps more accurately, the idea of understanding as something independent of action is denied by Dewey's pragmatism.

Dewey's Progressive generation faced a problem in the early twentieth century similar to what we now face in the early twenty-first. Historian Laurence Veysey points out that in the Gilded Age, "a life of virility and action seemed irreconcilable with the higher learning."[69] The university had to sell itself to the public to succeed, and it sold itself on utilitarian grounds that would appeal to the public at large.[70] Liberal education is under comparable pressure in our own time, as is clear from declining enrollment in conventional humanities programs.[71] It is not surprising that today's higher education is selling itself as a source of social utility and economic strength. We may have lost some of Dewey's democratic enthusiasm and optimism, but the case is again being made that, properly understood, liberal education is good vocational training.

Dewey is certainly right that aristocratic understandings of liberal learning can have more than a whiff of class snobbery toward economic life, and that such snobbery can reflect the sensibilities of the few who find themselves released from economic need. He is also certainly right that liberal education in a democratic society, that is, for the vast majority who do not have the good fortune to be immune to economic need, must include ingredients that are relevant to helping develop skills, understandings, and practices that will allow students to pursue their vocations not merely as necessities, but as elements of freely chosen, independent, and, one hopes, creative and satisfying lives. The demand for vocational relevance is an inevitable element of education in any democratic society this side of utopian plenty. Vocational needs are realities for all but a small handful of individuals and promise to continue to be so. To suggest that vocational choice and self-direction are irrelevant matters for free individuals is to consign the vast majority of democratic citizens to a world in which their free agency is severely constrained. Dewey inspires, in part, simply because of his faith in the possibility of building a humane and freely directed economic world. And though we may be more skeptical than he was about the degree to which economic institutions and practices may be democratized,[72] the preparation of students to choose their work and develop the skills to become self-supporting must be an element of any defensible democratic conception of education. Without this, such an education can't be fully liberal or freeing for most students in a democratic society.

Dewey clearly cannot be accused of any simple-minded vocationalism; his goal is less "job training" than educating people to play meaningful, by which he means democratic, roles within the vocations they eventually pursue. Even robustly understood, however, we may object to the degree to which Dewey reduces the scope and aims of education to the world of pragmatic, primarily economic, activity. We may worry that Dewey's emphasis appears to be significantly incomplete in its understanding of what our students need. A human life includes many important components—social, religious, familial, personal—in addition to the vocational, and all of these contribute in their way to our capacities for, or difficulties with, living freely. If liberal education is to educate for a freely lived life, there seems much more that must be included if we are to address the full array of our students' needs. Put bluntly, Dewey's view suffers from an economic reductionism. There are many realms of action beyond economic life that are seemingly ignored in his vision.

A second objection would protest that an education for action is often in danger of losing sight of the crucial normative question: Action to what end? Educated individuals must be capable of addressing, within reason, their vocational and material needs during their adulthood, but we also expect them to be able to critically reflect on these needs and the needs of the society at large in a way that allows for thoughtful evaluation of what is and is not appropriate, just, and liberating in our economic and other experiences. Simply being prepared for a vocation does not make an education liberal; all societies, regardless of how tyrannical they may be, must teach their citizens or subjects the skills required to contribute economically. Vocational training alone does not make an education liberatory. We expect a liberal education to at least offer elements that will help workers to be responsible and thoughtful, and not merely skilled or efficient.

We will return to the first of these objections—that there are human problems and interests independent of economic life that Dewey and his followers are less sensitive to than they ought to be—in chapters 3 and 4. Regarding the second objection, Dewey presents a more coherent, if ultimately unpersuasive, position than do many of his contemporary descendants who generally have less, or nothing, to say about this matter. Dewey holds that when one understands the full value of one's profession, and one contributes freely to it, the distinction between "private" and "public" interests dissolves; there is no meaningful distinction between oneself and the role that one has professionally assumed. Such roles are freely chosen since the individual has been educated to understand the full value and purpose—the liberating elements—of the activity and how these relate to her or his personal talents, interests, and commitments. The individual's personal interest is in no way incompatible with the demands of the profession. "Socialized disposition" is the disposition to understand oneself as serving the society and oneself by fulfilling the functions of a chosen profession.

The example Dewey gives of this process in the final chapter of *Democracy and Education* is about a physician who serves the sick and dying during a plague. Such service requires the doctor to prefer performing his social function over assuring his own safety. For Dewey, such a preference is not the result of choosing "virtue" over "interest," for the simple reason that a properly socialized and freely functioning physician has assumed the interests, indeed, the very sensibilities, of his professional role: "A man's interest in keeping at his work in spite of danger to life means that his self is found *in* that work; if he finally gave up, and preferred his personal safety or comfort, it would mean that he preferred to be *that* kind of self."[73] For Dewey, it is a mistake of individualist philosophy to imagine that our senses of self and our personal interests are distinct from our social roles and relationships. Thus, to formulate the problem as a choice between individual and social interest is to misunderstand the issue. The problem is, What kind of social role does one embrace to define one's sense of self? "Morals concern nothing less than the whole character, and the whole character is identical with the man in all his concrete makeup and manifestations. To possess virtue does not signify to have cultivated a few nameable and exclusive traits; it means to be fully and adequately what one is capable of becoming through association with others in all the offices of life. . . . The moral and the social quality of conduct are, in the last analysis, identical with each other."[74]

Put simply, the individual achieves his or her individuality through the free exercise of a socially useful vocation that enhances the interests and possibilities of an entire community: "All education which develops power to share effectively in social life is moral."[75] Dewey's language about this point is even more overtly moralized in *The School and Society*: schools should be "saturating" students "with the spirit of service."[76] A sufficiently liberal education, for Dewey, is an education in which we come to view our own interest as being identical with the interest of the beloved community. To the degree that this is so—and this can only be so to the degree that individuals are genuinely integrated into the awareness of and participation in solving the problems associated with the community—the tension between individual and society dissolves. Education, as Dewey understands it, produces the conditions for experiencing and embracing a moral life. This is another way of saying that it prepares us to live a fully democratic life in communion with other democratic citizens.[77]

The beautiful harmony of Dewey's vision does little to persuade us that democratic education paves the way for a democratic society in which conflicts between individuals and society dissolve, where individual wants and desires become fully congruent with the needs of society at large.[78] Many of us will remain skeptical; we will think the question of civic virtue, for example, remains unresolved even if we train our students for successful careers, and even if this training successfully integrates students into a professional ethic with which they deeply identify. We currently live in a society with remarkably well-trained engineers, scientists, and business school graduates, many of whom take their professional obligations and ethical responsibilities very seriously. We also suffer from profound political polarization, animosity, and moral disagreement. At a time when liberal education is under attack and finding much of its current defense in utilitarian and economic terms, it is notable that much of the conventional defense of such an education was less about its ability to train effective social actors than it was to encourage virtuous ones. Dewey clearly hoped to provide a bridge between his understanding of action and the promotion of civic virtue, but the utopianism of his formulations forces us to search (as we will in chapter 3) for other views promoting liberal education as a stimulus for civic virtue. Dewey's hope that reinvigorating liberal education as a form of action engaged with the economic realities of the contemporary world—and those who follow him in this general project—can't help but leave us worried about the nature of the engaged action being encouraged. In a world still a far cry from Dewey's democratic industrial economy, in which all participants are invested with a kind of equality of understanding and contribution to the common good, it is hard to imagine that training effective, even clever and committed, workers is alone a sufficient ideal for liberal education.

The physician who believes her professional obligations require her to face danger while practicing her profession still has, of course, the tug of other fears and other interests, concerning her personal safety, her obligations to her family and friends, her religious obligations, and so forth. Can we doubt that when faced with the choices presented in Dewey's example, a decision still must be made, that she will need to deliberate about this decision, that different physicians are likely to make different decisions about such matters, or that we have not only the capacity but even the responsibility to think about which decisions are praiseworthy and which are not? Even assuming Dewey is right that the physician must remain at her post when facing the dangers of plague, in his telling this choice is drained of its moral power by his implication that there is actually no real choice to be made. Yes, there is: there is a choice about whether to continue as a physician under these conditions. Choosing to do so cannot realistically be thought to be a closed question, even for someone who has previously accepted the ethic and responsibilities of the medical profession. To think that the question is closed is to unrealistically ignore or minimize the need for courage and virtue, or even the necessity of weighing multiple and not infrequently conflicting obligations, at such moments.[79] More needs to be said about how we are to gain the reflective capacity to make free and responsible choices and judgments in our vocational and professional lives. It will not do to simply claim that properly socialized individuals will see no tension between their professional and other interests. To claim that such tensions simply dissolve with proper socialization is to evade, rather than address, the question of moral responsibility.

■■■■■■ Liberal education, in short, can't help but ask the question, Action to what end? Dewey's educational and democratic theory hasn't provided as much guidance on this score as we would hope. "Socialized disposition" appears to promise more than it can deliver, leaving the normative choices confronting free individuals less addressed than defined away.

At its best, the emphasis on action in liberal education encourages a genuinely democratic interest in promoting students' future economic well-being and relative self-sufficiency (or, perhaps more accurately, personal vocational responsibility) as matters intimately related to the development of their personal freedom. Democratic education at all levels rightly aims to help students discover their interests and talents and guide them to meaningful and satisfying careers. Dewey rightly insists that part of learning to be a free individual is learning to care for the necessities of life, to gain the skills and knowledge needed to make one's way in the professional and economic world. Dewey's hopes were that such an education would cultivate a new moral sensibility guiding our economic lives and understanding of democratic culture. In practice, however, too much emphasis on action, and too narrow of a conception of the scope of action, can serve to deflect our attention from other matters of great educational importance. It is sobering to note that when Roger Geiger, one of the most distinguished historians of U.S. higher education, surveys Dewey's curricular contributions to twentieth century higher education, he identifies only bland notions of "education for life" (and even these modest influences were waning by mid-century).[80] How could such a rich democratic theory, committed as Dewey was to the democratization of modern economic life, have been reduced to life skills and homemaking classes? It seems that the wealth of Dewey's democratic theory was quickly jettisoned from the Deweyan educational inheritance. The education he hoped would produce democratic economic action has been reduced too often in the contemporary academy to action aimed at narrow vocationalism and conventionally understood professional success. We do well to remember Dewey's lesson that liberal education must include a commitment to preparing students for roles in the world of work, that such roles constitute a significant element in the experiences of free individuals. But Dewey's legacy cannot replace or eliminate our concern for other, even more significant, values in liberal education. A concern for action is legitimate, but it must not be allowed to replace or blind us to the need for addressing the virtues justifiable action requires, or to some of the broader range of problems confronting, and possibilities presenting themselves, to free individuals.

I have argued that there is a place in liberal education for a limited but meaningful focus on vocational matters. Stefan Collini, warns us, however, that in the context of liberal education "skills-talk" can represent a "failure of nerve" in the academy. For him, such talk "is an attempt to justify an activity not in its own appropriate terms, but in terms derived from another set of categories altogether, categories drawn from the instrumental world of commerce and industry."[81] The view defended in this chapter is that vocational concerns have "liberal" elements that need to be recognized and addressed. Yet, we would do well to heed Collini's warning about turning the enterprise of liberal learning into little more than training workers for the modern economy. The danger is that these vocational concerns can distract us from other essential, even more essential, components of liberal education.

THREE

Virtue

In late 2023, Jesse Wegman, a member of the *New York Times* editorial board, wrote a column about what he believed was the distressing number of lawyers in the United States, "some of whom once held prestigious posts in government and academia," who "were willing and eager to tell transparent lies and concoct laughable legal arguments to help a con man stay in the White House against the will of the American people." His comments conclude with the following claim: "To a degree many people didn't fully realize until the past few years, the functioning of American government depends upon honor."[1] Honor is an old idea that conveys a moral commitment to discipline self-interest to the demands of moral principle. Without such a commitment, Wegman fears, it is all too easy for us to become unprincipled opportunists.

Wegman's perspective provides a significant contrast with the view Dewey defended. Dewey hoped that by orienting education to the practices and problems of everyday life, especially in the economic realm, we could appeal directly to the natural interests of students and at the same time socialize them into a full understanding of the human community and social interdependency. The goal was not just to make education more relevant but to break down what he took to be false barriers between individual and group interests. Dewey was persuaded that by making our institutions more democratic, and by attacking the "individualistic" ideologies he believed functioned as rationalizations for unjust social and political relationships, students would be both more engaged and would learn to identify their own personal good with the good of the (just) society they participate in and contribute to. Educating for the world of primarily economic action, democratically understood and practiced, students would grow into a society where the antagonism between individuals and communities would dissolve. Citizens would become habituated, through their democratic education, to work as equals, regardless of their differential positions, in pursuit of the common good. The problem of virtue would dissolve, as individuals would no longer understand their own interests as competitors with others' or with the community's as a whole. Rather than teaching students, for example, to be "disinterested" in their ethical evaluations, much as Wegman's appeal to honor suggests, a democratic education would simply socialize students to a new understanding of their personal interests as harmonious with the interests of the group to which they belong and contribute. Education focused on action, properly understood and pursued, would make the need for virtue and honor moot.

Dewey's contemporary, Alexander Meiklejohn, was deeply skeptical about the likely success of Dewey's moral theory, on grounds very much like those implied by Wegman's recent reflections. Adam Nelson, his biographer, notes that "immersed in a thoroughly pragmatic age, Meiklejohn stood in direct opposition to his more famous contemporary, John Dewey."[2] Meiklejohn had a long and influential career in higher education that took him from a deanship at Brown University, to the presidency at Amherst College, the founding of an experimental college at the University of Wisconsin, and an adult education program, the San Francisco School for Social Studies, focused on democracy and "great books." He was, like Dewey, a liberal reformer. Unlike Dewey, the liberal education he advocated emphasized a renewed commitment to the humanities and a distrust of the dethroning of the humanities by science in the modern university. The arguments Meiklejohn presents against Dewey may sound, at least to some degree, eccentric to contemporary readers. In the final analysis, however, his views are less distant than they may at first appear, and they played a crucial role in working to reestablish the humanities as the foundation of liberal studies.

In a book published during World War II, Meiklejohn developed his critique of Dewey and the vocationally oriented educational tradition Dewey represented. For our purposes, the important point is that he locates Dewey in a tradition of "Anglo-Saxon" thinking about education that emphasizes education's pragmatic utility: "On the whole, learning is, for [John] Locke and for his fellows, a servant of prudence rather than of virtue."[3] Education, in this tradition, serves as "an instrument of worldly success."[4] Meiklejohn's observation is simply that Locke, and Dewey two centuries later, attempted to locate virtuous dispositions in an actor's self-interest. For Meiklejohn, however, such an emphasis may teach us sophisticated forms of prudence ("self-interest properly understood," we might say), but it is incapable of generating anything that he would recognize as genuine moral principle.

Developing this critique leads Meiklejohn to emphasize the contrast between his own moral idealism and Dewey's pragmatism. He notes that Dewey's Darwinism leads him to reject any dualism between body and soul or mind; for him, "a mind is an educated body."[5] Meiklejohn, in contrast, insists upon this dualism as the precondition for moral life. Bodies, he argues, can have interests, and complex, even morally justifiable, understandings of these interests can be imagined. But bodies cannot generate moral principle as Meiklejohn understands it. The only way to evaluate the moral attractiveness of a particular conception of prudence, for example, would be with a moral principle that stands above and separate from that prudence: "The time has come when we must face the fact that if a man is not a spirit, then it is not sensible either to admire him or to despise him. We have drifted into ways of thinking and acting which logically exclude praise and blame from our accounts of human nature."[6] The only way to understand human potential and excellence, and also human failure and degradation, is to "separate Man from Nature."[7]

We can see the problems Dewey's materialism pose, Meiklejohn believes, by looking at his pluralist theory of democracy. It is true that Dewey is committed to allowing citizens to form what he calls "publics" to protect and pursue their interests as they understand them.[8] Meiklejohn fails to see, however, how Dewey's political commitments can generate anything other than what we might today call "interest-group pluralism." Dewey hopes to see a greater democratic equality and unity among citizens within the context of pluralist competition than is currently found in U.S. society (with its racial, class, and gender imbalances of power and influence), but this does not mean that at the end of the day he can provide a moral perspective that transcends group-based interest: "We have seen that Dewey chooses to explain political institutions in terms of selfishness rather than of sympathy."[9] Although Dewey hopes to generate a shared or universal interest, Meiklejohn believes he can do no more than produce "the competitive clash of 'pressure groups,' each fighting for its own hand. . . . It is a bedlam of privately warring factions."[10]

He recognizes that Dewey has "a passion for democracy," but Meiklejohn concludes that Dewey has "no theory of it."[11] What he means is that self-interest, on the part of any given group of actors involved in the competition between groups or factions, is a weak reed upon which to build a commitment to democracy. In this way, Meiklejohn comes to a similar conclusion to what we reached in chapter 2: Dewey's educational theory of democratic socialization is inadequate to fully address the nature of and need for virtue, for ethical choice, in social action. In Meiklejohn's language, Dewey's theory can't move us beyond prudence to "sympathy" with others; it can't teach us when sacrifice and a transcendence of self-interest may be required. His democratic theory will promote the kind of fissures and conflicts it is intended to resolve and eliminate.

We see, then, that Meiklejohn rejects Dewey's materialism and embraces instead a form of radical dualism as a precondition for what he understands as an adequate ethical and educational theory. As material creatures, we all have distinct and often competing interests. As spiritual beings, we have a shared nature and interest in what Meiklejohn believes is a universal good: "Bodies we try to make happy. Spirits we try to make magnificent."[12] The "dominant fallacy of our scientific-industrial civilization" is its materialism.[13] It is certainly the case that contemporary society presents radically new material conditions for life, but it is a mistake to believe that these new conditions have fundamentally altered the spiritual problems and needs of human beings. These, Meiklejohn contends, are universal and ahistorical. The two greatest geniuses of Western civilization, he claims, are Socrates and Jesus. The problems raised and addressed by these great figures are as germane today as they were 2,000 or 2,500 years ago:

> "Are you," it will be asked, "recommending for an Age of Science forms and methods of thinking which men used in the ancient days before Science had been created?" And to this, if my courage will sustain me, I must answer with a plain "Yes." In my opinion, the devising of the new scientific methods has in no essential way affected our dealing with the problems which Socrates and Jesus faced. And these are still in changing forms our most fundamental, our most urgent intellectual problems. When faced with them the results and methods of the sciences and technologies are relatively superficial and subsidiary.[14]

The deepest problems of human life, and the moral principles required to guide us when considering them, are not relevant only to our historical moment, as Dewey and so many others would have it. On the contrary, the reason we continue to find inspiration in great art and literature from the past is precisely because of our shared human concerns, problems, longings, and needs. Historical and cultural changes and variety are obvious but, from a moral perspective, relatively unimportant. As moral creatures, we share a nature, a basic human condition, with all who live, have lived, and will live in the future.

This suggests, for Meiklejohn, that the problem of liberal education is not correctly understood as one that needs radical rethinking in the contemporary period. Nelson notes that Meiklejohn "hoped to recover the intellectual certainty and cultural stability of an older educational milieu."[15] He thought of liberal education not merely as the exposure of students to a wide variety of views, traditions, and perspectives; providing students with a menu of ideas for them to sort out on their own is not itself sufficient. On the contrary, educators must present an authoritative "pattern of culture," they must be committed to a set of beliefs, they must speak on behalf of some "social group" and be committed to "impressing its way of life."[16] Meiklejohn is not entirely clear about exactly what he has in mind. In *What Does America Mean?*, he suggests that all citizens must be exposed to and encouraged to study the "permanent and recurring problems of a social order."[17] A few years later, during the early years of World War II, he suggests that the "vital issue" is that "there is only one pattern of critical intelligence which is the same for all men."[18] That is, it isn't just topics of concern, and their proper understandings, that liberal education aims at; it is a more basic rationality, tested less by pragmatic problem-solving than by metaphysical philosophical reflection. Generously interpreted, Meiklejohn's position appears to be that those who seek understanding will discover that people have been confronted by more or less the same moral problems from time immemorial, problems, for example, having to do with meaning, with justice, with the reality of suffering and death. In addition, when people have thought about these matters, they find they have access to the same philosophical tools, the same reasoning capacity, across time and place. Meiklejohn "insists" that "humanity has . . . one intelligence," that this intelligence is still "in the making," is precarious, and "may at any time collapse."[19] The cultivation of this reason is necessary if we are to learn our full human potential. The importance of this assertion for liberal education is that it teaches us that "all human beings should have the same essential education."[20] For Dewey, democratic culture has yet to be discovered, and this discovery requires the cultivation of the pragmatic project we discussed in chapter 2. For Meiklejohn there is no break in the cultural evolution he identifies—we are still developing the ideas and rationality struggled with by earlier generations. The culture Meiklejohn identifies (which includes classics from Plato and the Bible to Shakespeare, to moderns such as Darwin, Marx, Emily Dickinson, and Henry Adams[21]) requires continued development, but he finds a classic philosophical and literary canon continuous with our ongoing needs today. What Dewey viewed as aristocratic and undemocratic cultural traditions to be cast off in favor of a new democratic sensibility, Meiklejohn views as an ongoing conversation about shared concerns across the experience of Western culture.

Who constitutes the "social group" referred to in the previous paragraph, the group that Meiklejohn suggests must inform the values of the philosophical views being promoted by a genuine liberal education? Answering this question makes clear the nature of Meiklejohn's idealism. In one of his early sets of essays, he suggests that "one cannot talk of education unless one knows the human spirit and its world."[22] A few years later he refers to democracy's commitment to "a unity of spirit among a multitude of persons who are made one by common ties of admiration and devotion to common ideals."[23] By the time his ideas solidify in wartime discussions of the role of liberal education in fighting the undemocratic forces of fascism and autocracy, he explains that the teacher "leads his pupil into active membership into a fraternity to which he himself belongs."[24] This fraternity is humankind as a whole, the universal and united interests of people in general. Just as we must be exposed to the one human intelligence, so must we be educated to become "citizens of the world."[25] He appears to mean this quite literally, suggesting that "fundamentally, education belongs to the world-state."[26] Again and again we see Meiklejohn suggesting that the moral universe is coherent, cosmopolitan, and accessible to all those educated to seek it: "To choose not to seek for that unity is to choose not to think."[27] Just as there is one reason and one set of problems and concerns shared by all people, so there is a single moral community and, perhaps in the future, a single political community.

This moral community is not established, for Meiklejohn, by appeal to a natural law with origins in divine will or intention. Rather, his perspective reflects Rousseau, or perhaps more accurately a variant of Kantianism, insofar as he believes that this common reason and the principles it generates grow entirely from human capacities. Moral life will find its completion as these capacities come to fruition in an increasingly inclusive democratic human community:

> Modern education must teach its pupils to participate, not in an intelligence which makes and controls the universe but in an intelligence which men are inventing as they seek to create meaning and value in an otherwise meaningless world. In that attempt mankind has no backing outside its own ranks. If individuals or groups are to find support, consolation, co-operation, they can find them only by standing together, by uniting with one another. The state, which takes charge of education, can have value and efficacy only as an agency of that attempt at human unity.[28]

Human beings have the capacity to unite as a single community, and the tools for such unity grow from our philosophical capacities rather than from our material interests. In fact, Meiklejohn believes that the science revered by Dewey, growing as it does from material rather than "spiritual" needs, is responsible for the chaos of modern ideas, the degree to which our different disciplines and perspectives appear unrelated to any common rationality or set of commitments.[29]

Meiklejohn writes that liberal education produces "men of power" who can "lead and dominate the men about them."[30] In this somewhat off-putting phrasing, what he's suggesting is that liberal education must produce strong leaders, but to what end or ends will they be dominating "the men about them"? This is clearly not a sophistic education, aimed simply at giving students the tools for whatever success they happened to want. On the contrary, Meiklejohn is consistent in arguing that the goal of the teacher is to provide the student with insights into the highest human goods and potentials, teaching people that they can live their lives "better than they would live them by mere tradition and blind custom."[31] He is confident that students, properly instructed, will seek "deliverance" from the "bonds" of conventional knowledge, "partial knowledge," and "self-interest."[32] Teachers will initiate their students into the world community of those aspiring to the most admirable purposes, and these students in turn will graduate from the liberal college and become forces in society to encourage all citizens to recognize and aspire to human excellence. Meiklejohn's hope, he wrote a few years later, "is that every American shall live the life of the spirit, that his activities shall be worthy of human admiration."[33] Nelson notes that Meiklejohn recognized that the high ideals of liberal education meant that in our nonideal world the teacher's life has a necessarily tragic element to it.[34] He nonetheless writes from a vision of a future world united by shared moral commitments and understandings of moral truth and human potential.

If Dewey wanted to tear down the walls around the ivory tower, to integrate the whole educational project from primary school to higher education directly into the workings of society at large, Alexander Meiklejohn wanted to reinforce the walls especially around colleges and universities to assure the integrity and effectiveness of his educational project. Meiklejohn agreed with Dewey that education was the central project for providing citizens with the knowledge and character to serve and defend democratic society. What he meant by a liberal education, however, was something much closer to the traditional intellectual exposure to the culture of the humanities than what Dewey had in mind. Dewey believed that conventional intellectual life was a class indulgence, the pretension of a ruling elite bent on preserving an undemocratic culture completely out of step with the needs and sensibilities of the democratic many. Meiklejohn thought of liberal education in more traditional intellectual terms, even if the content of the humane education he promoted would take on a more secular tone than the theological education of the nineteenth-century colleges. His goal was less to train people for the practical engagement with society than to provide a retreat from engagement for the sake of broad philosophical reflection. It is true, Meiklejohn writes, that "to teach young people is to make them ready for the world in which they are to live."[35] Engagement with practical affairs, with the world of economy and vocation, however, could and must wait. The preparation he had in mind could only take place when young people were temporarily insulated from such immediate concerns.

Meiklejohn's nonpragmatic sensibility could hardly be better captured than by his claim, in a book of essays published while he was president of Amherst College, that "to be liberal, a college must be essentially intellectual." What this means, he explains, is that the "college is primarily not a place of the body, nor of the feelings, nor even of the will; it is, first of all, a place of the mind."[36] The mission of the college teacher is to convince citizens of the "value of knowledge; not the specialized knowledge which contributes to immediate practical aims, but the unified understanding which is Insight."[37] For Meiklejohn, the task of liberal education is not geared toward the practical matters of how industries produce goods and services, or the particular skills required for a student intending to make a living in a given sphere of the economy, or any other vocationally useful information. Instead, colleges need to help students consider not how goods are produced, but rather, how such goods should be distributed and to what uses they should be put. That is, college is a time for considering matters of justice and the good. The liberal college is "expected to inform our people as to how the goods of life should be shared and how they should be used. These are the two fundamental aims of liberal teaching."[38] To focus on these tasks, the college must be able to give their students some "taste and insight" into these challenges. This can only be achieved, however, to the degree that college teaching remains "apart from the machinery of life," refuses to "be busy with it," and stands back to survey the social world without being immediately involved with or invested in it.[39] This environment can only be liberal insofar as it allows for the kind of reflection discouraged by the busyness, conventions, and common sense of daily life: "A college is our social and individual striving to escape the bonds which the world's work would fix upon us. It is the search for freedom from ourselves."[40] Yes, the purpose of education is to make young people ready for the world they will enter, but it achieves this purpose by allowing them the opportunity to assess and evaluate this world, and imagine other possible worlds, to assure that they will be truly self-directing when they leave the sheltered environment of the college or university. Meiklejohn took this principle seriously, arguing that "the college should be withdrawn from the world of affairs in order to remain entirely unbiased."[41] In fact, when an Amherst student enlisted in the Navy during World War I, Meiklejohn (unsuccessfully) attempted to deny him his diploma.[42]

In 1944, Dewey published "Challenge to Liberal Thought," in which he once again explained his views about education and distinguished them from more conventional understandings of liberal education, or contemporary versions such as Meiklejohn's, which attempt to build a canon of influential texts for study as a secular alternative to traditional classical/religious education. He reiterates his point that his ideal education "would make all who go to school aware of the scientific basis of industrial processes," and that a truly liberal, or liberating, education aims at "effecting a release of human powers."[43] As he does in so many other books and essays, Dewey stresses what he takes to be the equivalence of scientific and democratic method,[44] and criticizes any view as "reactionary" that would "urge that technology and science are intrinsically of an inferior and illiberal nature" compared to the humanities.[45] When he speaks of education's goal of cultivating and releasing "human capacities," he has in mind our abilities to act pragmatically in controlling the material world and bending it to our will,[46] rather than what Meiklejohn has in mind as the controlling and shaping of our own wills and desires apart from our material wants and needs. He restates his belief that education "must accept wholeheartedly the scientific way, not merely of technology, but of life in order to achieve the promise of modern democratic ideals."[47] He contemptuously suggests that the "idea that an adequate education of any kind can be obtained by means of a miscellaneous assortment of a hundred books, more or less, is laughable when viewed practically."[48] In fact, he suggests that to fetishize "great books" is to fall into a kind of medieval dogmatism, appealing to a canon of texts as morally authoritative, rather than cultivating and extending the tradition of reason pioneered by the Greeks.[49] For Dewey, any attempt to mine the literary and philosophical tradition for a unified conception of truth and knowledge is simply incoherent and a distraction from the attempt to build a new conception of liberal education aimed at successful action in the modern, scientific, industrial world. Worse, it is a form of reactionary and undemocratic politics; Dewey suggests that it is "no accident" that Europe has been engulfed in conflict, given that it provides a home for this older conception of liberal culture.[50]

In his response to "Challenge to Liberal Thought," Meiklejohn politely suggests that Dewey is insufficiently generous when he contends that interest in studying and teaching literature and ideas from predemocratic societies commits one to undemocratic politics: "I can find no basis whatever for the assertion that the study of the past implies the acceptance of the standards of the past as superior to our own."[51] In addition to insufficiently valuing what premodern writers might contribute to our own thinking, Meiklejohn objects, unsurprisingly, to Dewey's promotion of science as the model both for contemporary education and democracy itself: "To many of us Mr. Dewey's account of the 'scientific method' is very unsatisfactory, especially as it bears upon the difference between values and facts."[52] Meiklejohn simply doesn't believe that Dewey's pragmatism has sufficient philosophical resources for thinking seriously about moral issues. He also believes that Dewey has lost interest in precisely the philosophical and literary tradition that we need if we are to think productively about our contemporary obligations. Dewey suggests that democracy requires a whole new educational idea, focused on science and applied knowledge and overcoming the gulf between intellectual and productive life, but Meiklejohn protests that we need an exposure to a wide range of ideas and ideals if we are to have the resources out of which we can then make moral sense of our world.

The resolution of this exchange was far from satisfactory. Dewey denied, somewhat disingenuously, that he undervalues ideas from the past, and reasserted his claim that Meiklejohn's educational philosophy is at best an obstruction to the development of a democratic education and politics. Any dualism between humans and nature, between the mind and the body, "stands in the way of building up the attitude which in serving the needs of a genuinely liberal education will also serve the needs of our troubled and divided social life."[53] Indeed, in response to Meiklejohn's generous claim that perhaps they had misunderstood each other, Dewey made clear that any misunderstanding was on Meiklejohn's part alone.[54] For Dewey, these disagreements were versions of the fight for democracy being played out dramatically and violently on the world stage.

▬▬▬ Another significant contributor to the development of a "great books" curriculum was, of course, Robert Hutchins, the president of the University of Chicago. In many ways, he gives us an argument much like the one we find in Meiklejohn. In *Education for Freedom*, for example, published during World War II, Hutchins presents an argument that sounds very familiar after reading Meiklejohn. He argues that until we get our educational house in order, we will be unable to resist the antidemocratic forces currently unleashed upon the world;[55] he criticizes the preoccupation with science and scientific method in the country's academic life and suggests that we need to restore the central place for philosophy at the center of the educational project;[56] he criticizes the materialism of life in the United States and claims it has corrupted the university;[57] he insists on the intellectual nature of the educational mission and rejects broader purposes aimed at socialization and economic development;[58] he argues that in order to fulfill its mission, higher education must be set apart and insulated from the routine problems and concerns arising in civil society;[59] he contends, therefore, that higher education must develop and debate ideas that are not part of the "common sense" of democratic society, and that not being "popular" is part of its unique contribution;[60] that historicism has corrupted our intellectual life by giving us permission to ignore arguments simply by suggesting that they reflect a different time and place;[61] and that education to the intellectual life, as he understands it, is intimately tied to moral education.[62] In all of these ways, Hutchins makes arguments similar to those we find in Meiklejohn.

The first significant difference from Meiklejohn is Hutchins's view of the audience for a full liberal education. Meiklejohn thought this education was reserved for the few who would attend college; they would then assume leadership roles in society after their liberal education. They would use their philosophical training to guide democratic society. Hutchins, in contrast, makes the case for liberally educating all citizens. He writes that "the choice before us would seem to be clear: either we should abandon the democratic ideal or we should help every citizen to acquire the education that is appropriate to free men,"[63] and that "every man and every free citizen needs a liberal education."[64] In order to achieve this goal, he argues that an education in the great books is actually a project for secondary rather than higher education. Contrary to claims that such books and the ideas they contain are too difficult for younger students to understand, he suggests that "Mr. [Mortimer] Adler and I have found that the books are more rather than less effective the younger the students are."[65] Much like what we find in a recent book by Roosevelt Montás,[66] the argument is that liberal education addresses some of the most basic human questions and concerns, and the great books are those marked by the brilliance with which they raise and evaluate such questions. These are not concerns of an elite, but of all human beings. If all are to participate in the practices of freedom, they require the opportunity to be exposed to and wrestle with liberal learning. Dewey found such an education deadening, that it required imposing an archaic culture on uninterested and noncomprehending students. The social elite alone is interested in such things, and this interest grows more from cultural snobbism and social hierarchy signaling than because of any moral or philosophical need being met. In its place, he proposed an education not in the literary, artistic, and humanistic culture of the past, but what he took to be a truly democratic education aimed at integrating all future citizens as productive and socially aware contributors to the modern industrial economy. Hutchins is blunt in his critique of Dewey's view: "Looking at an industrial society, [Dewey] concluded that the young should understand it and that they should do so through considering the various economic activities of life in their moral, political, social, and scientific context. He also thought that this would be very interesting to them. His psychology appears to be false and his program impractical."[67] Dewey assumes that the natural interests of students are economic, that these matters constitute the most immediate and relevant set of concerns they are drawn to understand. Hutchins contends that this is a wild underestimate of the interests and concerns of people from all walks of life. In fact, to suggest that the conventional concerns of liberal learning are uninteresting or unimportant to the democratic many is itself a form of undemocratic snobbery. To be human, with a longing for freedom, is to yearn, in Montás's words, "to go beyond questions of survival to questions of existence."[68] Hutchins is often criticized as undemocratic, as the kind of snob Dewey criticizes,[69] but this significantly misses his point: in Hutchins's view it is Dewey who is being condescending toward the interests and capacities of average democratic citizens.

It is important to be clear about Hutchins's distinction between liberal and higher education. He was both optimistic and democratic about his conception of liberal education as an exposure to the great books with their various approaches to understanding moral and civic life. Dewey wishes to avoid metaphysics, or conventional philosophical commitments to "first principles," which he took to be a dead-end inevitably leading to dogmatic assertions about the nature of ultimate reality. In contrast, Hutchins believes such philosophical commitments, explored and debated in classic texts from the Western tradition, are unavoidable. Like Meiklejohn, Hutchins sees no reason to be convinced that pragmatism avoids the need for such assumptions, such philosophical starting points, even if pragmatists such as Dewey ignored their own unexamined assumptions. The study of such matters, Hutchins holds, should be available to all normal people in the course of their secondary education. On the other hand, Hutchins believes college education should be limited to that minority of individuals who are drawn to purely intellectual work and scholarship. Some commentators today, including Andrew Hacker and Claudia Dreifus, look forward to universal access, or near universal access, to higher education.[70] Hutchins, however, thinks higher education should be restricted to those who wish to specialize in scholarly pursuits beyond general or liberal education: "Democracy does not require . . . that the higher learning should be open to anybody except those who have the interest and ability that independent intellectual work demands. The only hope of securing a university in this country is to see to it that it becomes the home of independent intellectual work. The university cannot make its contribution to democracy on any other terms."[71]

Hutchins thus promotes universal access to liberal education, but not to higher education.[72] He believed that higher education was being hijacked by vocational education, and by the extracurricular elements of "college life," precisely because higher education abandoned its intellectual mission in order to become a "service-station" to society.[73] The pursuit of money in the academy leads to the adaption and development of anti-intellectual projects and activities that threaten to overwhelm its academic integrity. To criticize Hutchins for not supporting a democratically accessible higher education points to a truth about his exclusionary view of college, but the point can blind us to the democratic foundation of his promotion of liberal education. To miss this point is to miss the depth of his democratic commitments, the degree to which his promotion of liberal education was embedded in a deep democratic faith in the capacities of all citizens.

The distinction between liberal and higher education, for Hutchins, leads to an ambiguity in his understanding of the substance of liberal learning. He proposes that we complete secondary, or liberal, education at the equivalent of the end of the sophomore year of college (by age twenty).[74] True collegiate work should only commence after this, and then as a specialized rather than a mass form of education. The goals of the two schoolings would be different in an important way. The higher learning, as he promotes it, is closer to what we would today think of as graduate education: "As education [higher education] is the single-minded pursuit of the intellectual virtues. As scholarship it is the single-minded devotion to the advancement of knowledge."[75] This level of education pursues knowledge as its own reward, for its own sake, and will not necessarily lead to consensus. In fact, the scholarly life is likely to be contentious even when, perhaps most especially when, it is most healthy. Education at this level, Hutchins suggests, is "a conversation aimed at truth," but the "object" of this conversation is "not agreement but communication."[76] Universities are needed by democracies precisely because they will produce controversies, that is, differences of opinion and viewpoint, "as an 'end in itself.'" "A university that is not controversial is not a university."[77] The idea is that scholarly life will lead to vigorous debate, a shared commitment to the rules of intellectual integrity for all those involved in this debate, but not necessarily a consensus opinion or resolution to the debate. On the contrary, controversies without end are the expectation, as is the intellectual integrity required to navigate and contribute productively to these controversies. Truth is the goal, and even if truth cannot be reached in any final or completed sense, the faith underlying this activity is that it can continue to be approached. The university is satisfying to its participants simply because of their love of this process. Its job is to "turn out graduates who are capable of independent thought and criticism . . . who are committed to the fullest development of their highest powers and who can do their part as responsible citizens of a democratic state."[78] The democratic society within which universities are housed benefits by having its own biases, opinions, and common sense challenged by philosophical inquiry, broadly understood. This is the civic contribution of the university, well above, say, the utilitarian fueling of economic development (which Hutchins would leave to industry and other institutions of civil society).

Hutchins's comments about collegiate education stand in sharp contrast to his arguments about liberal learning. If the goal of university life is the pursuit of intellectual controversy and debate, the goal of liberal education is the creation of consensus. The United States, he believes, is not yet, at the time of World War II, a country committed to "the achievement of the common good through reason," but that should be our goal.[79] To be educated liberally is to be educated for what Hutchins calls "civilization," and "civilization is the deliberate pursuit of a common ideal." The project of liberal education is the "deliberate attempt to form human character" in relation to this ideal.[80] Here we appear to be back at the position defended by Meiklejohn. This ideal is not merely to promote a set of intellectual virtues, but it will include these to the degree that students will be educated in "rationality." There appear, however, to be additional substantive moral commitments that such an education must teach: a proper understanding of the foundational principles of democratic civic life, for example. Democratic education begins with the liberal principles and ideals of democracy and its philosophical and moral inheritance. This will presumably aim to produce a citizenry with a shared commitment not just to principles of reason and honest debate but also to substantive civic doctrines. We find here very much what we find in the Report of the Harvard Committee, *General Education in a Free Society*, that general education, or liberal education, concerns primarily the "question of common standards and common purposes."[81] The struggle against tyranny in World War II generated the promotion of a mass educational program designed to introduce all (future) citizens to the classic texts and ideals informing our political order. The assumption, not at all persuasive in retrospect, was that this philosophical and cultural education would succeed in generating a universal or near-universal understanding of the nature of democratic values and a commitment to liberal democratic principles and practices in the face of challenges from autocracy and various forms of political chauvinism and racialist nationalism.

It is Hutchins's collegiate argument, however, which he did not intend for the general education of the entire citizenry, that actually helps us formulate an alternative position to that presented by Meiklejohn, the Harvard Committee, and others involved with redesigning and reinvigorating the humanities and liberal learning in the early and mid-twentieth century. The two weaknesses of the "consensus" project concern, first, the unlikelihood that intellectual exposure to a set of ideas will lead to a universal set of responses to them and, second, the danger that this intellectual project will be corrupted by political considerations. In the first case, there is simply no reason, given everything we know about the wide diversity of defensible intellectual responses to virtually any set of ideas or any conventional texts, to believe that free and informed responses to these ideas and texts will generate anything approximating consensus. The breadth of literary and philosophical interpretation testifies to the contrary. In the second case, the challenge presented by a diversity of views will tempt the educator to evaluate the student's success by political rather than philosophical or intellectual standards. Consider alone the problem of selecting materials to be incorporated into the curriculum. In the American tradition, for example, should the writings of the Founders and a few later political leaders be the only voices to which students are exposed, or will the women from Seneca Falls be included, and the speeches and pamphlets of abolitionists? Will Malcolm X be read, or William F. Buckley Jr., or Betty Friedan? These, of course, are questions of great significance, and have been (and continued to be) answered differently by different citizens, politicians, and educators. Questions about whom to include and exclude cannot be avoided by simply suggesting that "the best" or "most important" texts will be selected.[82] Any claim that these choices are self-evident either intentionally or unintentionally threatens to hide political loyalties behind professed intellectual commitments. The alternative position, captured occasionally in Meiklejohn's writings but more clearly in Hutchins's defense of collegiate education, is to promote vigorous debate within and between philosophical traditions. The ideal here would be less to promote a substantive moral perspective than to cultivate the skills, virtues, and commitments of intellectual investigation and conversation. The goal of liberal learning, in this second incarnation, is to provide students with a rich background of ideas and perspectives that have played significant roles in our history, along with the skills to assess, compare, and come to rational judgments about them. The task is less to teach students the substantive normative truth than to expose them to the significant debates relating to such matters, along with the skills and disposition required to come to defensible independent consideration of them. The position here is much like that defended by Mill in his St. Andrews address, as we saw in chapter 1.[83]

Hutchins's promotion of great books to achieve these goals, at least in the context of collegiate education, was famously confined to what he (and his collaborator Mortimer Adler) took to be the Western canon, and this focus continues to be championed by some today.[84] In principle, however, there is no reason why a proper liberal education need be confined to this tradition. Henry David Thoreau, in the nineteenth century, took inspiration from the Confucian and Hindu traditions just as he did from his beloved Greek and Roman classics. The demand of the last half century of humanities scholarship that non-Western voices, and the voices of groups and individuals who had been silenced or ignored within the West (e.g., woman, people of color), be included in a proper liberal education has greatly expanded the possibilities for probing the human experience and exposing students to a greater variety of important perspectives than they could have experienced under Hutchins's, or Allan Bloom's, prescribed curriculum.[85] The point here is simply that the Western or "Eurocentric" perspective in

Hutchins's argument doesn't negate the power of a more expansive version of this argument. One can, and many of us believe we must, develop a more inclusive and cosmopolitan view of great books than that promoted by Hutchins, Bloom, or Anthony Kronman, and still believe that the point of a liberal education is to introduce students to the greatest literature (broadly conceived) and insights of world cultures.[86]

▬▬▬▬ Viewed from our own time, it is hard not to admire the enthusiasm and optimism of Dewey and his critics, all of whom were convinced of the central role education would play in supporting democracy as it faced profound challenges. They represent a heady time when our university system was young, and it was assumed that it would play a critical role in promoting democracy's health and prosperity. At our moment of increasing cynicism and despair about the potential of liberal education to play a critical role in a democratic society, we might find inspiration and renewed energy simply from the example of commitment and hope among the modern university's founders.

It is also true, however, that the gap between Dewey's desire to educationally engage with society and Meiklejohn's and Hutchins's promotion of the great books was great and the debate between them unproductive. The latter two were deeply critical of too much focus on "action" in liberal education, suggesting that the educational question should begin not with action, but with reflection on morally defensible understandings of what action is required. They feared that applied knowledge was crowding out the necessary study of the preconditions for responsible engagement. As this brief survey of Meiklejohn's and Hutchins's ideas and commitments makes clear, it is hard to overestimate the normative energy of their writings. They write in defense of their secular values with as much moral enthusiasm as their Puritan forebears wrote from their theological commitments. Meiklejohn's vision of moral unity, the idea that all knowledge is one, recalls Cardinal Newman's position, a position much easier to fit into Newman's Catholicism than into the secular perspectives of the modern research university. Meiklejohn also had a good sense of the weakness of Dewey's most sophisticated defense of the social engagement of the modern university. He shrewdly observes that the pragmatic desire to serve each student's personal interests, to discover and appeal to what they find relevant, leaves the teacher more concerned with teaching methods than with establishing the content that is required by all students: "Having nothing to teach, we have discussed chiefly methods of teaching."[87] When a focus on method replaces a focus on content, we are moving down the road to the science of administering education, rather than cultivating the humane art of teaching. First and foremost, Meiklejohn insists, we must instruct students not simply in what they find relevant or engages with their personal interests. We have an obligation to bring them the best and most important ideas available to us for the purpose of instructing them on their moral obligations and cultivating moral virtues among them.

Simply to raise the concern about "education to what end," however, raises an immediate objection: How can we take seriously any claim linking liberal to moral or civic education when the world is so clearly full of liberally educated individuals without any obvious moral virtues? Stanley Fish, to whom we will turn in chapter 4, claims that academic skills and moral capacities have no obvious relationship to one another, and when we reflect on the poor behavior of the liberally educated, we are likely to think this may be an understatement.[88] Citizens of my generation may recall that key architects of the morally and politically catastrophic U.S. war in Vietnam, Secretary of Defense Robert McNamara and Secretary of State Dean Rusk, both received excellent liberal educations (McNamara studied economics, mathematics, and philosophy at the University of California, Berkeley, and Rusk earned an appointment as a Rhodes Scholar at Oxford University on the strength of his undergraduate work at Davidson College; both men were members of Phi Beta Kappa, among the most prestigious achievements of the liberally educated). Contemporary citizens will certainly look at the cadre of powerful senators with Ivy League degrees and wonder how we could possibly believe that this education has been morally ennobling for them. Jason Brennan and Phillip Magness suggest that there "is little evidence higher education does much to foster students' moral virtue,"[89] and Daniel Cottom observes "how massively counterintuitive" any such expectation "must be to anyone who has ever spent any considerable period of time in the company of academics."[90] Addressing the incoming undergraduate class at the University of Chicago in 1997, political scientist John Mearsheimer raised a few academic eyebrows when he suggested that the university would not "provide you with moral guidance." Indeed, he claimed that the university is a "remarkably amoral institution," pursuing intellectual rather than moral education and purposes.[91] One is tempted to think this is as it should be, given our often appropriate democratic skepticism about elite professions of moral virtue: What are we to make of implications that a form of higher education pursued by only a minority of U.S. citizens would promote moral insight not available to the majority? At the very least, the claim of liberal education leading to virtue could offend our sense of civic equality unless and until we succeed in bringing this education to all. At its worst, the claim could feed populist fires of resentment toward higher education and the liberally educated. It is not a long step to take from observing the hypocrisy of claims to moral virtue to suggesting that the university is engaged in immoral and subversive activities and the indoctrination of our youth into unprincipled and un-American ideologies.[92]

Despite these obvious objections, however, claims about the morally ennobling qualities of liberal education appeared in its earliest defenses and are consistent elements in its promotion since that time. Aristotle assumed that such an education was essential for the responsible exercise of civic liberty. C. Wright Mills rightly observed that the "function of education as it was first set up in this country was political: to make citizens more knowledgeable and better thinkers."[93] It is true that this purpose shifted, over time, to economic concerns and job preparation, to "train people for better paying jobs."[94] The critical point is that most of what we think of as a broad, nonvocational education, which has played such a crucial role in the United States, was first justified primarily on the grounds of promoting skilled and responsible citizenship, and only later did our focus shift to that which is so common today, of promoting robust economic well-being. In fact, some of the educational thinkers from the founding era were so committed to civic education that they were less than fully committed to what we might think of as the liberal elements of an appropriate education. Benjamin Rush, for example, wrote, "Let our pupil be taught that he does not belong to himself, but that he is public property."[95] In chapter 1, we saw that the early colleges also thought of themselves in highly moralized terms; in the early years after its founding, Harvard graduates were referred to as the "Sons of the Prophets."[96] The provost of the College of Philadelphia (later the University of Pennsylvania) wrote that "Thinking, Writing and Acting Well . . . is the grand aim of a liberal education."[97] The colonial colleges were aimed at producing "Christian gentlemen" committed to "public service."[98] In the first century after the Revolution, the vision of Henry Tappan, the president of the University of Michigan, continued this commitment to the moral development of a social and political elite. The university, he claimed, would prepare "thoroughly-disciplined men to go forth into the world as ministers of truth and virtue."[99] Almost two centuries later, Ronald J. Daniels, president of Johns Hopkins University, suggests that universities today "can teach the art and science of citizenship," and are obligated to do so.[100] Such moral and civic ambitions are ever-present throughout the history of our higher education, from the colonies to the present.

The moralized justifications for the colonial and nineteenth-century college system are not surprising, as their primary purpose had grown from the need to supply clergy to the colonies and then to the new nation; of course, there would be a significant moral component to the training of this particular professional caste. Small wonder, we might say, that the Puritan colleges believed, in the language of a seventeenth-century text, that "the main end of [a student's] life and studies is, *to know God and Jesus Christ which is eternal life.*"[101] Although students from the colleges entered professions other than the ministry, such as law or commerce, the core of the classical training was aimed at the needs of the clergy above all others. The ancient literatures, from the Bible to the Greek and Roman classics, were studied for their spiritual and moral guidance. The classical training provided by the colleges allowed aspiring ministers to develop skills that were not just intrinsically valuable but critical for the study and reflection required by the professional life of parish ministers.

The modern university, with its scientific orientation and desire to be more integrally engaged with the economic and cultural life of our society than the colleges had been, found itself in need of justification as both an economically and ethically useful institution. We saw in chapter 2 that the modern university had to be sold to the public by the first generation of its leadership.[102] It did so by making higher education useful to the ends of the dynamic, technological, increasingly heterogeneous and capitalistic society. Rather than training a disciplined and pious clergy, as had been the focus in the nineteenth century and earlier, the task was now to develop a university system that would become a "powerful agent of social change in its own right."[103] It was not only in terms of economic utility, however, that the university justified its new role in society. It was also to serve what were taken to be the democratic values of this energetic and quickly changing society. The modern university would attend to the needs of democratic society through its engagement with all fields of learning and all professions, through the admission of students representing a broader swath of U.S. society than had been found in the colleges, and through the wide diffusion of knowledge throughout society.[104] Most importantly, the university would provide citizenship education and graduate alumni committed to work that would serve the public good.[105] The university aimed to become both economically and civically indispensable. The benefits of disinterested and scientifically informed management and administration would be brought to every corner of society by graduates of the university system. The university was promoted as an institution particularly well poised to promote virtuous citizenship and responsible democratic leadership.

It is within this context that Meiklejohn provides us with a clear and simple model for thinking about how modern liberal education should promote virtue among its students—by instructing them directly to this virtue. One is reminded of Catharine Beecher's demand that "the American people are to be educated *for their high duties*."[106] It is difficult, however, for us to take this demand entirely seriously. After all, such a demand assumes, in Meiklejohn's language, a "unity of knowledge," including moral knowledge; in Beecher's terms it assumes an ability to make a confident claim about the nature of our "high duties." All such moral certainty, however, challenges our recognition of the obvious moral pluralism within our society, even if we ignore the moral skepticism about the "truth" or "reality" of moral principles shared by many.

Yet, before we dismiss Meiklejohn's position out of hand, we need to recognize the degree to which it becomes more intuitive and attractive when we think less of Meiklejohn's specific moral theory than the moral theory that seemingly appeals to a broader sector of the academic universe. It was not at all unusual among college students of my generation, for example, to believe that if only we could teach people the truth about a particular matter, we could transform them from ignorant vice to informed virtue. Recall the roll of the "teach-in" during the Vietnam War and the civil rights movement, and of political movements (e.g., divestment from South

Africa, opposition to nuclear power and weapons) in the decades that followed. The assumption behind the model was simply that the truth about a
particular issue—the war, racial equity, environmental sustainability—was
not being made available to a sufficiently large civic audience. Presumably,
in the eyes of those organizing such teach-ins, if more people knew these
truths, it would be much more likely that broader swaths of the public
would change their opinions from counterproductive to productive, from
retrograde to just. Such an attitude has informed the creation of required
courses related to topics of significant public concern in many colleges and
universities: my own university, for example, requires students to take
coursework focused on matters relating to both social diversity and environmental sustainability. Although few of my faculty and administrative
colleagues would think of themselves as committed to the same high-
pitched Kantianism found in Meiklejohn's writings, significant numbers of
them believe we can at least hope for morally positive outcomes by exposing
students to such requirements. This is why, for example, activists will not infrequently demand "training" for faculty on matters such as racial or gender
and sexuality matters. Hope reigns supreme, it seems, that if we can simply
expose people to the right and the true, we will succeed in recruiting them
to these commitments. The assumption behind the hope is that unjust behavior grows less from interest and power than from ignorance, which will
be cured by exposure to the truth.

Aside from questions of naïveté related to this position, there are obvious dangers to thinking of the teaching of virtue in such a straightforward
manner. It assumes a kind of expertise on the part of the faculty that many
(including many of the faculty) will be skeptical of. To be an expert in an
academic discipline may require certain intellectual virtues of honesty and
industriousness, but it does not require a person be a paragon of the moral
or civic virtues more generally. Nor does it even require a certainty about
the moral lessons of what one studies. Honest scholars have, in fact, been
known to change their minds about such matters over time. Historians offer
new interpretations in light of new information, philosophers change their
minds and find opposing arguments more compelling than they previously
had, and literary scholars become more or less sympathetic to an author
they had felt quite differently about upon earlier readings. These are mundane realities for all scholars who spend their lives committed to study.

To assume deep and stable truths, including moral truths, that are available to scholars to convey directly to their students is likely to misunderstand the nature of scholarship.

This is not to deny the obvious, however, that expertise generates knowledge unavailable (by definition) to the inexpert, and that such expertise can significantly influence our normative perspectives. To use an example from our day, we are currently experiencing a populist resistance to a frank and honest reckoning with the realities of U.S. history. Serious and highly regarded historians offer differing, sometimes conflicting, interpretations of the past,[107] of course, but all serious scholars would recognize any attempt to remove or significantly diminish an understanding of, say, slavery, or the murder and forced migration of native peoples by European populations migrating to the Americas, as an attack on a true and justifiable understanding of the American historical experience. We can expect an honest historical accounting to challenge any simplistic heroic or hagiographic historical narratives, and it is axiomatic to the scholarly enterprise that teachers must provide a truthful account of their subject to their students. This may not assure morally appropriate or praiseworthy responses to this knowledge by students, but it will certainly serve to mitigate the effect of false or radically incomplete narratives to support specious moral arguments. We have good reason to be wary of any overly aggressive defense of the normative value of scholarly expertise, but we also have reason to value it with some modesty and care. Any justifiable moral account of our obligations and options in public policy, we might say, must take place within the parameters of historical and sociological realities. The fact that some of these realities disturb us or suggest the injustice of certain contemporary institutions or civic relationships speaks to the power of truth and the need to do all we can to be honest about it. To resist the truth because it calls into question certain privileges or realities we would prefer not to question speaks more to a political problem than an ethical problem for liberal education. The educator's obligation is to teach the truth as accurately as she or he knows how. It is at least imaginable that exposure to some such truths will have normative constraints on student opinions.

In this way, we can hold out a somewhat limited hope for what we might call the "didactic" model of promoting virtue. Yet, we are rightly skeptical about simply explaining the moral virtues to students and demanding, as a condition of academic success, that they adopt and embrace them. What could possibly make us think that they would respond well to such demands in the first place?[108] We might expect such a program to produce dishonest responses by students who simply convey to their teachers what they believe they expect, all the while growing cynical about the entire educational project. However, we can expect that students' moral sensibilities could and perhaps should be shaped to some significant degree by their increasingly sophisticated understanding of the nature of the world around them. The moral content of this shaping is clearly less precise and exact than a more obviously didactic approach (along the lines seemingly promoted by Meiklejohn) would aspire to, but it should be significant nonetheless. There is no assurance that students will become either more "liberal" or "conservative" in conventional political terms because of this experience. We can hope, however, that regardless of their ultimate moral judgments, students' understanding of their moral and political values will be both more sophisticated and morally defensible than they would have been without a liberal education.

I suggested above that a danger of this understanding of how liberal education can promote virtue is that it can be viewed as arrogant and undemocratic, especially outside the academy. It is well known that the professoriate skews liberal and Democratic, and Republicans have become increasingly vociferous in their attacks on what they take to be the liberal bias at the heart of higher education, especially in the humanities and social sciences. The core of liberal education, simply, is accused of being politically partisan. The charge is that the academy uses its position as gatekeeper for elite positions in society to indoctrinate those who will wield power with opinions and values that run counter to the sensibilities of the public at large. The attack on the academy, for example, by Governor Ron DeSantis in Florida, is an attack on what is taken to be the unvarnished contempt of an undemocratic academic elite for what is best and most valuable in U.S. society. This culture war represents an attack both on the idea of expertise[109] and on what is taken to be the corrupt politics of experts. The political effectiveness of the attack illustrates a structural problem for liberal education in a democratic society. The liberal academy provides a place for study and reflection beyond what is found in the daily affairs and spaces of democratic civil society. As such, it is always in danger of promoting thoughts, findings, arguments that challenge common sense and conventional wisdom. In moments of great populist distrust and conspiracy paranoia, it is not surprising that the academy, to the degree that it represents free inquiry, can be perceived as an insult to democracy. Even the sciences are not exempt here, insofar as they uncover evidence to suggest that the free behaviors of individuals in society may in fact be destructive or counterproductive. Climate scientists can attest to the degree that they are viewed with (at best) suspicion in many corners (especially conservative and Republican) of society.

At moments like this, claims that liberal education will speak truth to ignorance can seem to throw fuel on an already brightly burning fire. It takes a great deal of "social capital," or trust, among citizens of different perspectives and belief systems to listen to even expert claims when what is being claimed is that what we believe to be right and good may in fact be wrong and bad. To defend liberal education on the grounds that it promotes virtue by a class of highly trained professors who will enlighten the benighted many is, of course, a recipe for exacerbating rather than overcoming distrust. Even so, there is a modest sense in which it may in fact be true that virtue is promoted when students and teachers interact in a healthy educational environment. In that case, climate scientists will help their students understand the truth about our changing environment, just as historians will help them understand the truth about the complexities of our nation's history. In both of these cases, and an infinity of others, a fruitful educational context will almost certainly shape not only students' understandings of the nature of the (natural and social) world but will likely shape their normative understanding of their relationship to it. To the degree that liberal education takes place, it is hard to imagine that it won't have at least some moral content or influence. The truth as we see it will inevitably shape our values, at least to some degree.

This is not to say that the way this shaping takes place is predictable in any exact sense. On the contrary, education to the nature of things, to the truths about the world we inhabit, will only shape moral sensibilities within broad parameters. And, in fact, we know that a certain degree of success in our education can lead to quite unpredictable, or at least unpredicted, outcomes. Recall the promotion of "general education" by the report of the Harvard Committee of 1945. In *General Education in a Free Society*, the committee recommended a broad liberal education, including exposure to a set of "great books" in the Western tradition. They argued that such an education would promote a set of "traits of mind," including the ability "*to think effectively, to communicate thought, to make relevant judgments, to discrimi-nate among values.*"[110] We noted in chapter 1 that "one of the aims of edu-cation is to break the stranglehold of the present upon the mind,"[111] and to promote "responsible private judgement."[112] It is clear, they suggest, that it is "impossible . . . to separate effective thinking from character," and therefore that general (liberal) education in both the secondary school and the college should be "oriented toward moral character."[113] Above all, the greatest moral aim of the Harvard Committee was to promote among students "a unifying purpose and idea," an "enlargement of the common concern," which is "in-deed the distinctive character of our age."[114] Students should be exposed to a canon of works that can be thought of as constituting a core set of histori-cally influential texts from which modern liberal democracy evolved and which are reflected within the practices of free government. The Harvard Committee report hoped general or liberal education would strengthen lib-eral democracy in the face of aggression by communist totalitarianism. General education, they held, should promote a deep understanding of the intellectual roots of free government, thereby promoting a bond of shared commitments among the country's citizens.

The cultural education envisioned by the Harvard Committee (and the Truman Commission soon thereafter), and widely adapted in the postwar period, did not produce the kind of calm and determined solidarity its pro-moters had in mind. On the contrary, when the students became restless and rebellious in the 1960s, it was at least in part a response to the hypocrisy of society when seen from the perspectives of our founding ideals (consider both the deep inequalities built into our domestic racial heritage and our imperial actions abroad), and from the "provincialism" of viewing our own tradition as somehow morally privileged over all others. The general edu-cation cultivated after World War II had important effects on the student bodies of the 1950s and 60s, but these effects sometimes encouraged more rebelliousness than solidarity.[115] This certainly looked like a perverse out-come to many (recall the outrage of Bloom's evaluation of the students at Cornell in the 1960s in *The Closing of the American Mind*), even if to others re-bellious students represented a moral awakening of the nation's conscience (contrast Bloom's screed with Herbert Marcuse's praise for the student rebels in *An Essay on Liberation*). The point is simply that the kind of moral out-comes liberal education may produce are not necessarily what a teacher has in mind. This is actually as it should be, given that we are educating for freedom.

The lessons will be learned and applied by free individuals, making their own choices rather than mimicking the choices of their teachers. Even when these choices seem perverse, they may, in fact, reflect a much greater virtue than the teachers themselves recognize. To attempt to produce a more controlled and predictable outcome would require teachers to become didacts. Instructing students in the specific and particular moral lesson of this broader education would be to move in a direction both less morally defensible and less likely to be effective.

The ideal of liberal education we find in Meiklejohn's early writings is one in which the Protestant theology of the liberal education found in the colleges in the nineteenth century and earlier was replaced by Kantian philosophy and ethics. This move is less objectionable than we might at first think, when we consider various ways we do expect disciplinary information to influence the moral development of students in liberal arts programs. Yet, insofar as this approach promotes the didactic presentation of a moral perspective as the perspective to be adopted by the student, this approach is objectionable beyond the concern that the lessons being taught may be rejected by significant portions of the democratic citizenry. Populist anger alone doesn't seal the case against it; it is certainly to be expected that liberal education may promote ideas and perspectives contrary to the common sense of some significant element of public opinion, and, in many cases, this may be a good thing not just for the student but for public opinion. The stronger objection is that we might contend that such a didactic education is not liberal in the first place. If the goal is to promote students' freedom, the task is to give them resources to help them develop their own defensible moral judgments. The point isn't to tell them what to think, but rather to help them to think well and responsibly.[116] Meiklejohn and Hutchins were often in danger of promoting didacticism. Despite this, the kernel of a defensible view of how liberal education, properly understood, is related to the promotion of virtue is found in the tradition they helped pioneer.

███ A general objection we encounter to the perspective I'm defending is that it is simply too promiscuous to be helpful. Some will think that by opening liberal education to a plurality of cultural and normative traditions, the student is left with no significant grounding in any of them.[117] Others will worry that such an approach threatens to treat all traditions or perspectives as equivalent, opening the door to a vacuous and dangerous relativism.

Regarding the first objection, Patrick Deneen claims that liberal education, as understood and practiced in the academy today, is incapable of promoting the qualities of character required by free, self-governing individuals. Deneen holds that liberalism has failed as a public philosophy because it promises to release individuals from all constraints; it teaches us, he believes, that such a release is the very meaning of liberty. Liberal political theory assumes we are born free and that the demands of community life are a limitation on, even a threat to, our freedom. Individuals struggling to assert their freedom will naturally be in conflict with collective needs and goods, and the good society is one in which as much of this natural freedom as possible is secured for individuals against the imperious claims of society. For Deneen, this liberal view fails for at least two reasons. First, it simply misunderstands the nature of human freedom. Rather than an escape from external demands, freedom requires the acceptance of the limits imposed by a tradition: "Above all, liberal education [in classical political thought] did not so much 'liberate' students from the limits of their backgrounds as it reinforced a basic teaching embedded deeply within their own cultural tradition, namely an education in limits."[118] One cannot be meaningfully free alone, because we are utterly dependent upon the web of human connections required to not only sustain our lives but also for any significant human flourishing. Meaningful freedom can only be developed within the context of a living community: "The one thing needful in our time—an education in self-restraint, limits and tradition, the lessons our colleges and universities were designed to reinforce—is the one thing that our great universities are no longer well-designed to provide since our elders generally agree such an education is undesirable."[119] Only when individuals learn to embrace a rich communal tradition will they find the opportunity for the free and responsible release of their creative energies. To learn civic freedom, to become a freely contributing member of a community, one must first learn to suppress one's "natural" inclination to satisfy impulse. Impulsive desire, after all, is not itself freely chosen. Only when we understand the richness of our life as constituted by the submission to the requirements of a community will we be able to freely contribute to our world. Freedom comes from submitting to the limits of community, and then embracing and contributing to that community. Liberalism, in Deneen's view, profoundly distorts this truth about human freedom.

The second failure of liberalism grows from the first: when a group within society seeks its liberation as a lack of restraint, it turns individuals in this group into tyrants who view the rest of the world, including other people, as objects to be used for their own purposes and pleasures. Such a perspective may allow a certain class of individuals an unrestrained life, but this will invariably come at the cost of freedom to others: "We can either elect a future of self-limitation born of the practice and experience of self-governance in local communities, or we can back inexorably into a future in which extreme license coexists with extreme oppression."[120] Deneen's point is similar to Thoreau's observation that the "luxury of one class is counterbalanced by the indigence of another."[121] Deneen writes, for example, that in elite colleges, children of privilege learn "how to engage in 'safe sex,' recreational alcohol and drug use, transgressive identities, cultural self-loathing, how to ostensibly flaunt traditional instructions without bucking the system—all preparatory to a life lived in a few global cities in which the 'culture' comes to mean expensive and exclusive consumption goods, and not the shaping environment that governs the ambitious and settled alike."[122] It is precisely the norms of traditional communities that this environment attacks, nurturing an elite who will be unconstrained by such norms and protected by their wealth and social power as they indulge, as a matter of professed right, their desires. All the while, less privileged individuals are not only insulted by such attacks on the religious and cultural values they hold dear, but they are also significantly more vulnerable to personal calamity if they reject these values, as elites encourage them to, because their lack of wealth and social standing will never protect them from the consequences of irresponsibility the way elites and their children are protected.

The ideal of progress that informs the modern university, for Deneen, is an ideal of ever-increasing wealth, safety, and liberation from responsibility and accountability. Self-invention and consumer satisfaction fuel the elite attack on the cultural systems that shape and give meaning to the vast majority of nonelite citizens: "Thus, universities are among the primary places where a pervasive commitment to *progress* means that existing social institutions must also be constantly upended, transformed, changed, and altered in line with the fundamental aim of progress."[123] If Deneen's first point is that liberal education as currently understood in liberal society promotes a flawed understanding of liberty, his second elaborates on the destructive power of such a mistake. This is not a threat merely to the well-being of individuals but an assault on the structures and values of communal life that allow for the very possibility of a responsible and rewarding liberty. Deneen rehearses the right-wing populist attack on multiculturalism and identity politics as decadent and self-serving assaults on "any shared understanding of justice as a constraint upon tyrannical power" and "the assertion of the priority of individual and group experience of offense, harm, and injury as the criterion for assessing how to allocate political power and resources."[124] The crucial point for us is simply that he gives reasons to think that a broad cosmopolitan liberal education would defeat the possibility of being educated into a *particular* cultural practice. Released from the constraints of such practices, liberal education unleashes elitist attacks on all that might constrain such destructive arrogance and selfishness.

Deneen's critique of liberalism includes a great deal of caricature and polemic (one senses not so much that liberalism has no virtues, but that Deneen has significant hostility toward the liberal virtues of toleration and respect for plurality). He is right, however, that liberalism, to the degree that it pursues liberal education, *does* place traditional forms of authority in jeopardy. There is simply no way around this, and it is important to be clear and honest about it. When liberal education promotes exposure to a wide array of ideas and values, it puts every established order in jeopardy. How could it be otherwise? In chapter 1, I noted the modern Greek dictator Ioannis Metaxas's demand that no student governed by his regime should have ideas contrary to those promoted by the state.[125] Deneen would rightly object that he is not promoting the kind of statism that Metaxas is promoting, but instead envisions a more decentralized (and in his view, democratic) localism.[126] The point, however, remains: if we take Socrates as the guiding founder of liberal education, we must recognize that there is inevitably a disruptive and even a radical potential to the philosophical project. There is simply no denying that it places opinion and convention under scrutiny. There will be those who will be led, such as Michael Oakeshott, to conservative conclusions from exposure to this project. Others, such as the liberal democratic theorist Danielle Allen, will be led to quite different conclusions.

The farmer, poet, and conservationist Wendell Berry, with Deneen, objects to the way contemporary education undermines local communities. Berry suggests that our schools serve the economy promoted by our government, rather than our communities, by encouraging students to leave home and pursue careers in the broader (usually urban) society: "The local schools no longer serve the local community; they serve the government's economy and the economy's government. . . . Our children are educated . . . to leave home, not to stay home."[127] As an essayist, Berry's claim is powerful and punchy, a rhetorical plea to educate students for return to their local communities rather than to prepare them for careers in the broader capitalist economy. As a novelist, however, Berry presents a more subtle view. Hannah Coulter, the remarkable protagonist of a novel by that title, reflects on the fact that her children grew up and left the land they were raised on: "We wanted them to have all the education they needed or wanted, and yet hovering over that thought always was the possibility that once they were educated they would go away, which, as it turned out, they did. We owed them that choice, and we gave it to them, and it might be hard to argue that we were wrong. But I wonder now, and I wonder it many a time, if the other choice, the choice of coming home, might not have been made clearer."[128]

People sometimes leave home, of course, for completely selfish and morally compromised reasons. They also sometimes leave their homes and traditional communities for completely responsible, even admirable reasons: to become teachers or artists or scientists or civil servants; to marry and share their lives with the person they love; because they are committed to their crafts and professions that take them elsewhere. When we educate our children liberally, we open up a world of possibilities beyond the horizon of the local, no matter how much this distresses us, and there is a chance that free individuals will chose to live in a place and a manner different from what they experienced in their childhood. Perhaps Hannah Coulter could have made the opportunity for return clearer to her children. But she admits that she was not wrong to allow them an education to a world beyond the local and conventional. For all the disturbing bluster and polemic of Deneen's attack on liberal education (e.g., students are currently taught "cultural self-loathing" in college), he is right that liberal education as it is currently practiced is potentially disruptive. But this is not because it is a perversion of liberal education; his criticism is true to the degree that we honor liberal education. Such an education is not inevitably disrespectful of traditional communities, but it does promote moral inquisitiveness about all communities, cultures, and points of view. To probe is not to reject, but it does make rejection a possibility (and even a moral requirement, of course, in certain circumstances). Deneen's understanding of liberal education significantly distorts the critical power of this form of education not only as it is understood in our contemporary society but as it was born in the Socratic tradition 2,500 years ago. Socrates chose, even at the cost of his life, to remain in Athens (he had the opportunity to escape prison with support from his students and admirers). He did so, however, as a "gadfly" who enraged a significant number of his fellow citizens, who viewed him as corrupting and impious. One can hear echoes of these citizens in Deneen's charge that universities teach students to hate their own cultural inheritance.

In addition, the world as we experience it today is so interconnected that it would be irresponsible to focus a liberal education only on national or Western culture. How can we expect our own citizens today to be responsible if they know nothing about Islam, or about contemporary China, or about the effect of climate change on the political stability of the developing world? We can't any longer, in good faith, prevent a student from being exposed to a broad array of views and perspectives. We may prefer to live in a world less connected to such a diversity of cultures and perspectives, but that is not our world or the world our children will have to negotiate as informedly and rationally as possible. Contrary to critics such as Deneen, a liberal education appears to be necessarily a cosmopolitan education. Again, such an education does not guarantee the efficient or effective socialization of students into a rich local cultural tradition, and may, in fact, destabilize such traditions. This would appear, however, to be the consequence of the liberty of those liberally educated to self-rule, rather than a pandering to a desire to escape limitations and restraints on impulse and self-interest. We may hope our children choose to return to the life we raise them to, but the danger of a free education and a free society is simply that they may choose otherwise, and for good reasons. This is a very real burden that any free generation bears in relation to the next.

Finally, there is the concern that a liberal education committed to exposing students to a wide variety of ideals and traditions is likely to stimulate moral relativism. It is not unimaginable that students may reach the conclusion that since the world is full of many ideas, many of which have articulate defenders, many of which have large numbers of adherents, that it is impossible (and perhaps even unacceptably intolerant) to make significant moral distinctions between or judgments about them.[129] Such an outcome, of course, would undermine the fundamental project of liberal education by devaluing reason as a powerful force and leaving us with nothing but power to mediate moral disagreements. Wendy Brown has recently asserted, regarding this concern, that "tolerating all viewpoints" in the classroom is a mistake.[130] This is almost certainly correct, but it is difficult (and Brown offers no guidance here) to know how to draw the line between views to be scrutinized and those to be rejected as unworthy of consideration. Clearly, standards of moral defensibility are insufficient for generating this distinction: Carl Schmitt was an unrepentant Nazi who continues to be studied and discussed in university courses today; the final passages of Marx's "On the Jewish Question," to say nothing of Nietzsche's *Genealogy of Morals*, traffic in the ugliest anti-Semitic stereotypes and caricatures. In fact, appalling political ideas are as abundant in both the present and the past as are appalling politics, and the student of political thought is necessarily awash in them. Many of us believe, nonetheless, that we must teach Nietzsche and Marx and Schmitt not despite the variety of their views, but precisely because of this variety. Texts for liberal study must be selected not only for the cogence or attractiveness of their arguments but also for their historical importance. By exposing students to a tradition of ideas, without didactically promoting one over others, the teacher seems to be attending to the obligations of liberal learning. They must also be helping students to evaluate and make judgments about these ideas as reasonably and responsibly as possible.

■■■■ The hope of promoting virtue through the practice of liberal education is a hope with a paradoxical character. Training students for careers is clearly not all we wish for from such an education; we also want to educate good citizens, free and responsible members of a democratic political order. The temptation, of course, is to teach this goodness directly, which undermines the project (or at least threatens to undermine it) from the start. Instead, I have suggested exposing students to significant cultural and intellectual traditions, and giving them the intellectual tools to confront, imagine, and to evaluate these materials. If we successfully build a "moat between academic and political life," as Wendy Brown sensibly recommends,[131] we are left primarily with the project of teaching students to read carefully, sympathetically, yet thoughtfully and responsibly. Our goal will be for them to become as "philosophical," broadly understood, as we can encourage, model, and teach them to be.

Will such an education produce virtuous citizens? There is no assurance whatsoever that it will. We can reasonably hope, however, with John Agresto, that such an education will make it less likely that students will be moved by demagogues or "ruled by slogans or unexamined opinion" in the future.[132] Presumably a good liberal education will teach them to distinguish between what is reasonable and what is rot.[133] We may even hope that it makes students take their moral and civic obligations seriously, that it makes them not only law-abiding but engaged and responsible citizens. We may hope that it imparts at least a modicum of virtue.

It is reasonable to aspire to such, to hope that this could be the case in a significant sense. We must also recognize, however, that the very possibility of stimulating virtue generates the opposite possibility. Heaven knows that our public life is today populated by a fair number of individuals with exceptional liberal educations who have turned their intelligence and knowledge to work for less than virtuous purposes and in less than admirable ways. Cynicism and demagoguery may grow among the liberally educated, just as virtue and responsibility may. There is no assurance that one will be produced rather than the other. Such is the nature of freedom: it doesn't guarantee wise or ethical behavior among the free. Yet, despite this, liberal education is not only compatible with, but perhaps even required by, a free citizenry. It is also an educational tradition that has a particularly deep relationship to the growth of liberal democracy in the United States. In the final analysis, this commitment is both required by a free political order and built upon a democratic hope and faith rather than a science of pedagogy. There are no certainties here, but this is the only educational option compatible with civic freedom and personal responsibility. The temptation to impose a political outcome on the educational process is a temptation to violate the liberty informing the system in the first place. We can't teach virtue, but we can hope for it and encourage it. That's pretty much all we've got.

FOUR

Delight

We saw in chapter 2 that despite legitimate concerns regarding the contribution of liberal education to the vocational opportunities for and skills required by students, this alone was an insufficient set of purposes to fully guide our understanding of what a liberal education should look like. It turns out that focusing on the civic potential for liberal education likewise appears to be an incomplete goal, even when combined with vocational elements, of all that we would hope for from a liberal education. A free individual must be able to care for herself economically, and must be aware of her social relationships, duties, and obligations. But there appears to be one more key element to becoming a fully free individual.

Consider the opening paragraph of Plato's *Apology*. This, according to Plato, is how Socrates opens his response to the prosecution, which had already addressed the jury. It will be helpful to see the comment in full:

> I do not know what effect my accusers have had upon you, gentlemen, but for my own part I was almost carried away by them; their arguments were so convincing. On the other hand, scarcely a word of what they said was true. I was especially astonished at one of their many misrepresentations: I mean when they told you that you must be careful not to let me deceive you—the implication being that I am a skillful speaker. I thought that it was particularly brazen of them to tell you this without a blush, since they must know that they will soon be effectively confuted, when it becomes obvious that I have not the slightest skill as

a speaker—unless, of course, by a skillful speaker they mean one who speaks the truth. If that is what they mean, I would agree that I am an orator, though not after their pattern.[1]

Socrates's irony is designed to illustrate the difference between himself and his accusers. They use words effectively but falsely. In contrast, he claims that he will use words truthfully. Both usages require skill, but his is of a different nature than the skill of those who spoke before him. Socrates's contrast, however, is not simply between lying and telling the truth, even though, of course, it does include that. In addition, he is drawing our attention to a contrast between two different activities, philosophy and politics. Soon after these opening comments, he notes that "this is my first appearance in a court of law, at the age of seventy; and so I am a complete stranger to the language of this place."[2] He makes clear during the course of his "apology," in fact, that it is political life as a whole that he has refrained from, and not only the world of the law courts.[3] The rhetoric of public life is designed to persuade by appealing to an audience's passions. The language of philosophy appeals only to reason, Socrates is suggesting, and is designed to convince, we might say, but not persuade—if by convincing we mean appealing to reason, and by persuasion we mean appeal to emotion. Public life is driven by the interests, and therefore the passions or desires, of citizens. Public speech is designed to disguise naked self-interest by flattering and appealing to the interests of the audience. Philosophy, in contrast, appeals to what is true, to the degree that it can, regardless of the interests involved.

Socrates explains why so many prominent and respectable Athenians have grown to hate him over time. The actual charges against him, that he is guilty both of impiety and of corrupting the young, are, he contends, very weak and almost thoughtless claims. What is really at work, he believes, is a hostility that has grown as he has encouraged his fellow citizens to think more about what is just and true rather than how to pursue their own material interests. How could it be that the accusers are persuasive even though they are telling untruths? Because they have appealed to the bias against and hostility toward Socrates. They were doing what politicians do routinely: whipping up the crowd by telling them what they want to hear. The audacity of Socrates's claim in the opening paragraph of the *Apology* grows from an observation that is actually all too common and obviously true: that political rhetoric is not often distinguished by its direct and clear appeal to the truth. Even the flip side of this observation, that there is a recognizable, even demonstrable, truth that is often different from the claims being made in public life, is a commonplace. Anyone who has ever taken an "effective public speaking" course or listened to a debate knows that the techniques of persuasion are far less concerned with calm and dispassionate explanations than with appealing to the broader psychology, the loves and the hates, of audiences. What could be more obvious in our own political moment, when a postmodern appeal to "alternative facts" has done nothing to diminish the appeal of rhetorically skilled and audacious politicians? Truth is less persuasive, less interesting, in fact, than the stoking of biases and hatreds.[4] Even in calmer political moments we have understood the need to beware of the power of rhetoric to hide unspoken interests. We do not need to be persuaded that Socrates is committed to the truth over rhetorical persuasion (not all readers find Socrates as trustworthy as others do) to recognize the plausibility, even the commonplace nature, of the distinction he is making.

We should also note that the distinction leads to another distinction relevant to educational philosophy: Is our intention to teach people the skills required for worldly success, or is our intention to encourage a commitment to truth? If the former, we would want to teach students to use language (in our case, both written and oral) effectively, to speak and write clearly and persuasively. If the latter, we would be more concerned with what it is that the student hopes to communicate, the moral content of their commitments and ambitions. The professional teachers in Socrates's world were called "sophists," and they taught the male children of citizens the skills they would need to be successful in Athenian public life. Socrates, as portrayed by Plato, was at pains to distinguish his own philosophical instruction from sophistic instruction: he denied that he was simply teaching skills for success, and instead claimed to be guiding fellow seekers in the pursuit of what is good and true. His own view was that a purely sophistic approach to education was akin to giving people the skills to do both good and evil, without encouraging them to be good.

It is not surprising, then, that it is within a Platonic dialogue named for a famous sophist, Gorgias, where Socrates develops the distinction between philosophical and political values. The climactic exchanges here are between Callicles (an ambitious and talented young man) and Socrates. Callicles defends the conventional view that power is good in itself, and that political skills such as oratory must be developed if one is to become adept at gaining and exploiting power. Socrates defends a philosophical life of self-discipline. Each claims his own methods will lead to the free and happy life. Callicles suggests that the man with great political skill will be able to satisfy his great appetites; Socrates suggests that only the orderly and disciplined individual is free. Callicles aggressively defends power as the means by which an individual can "do what he wants," and he thinks Socrates's position implies that corpses and stones would be the happiest beings since they were never tormented by desire.[5] Socrates's answer to Callicles is that a person who simply submits to his desires is not a free person. This is the key point for our purposes. Socrates's claim is that to be driven by appetite puts us at the mercy of chance, at the mercy of whatever appetites we happen to have. He had early in the dialogue suggested, to the incredulity of his audience, that a tyrant was the least, rather than the most, powerful individual in a city. His point is that a tyrant is not in control of his own desires and finds himself enslaved to impulse. This makes him need to control those around him, so it continually makes him vulnerable and dependent. Socrates is arguing that only those who have reflected on what they want, rather than simply submitting to their impulsive desires, are the individuals in control of their lives. Only such individuals, we might think, are free.

If Socrates is right in his exchange with Callicles and others, a complete and liberal education, an education designed to make us free, cannot ignore philosophical concerns, broadly understood. It is not enough to be trained for work, no matter how essential economic independence is to our freedom. Nor is it sufficient to teach us our proper relations and obligations to others since our civic world is always touched by injustice and self-interest (Aristotle, Plato's student, famously noted that there is a distinction between being a good individual and being a good citizen[6]). In addition, individuals appear to require some instruction in philosophy, guided reflection on the truths that allow them to live free and satisfying lives. How else would we be able to distinguish between desirable and undesirable wants? Between impulses we should suppress and those we can (and perhaps should) rightly indulge? A free person must have some preparation for thinking seriously about what they should pursue, both for the sake of their own happiness and for the sake of justice to others. Most importantly, without such knowledge, one will not be fully autonomous, fully self-determining, fully free.

I have noted already a modern perspective, building on the legacy of Francis Bacon, that thinks of knowledge as a source of power. We might say that the entire modern scientific and technological project has grown from this commitment and has produced a singularly explosive development of "applied" knowledge. This activity stands in contrast with more contemplative (and distinctively premodern) forms of speculation. In this Baconian sense, the American pragmatic focus has been on addressing what John Dewey called the "problems of men."

There are three objections that the Socratic tradition can raise to this modern, and very American, sensibility. The first concerns the narrowness of the conception of "problems" and "usefulness" that is associated with the tradition. We might accuse pragmatists such as Dewey of discounting cultural and intellectual traditions that address what we can think of as "existential" or universal human problems, those anxieties and confusions and investigations that arise not from the particular moment in which we happen to live, but from the basic facts of human life that confront all individuals, one way or another, across time and place—problems about meaning, about love, about death, about the unseen, about human purposes.[7]

A second possible objection is simply that this tradition takes its philosophical commitments for granted, rather than reflecting on them and subjecting them to investigation. Quite simply, the Baconian perspective simply assumes our wants and desires and sets to work on satisfying them. We might think, however, for reasons already suggested, that these wants and desires themselves require scrutiny. There is a modern tendency to reduce all value to utility of the simplest and most obvious kind. To do this, however, is to beg the philosophical question: When is utility the proper moral standard, and when are there other considerations to be taken into account? To take our values for granted is to fall victim to precisely the kind of unconsidered life and action that a free individual aims to avoid.

A third possible objection concerns the possibility that some knowledge is valuable as such, that it supplies its own delights and should be made available to each generation not only as a source of power and freedom but as a source of pleasure (or comfort or satisfaction) in and of itself. The word "philosophy" (*philos* + *sophia*) means "love of wisdom," and suggests one is drawn toward it not for its usefulness but because it provides its own gratifications and is a source of delight. A more democratic sensibility than Plato's might contend that such a love, and the pleasures that grow from it, are widely sought by the many, by average people. The historian Carl Becker disagreed, as did Plato, once dryly commenting that the "average man does not hunger and thirst after knowledge any more than after righteousness."[8] Contra Becker, we might think that the evidence suggests that people delight in both "aesthetic" and "philosophical" experiences, where they are moved by art (painting, sculpture, music, film, literature) and by understanding something about the world that had previously puzzled or confused them. Think of the delight we express to others when we tell them how we love a song or a story. In this common, almost daily experience, we express the intrinsic pleasure of the arts.[9] Think, also, of even wildly untrue popular beliefs, such as today's political conspiracy theories. As wrongheaded as these may be, they nonetheless express a strong desire on the part of everyday people to explain and understand a world that otherwise appears deeply mysterious and confusing. Becker's cynicism would seem to take aim more appropriately at the content of popular belief than the very widespread desire to understand, a desire strong enough to make men and women grasp at straws. The problem, from this perspective, is less one of character (that is, an indifference toward understanding) than of education (that is, that many people understand very poorly and unskillfully).

If any of these concerns about the Baconian preoccupation of contemporary education are persuasive, a complete liberal education will require not merely vocational and civic components, but more broadly cultural and philosophical elements, encompassing the full range of arts, humanities, and sciences. This is necessary in part because civic and vocational commitments raise deeper philosophical commitments that can't be wished away. It is also necessary because learning can provide its own satisfactions to individuals beyond the social benefits we also seek.

████ Liberal education as a good in itself has always been a hard sell in the modern university, with its commitments to economic and civic goods.[10] For Dewey, such an appeal was simply decadent, promoting the pastimes of an exploitative leisure class. Recall economist Harry Gideonse from chapter 2, one of Robert Hutchins's faculty members at the University of Chicago (soon to move on to the presidency of Brooklyn College, and eventually to the chancellorship at the New School for Social Research), and how he captured the Deweyan ethos of the time by writing (against Hutchins) that universities "must seek to train men who will use learning in the service of the society about them," and that university curricula must be developed to include only what has "significance for living in our society."[11] There were dissenters, such as Thorstein Veblen, who argued that the university, properly understood, was "a seat of learning devoted to the cult of idle curiosity."[12] Veblen, in fact, believed universities were being corrupted by the "enemies of learning," surrendered to commercial and utilitarian concerns deeply at odds with the true nature of scholarship.[13] In contrast to "captains of industry," he promoted "captains of erudition" and a devotion to "a disinterested pursuit of knowledge."[14] For all the genius and flair of his indictment of the direction being taken by contemporary university presidents, the powers behind these new and growing institutions, Veblen's was a voice in the wilderness.[15] Today, in a significantly less polemical tone than Veblen's, Danielle Allen suggests that there are "eudaemonistic" goods (having to do with human flourishing), along with utilitarian goods, to be gained by a proper education, and the former include intrinsic pleasures and happiness that can grow from increased knowledge and understanding. Her primary focus is on the goods of civic life, but she nonetheless is sensitive to the full breadth of human flourishing that includes preparation for not only public but also for private life.[16] Gideonse's comments are much more representative of the ethos of the university in the United States in its first generation or two, just as the promotion of vocational and civic goods are today much more common than is an emphasis on the purely intellectual, philosophical, or aesthetic values of liberal learning.[17]

Among those who value what we might think of as the philosophical, and not just the utilitarian or civic, elements in a sufficient liberal education, it is common to think of these intellectual values as being in opposition to the values and sensibilities of democratic society. Advocates for this more philosophical content in liberal education, in all honesty, often view such goods as significantly threatened by, or at the very least not related to, democratic values. Veblen certainly thought capitalist society was a threat to the academy, and others share his desire to insulate and protect the academy from such popular influences. It is perhaps not surprising that one of the most articulate recent defenders of a purely intellectual liberal learning is an influential Englishman, Michael Oakeshott, rather than an American.

Oakeshott has nothing but contempt for the practical and utilitarian emphasis of the modern university (and modern society as a whole): "This world has but one language, soon learned: the language of appetite."[18] Bacon may have inspired much of what we think of as a modern university, but he has done so by destroying the actual purpose of liberal learning and replacing it with an apprenticeship to "domestic, industrial and commercial life."[19] An "engaged" or "relevant" university is one that has given up its true mission by simply "satisfying the contingent wants" generated by this society.[20] Learning, in this context, is reduced to "socialization" into, or a "recognition" of, the society around us.[21] The modern university is under assault by "men who are convinced only that 'knowledge is power.'"[22] Such universities serve the powers that be, rather than cultivating the means to judge and evaluate these powers.

A true university must be set apart from "the tyranny of the moment and from the servitude of a merely current condition."[23] The world around us is very powerful, "wealthy, interfering and well-meaning. But it is not remarkably self-critical; it is apt to mistake itself for the whole world."[24] This is the crux of the matter: when our education serves the forces in control of the contemporary world, it loses its liberal qualities, its commitment to cultivating individual freedom. Such freedom comes from independent judgment, not from understanding how to function satisfactorily in the current society, which requires only conformity and successful "socialization." Judgment requires a certain distance from the demands and sensibilities of the given world: "It has nothing to do with organic survival and much of it has little to do even with that selective 'getting on in the world' which is the human counterpart of organic homeostasis."[25] Rather, it is concerned with "adventures in human self-understanding."[26] These adventures require "conversational encounter" with "culture," or what "men from time to time, have made of this engagement of learning to be a man."[27] Liberal learning is learning to understand and perhaps even participate in a conversation that transcends a particular moment, a conversation that reflects on the human condition from a wide variety of times, places, and perspectives. Only this learning creates the possibility of free judgment, since only this learning gives us a range of human possibilities that true judgment requires. In Oakeshott's language, liberal studies in a university provide a student with "the gift of an interval" in which she or he may reflect not just on how to make a living but how to live a "more significant life."[28]

Oakeshott's views remind us of the Platonic theme of hostility, or at least tension, between this most philosophical understanding of liberal learning, on the one hand, and democratic commitments and sensibilities, on the other. There is nothing in Oakeshott's views that exclude egalitarian opportunities for pursuing the intellectual education he champions, just as we find in Plato's *Republic* a recognition that children within the laboring classes may occasionally be born with the disposition to receive a philosophical education and must therefore be provided with one out of respect for the natural order. That is to say that there is nothing in Oakeshott's views to suggest any hostility toward what we today call "meritocracy." His views do suggest, however, that democratic culture is itself hostile to liberal learning, and that liberal learning challenges and opposes democratic sensibilities and values. Even if liberal learning should be open to all who might receive it, it appears that this group will always be both a minority and in relative tension with democratic society. Oakeshott believes the world of power and utility is the world of democratic society, and that a university can never become a partner with this world and retain its character as a location for liberal learning. Teachers of liberal studies are concerned with "the pupil himself, in what he is thinking, in the quality of his mind, in his immortal soul, and not in what sort of a schoolmaster or administrator he can be made into."[29] Universities, proper, will "cease to exist" when learning has "degenerated into what is now called research" and "its teaching has become mere instruction."[30] Everything the modern university was becoming in the United States in the early and mid-twentieth century, we can see, threatens, from Oakeshott's perspective, to crush the learning that would actually allow students to become free and independent individuals in the sense that matters most. Democratic values are competitors, from this perspective, with liberal—or "liberating"—values.

Oakeshott's argument, in fact, comes very close to re-creating Nietzsche's argument in "On the Future of Our Educational Institutions," in which Nietzsche exercises no restraint in emphasizing what he takes to be the undemocratic nature of true learning. He assures us that "by the very nature of things only an exceedingly small number of people are destined for a true course of education."[31] The reality is that only rare individuals are suited for an education in "culture," that is, an education for understanding and appreciating the great and lasting works of art, literature, and philosophy. Such an education, by definition, is aristocratic, because true culture is itself aristocratic, confined by nature to the few of genius.[32] The many, on the other hand, are "stupid, dull masses, acting by instinct."[33] Nietzsche pulls out all the stops when it comes to describing the incapacity of the many for real and meaningful learning: modern students are "unsuited to and unprepared for philosophy," have "no truly artistic instincts," and such a student "is merely a barbarian believing himself to be free."[34] The idea of democratic liberal learning, for Nietzsche, is a contradiction in terms.

Given this reality, it is inevitable that mass education in an increasingly democratic world is an abomination, an insult to true learning and culture. Nietzsche understood perfectly well what democratic educators such as Dewey would demand in the years to come. They will "regard as their goal the emancipation of the masses from the mastery of the great few" and "seek to overthrow the most sacred hierarchy in the kingdom of the intellect—the servitude of the masses, their submissive obedience, their instinct of loyalty to the rule of genius."[35] Indeed they would. But what would these democratic educators have to offer the many if a real education is not available to them? The answer to this is twofold. Most obviously, education will inevitably be redirected away from culture to "teaching how to succeed in life," by which Nietzsche means aiming at utilitarian goods: "Utility is made the object and goal of education."[36] He admits that there is much to learn if we are to successfully participate in the "struggle for existence." Such learning, however, has "nothing whatever to do with culture,"[37] and culture alone is the object of a meaningful, liberating education. The second aim of mass education, not unrelated to vocationalism, is the protection and promotion of the interests of the modern state. Democratic education's hostility toward the few and the great will drive such individuals into "self-exile." In their place, the many will be "persuaded that they can easily find the path for themselves—following the guiding star of the State!"[38] Where the many once instinctively followed the great, they must now be trained to follow the state, which has replaced rule by aristocrats. As if he had read Dewey, Nietzsche suggests that publicly controlled schools will become "nurseries of a reprehensible culture which repels the true culture with profound hatred."[39] He was absolutely right that democratic educators would suggest that the economy itself would become the locus of a new democratic culture, and that it would look on the older humanist culture with the most profound distrust and hostility. He only differed from Dewey in his horror of this prospect.

Nietzsche is brilliant at exposing the sentimentality, the kitsch, of democratic sensibilities, the ease with which democrats can write off the historic traditions of culture and learning, the ease with which they can also romanticize the many. It is also true, however, that he is himself captivated by a comparable aristocratic kitsch. He writes that a democratic education would purge from the student "everything which might tend to make him strive after higher and more remote aims," while a true cultural education would allow a student to "rise above the transient events of future times as the pure reflection of the eternal and immutable essence of things."[40] Many of us have a much greater respect for the grand traditions of literature and philosophy than did Dewey, yet we still refrain from suggesting that aristocratic culture was itself committed to the "eternal and immutable essence of things" to a greater degree than other cultures (including democratic cultures) are.[41] One comes away from reading Nietzsche thinking that democratic society has a monopoly on vulgarity, narrowness, materialism, and ignorance. In truth, all human societies and all social classes have displayed these traits in plenty. Aristocracies may have left us cultural artifacts to value and from which we can learn, but Nietzsche's insistence that democratic society can leave us nothing of this sort looks less like insight than bigotry and spleen.

Almost a century after Nietzsche's lectures, Leo Strauss offers a more moderate and diplomatic elaboration on these themes in two lectures of his own. Originally, he suggests, democracy implied an aristocracy of the many, but as it has come to be practiced, it has instead become an elite representation of what he calls (reflecting the concerns of the 1950s and early 1960s) "mass culture." By this he means "a culture which can be appropriated by the meanest capacities without any intellectual and moral effort whatsoever and at a very low monetary price."[42] In short, this is a society driven by the most basic desires and wants. On the whole, modern philosophy has evolved to serve these wants. Reflecting this development, the Baconian concern with the "relief of man's estate" has replaced the older philosophical project, "what one may call disinterested contemplation of the eternal."[43] Science, rather than the older philosophy, has become the only undisputed authority of our age (a claim, we might note, not easily made today), and science has itself become "incompetent to distinguish between good and evil ends."[44] The educational world, under these conditions, is controlled by the "insufficiently educated."[45] Strauss agrees that philosophy and science are no longer viewed as ends in themselves, but as powers "for making human life longer, healthier, and more abundant."[46] The project of the modern world is to allow people to "live as they like,"[47] that is, by impulse, rather than as free individuals who study and evaluate goods and values beyond those given by our desires. The classical understanding of education as the formation of character is replaced in our world by "enlightenment," or self-interest rightly understood, by which he means the prudent pursuit of our wants.[48]

Liberal education, as Strauss understands it, "is the counter-poise to mass culture" and its "corroding effects." Rather than focusing on satisfying our desires, our economic and other utilitarian needs and wants, liberal education is an education "in culture or toward culture." It is a "liberation from vulgarity" and an invitation to "experience in things beautiful," providing an escape from mass culture by offering exposure to "human excellence" in the form of the greatest ideas captured in the greatest books.[49] It is clear that this education can never become fully democratic; it will "always remain the obligation and the privilege of a minority."[50] Strauss does distinguish, however, between two groups for whom liberal education can be provided even within a democratic society: gentlemen and philosophers. Gentlemen are created when liberal education shapes their "character and taste."[51] This character education encourages them to aim for higher purposes than the many, but they learn to emulate this aspiration more than to understand it. They are driven less by a love of knowledge itself than a concern with a kind of honor earned by their disciplined characters. Philosophers, on the other hand, look to truth and understanding. Both groups require a liberal education, but this education leads them to different ends. By nature, there are more potential gentlemen than philosophers.[52] Gentlemen aspire to responsibility and honor; philosophers aspire to truth. This suggests that although the interests of these groups overlap, insofar as they both aim to mitigate and resist the most vulgar impulses of mass culture, their interests also diverge significantly enough that their potential for shared purposes is limited. Liberal education brings to gentlemen a taste of and for human excellence: "Education to perfect gentlemanship, to human excellence, liberal education consists in reminding oneself of human excellence, of human greatness."[53] In the first of these two lectures, Strauss assumes that none in his audience could be philosophers, even though they could aspire to philosophize in full awareness of their limitations. In the second, he notes the distinction between philosophers and gentlemen:

the latter are groomed for leadership; the former seek eternal truths. True liberal education is out of favor in democratic society at large, and in the modern research university that serves this democratic society. Even here, however, there can be enclaves of commitment to this education for character and exposure to the greatest of the classical philosophical tradition (that is, the tradition before its turn toward power and utility).

Strauss obviously shares with Oakeshott and Nietzsche a deep distrust of democratic sensibilities and suggests that liberal education can only succeed when it is at least in part protected and isolated from the broader democratic culture. His reflections on the distinction between liberal education and democratic society are eloquent and worth quoting at length: "Liberal education is concerned with the souls of men and therefore has little or no use for machines. If it becomes a machine or an industry, it becomes undistinguishable from the entertainment industry unless in respect to income and publicity, to tinsel and glamour. But liberal education consists in learning to listen to still and small voices and therefore to become deaf to loud-speakers. Liberal education seeks light and therefore shuns the limelight."[54]

One needn't ascribe to Strauss's distrust of democratic culture and sensibilities to find power in this comment from the mid-twentieth century as the university system was fully coming into its own. Now, in the twenty-first century, it is clearer than ever that the university in the United States is almost entirely captured by a corporate model, full of publicity and even more tinsel and glamour than Strauss could have imagined in 1960. We needn't share his understanding of democracy to think his comments rightly warn us of the difficulty of pursuing a liberal education aimed at the investigation of truth within the university as it has evolved and developed in our time.

▬▬▬▬ Strauss is clearly echoing, as do Nietzsche and Oakeshott, an ancient perspective on the tension between opinion and truth, the views of the many and the perspective of philosophy, the tension between liberal education and democratic society. There is a quite different, and modern, and in many ways very American, version of this story, however, captured in Stanley Fish's provocative work. Of all those who have contributed to the outpouring of criticisms of contemporary higher education, Fish has a uniquely polemical message. He joyfully lampoons what he once referred to as the contemporary "woe-is-us" books on higher education.[55] He shares with conservatives the belief that the humanities have been seriously weakened by politicized understandings of both scholarship and teaching. His charge to his professorial colleagues is that we should "save the world" on our own time, rather than on the university's. Scholarship, the proper work of the faculty, is only justified to the degree that it aims at the truth, as such truth is defined and revealed within academic disciplines. Professors are trained within these disciplines, with their methods and boundaries, and are only professionally justified in pursuing and teaching knowledge defined and constrained by these methods and boundaries. Fish has no sympathy with claims, such as those made by Strauss, that liberal education is primarily aimed at the development of character. The academy has nothing what-soever to do with character development, outside of a narrow range of intel-lectual and professional virtues. The faculty's job is to pursue truth in the disciplines within which they have been trained. They must not leverage their positions for the sake of promoting a particular politics, or even in the attempt to make students better people. To pursue moral projects beyond their professional training is to demean their discipline and pretend to au-thority and expertise that academic training simply does not give. It is, bluntly put, a form of corruption.

Central to Fish's claim is the idea, contrary to much contemporary con-ventional academic wisdom, that avoiding politics in the classroom is both desirable and easy to do. He notes that universities market themselves with preposterous claims about their ability to solve virtually all social prob-lems,[56] despite the fact that academic skills, as he understands them, have no correlation with moral capacities beyond the virtues required to pursue a discipline accurately and honestly.[57] What colleges and universities *can* do is introduce students to bodies of knowledge and provide them with ana-lytical skills that will help them understand and engage these traditions and perhaps even pursue disciplinarily defined research. That's all. "If you're not in the pursuit-of-truth business, you should not be in a university."[58] He is opposed to giving academic credit for a host of other activities, such as internships and community service, since these aim at goods other than truth—that is, other than academic goods. What we need to do in the academy is "academicize," which is to speak of subjects in ways an academic discipline is designed to study them. Any normative issue, including political issues, can be investigated within the structure of an academic discipline. But this must take place as a purely academic exercise, rather than as an exercise in normative advocacy. Only then can faculty remain within the limits of what they have been trained and hired to do.[59] To be employed to teach, say, political theory requires introducing students to the literature of political theory, the main ideas found and debated within this literature, the ways in which the literature has been read and evaluated by others, and the like. That is what a PhD in this field qualifies one to do. What such a professor is not qualified to do, in Fish's view, is to use his or her professional platform to advocate for a particular political program.

Fish makes two central claims in this discussion. The first answers those who think that *whatever* we do in the classroom, we are engaged in a political act. From that perspective, Fish's analysis is nonsensical and asks us to do the impossible. We have seen, however, that Fish believes that to politicize our classrooms demeans the academic life and underestimates our obligation to separate our life as citizens from our life as scholars: "Teachers who prefer grandiose claims and ambitions to the craft are the ones who diminish it and render it unworthy."[60] They also fail to appreciate the ease with which we can remove our politics from our pedagogy. In truth, Fish argues, it is not difficult for the professor of political ideas to teach the history of political thought without students learning anything about the teacher's personal political values—indeed, we might think that one would have to either become very sloppy in presentation or intentional in one's political advocacy in order for the students to learn anything about this at all. Nor is it impossible to hold students responsible for developing a knowledge of this literature without ever asking for their opinions or judgments about it—indeed, we might think, with Fish, that that is exactly what we should be doing. That is what educating them in our disciplines means. In Fish's pithy prose, "Only bad teaching is a political act."[61]

Fish's second claim is that it is simply false, and contrary to human experience, to believe that an excellent college or university education is in any way related to being a good person. It is related, rather, to the student's knowledge, skills, and abilities within the disciplines she or he studies or studied. These academic qualities are what determines success or failure in higher education. Individuals' moral development, the qualities of their character, are appropriately shaped by a host of institutions and relation-ships other than the academy—families, religious institutions, peer groups, and so forth. The academy may only rightly insist on those moral virtues re-quired to pursue its particular goals: honesty, thoroughness, perseverance, and other intellectual virtues.[62] It is a mistake to believe that these demands should be extended to include political or other normative virtues and com-mitments. In truth, educational and democratic values are distinct and separate. Our integrity as educators depends upon maintaining this distinc-tion. It also requires that we not ask of education what it cannot give with-out corrupting its true mission: that we produce democratically or other-wise morally excellent graduates. To insist on this is to promote a fiction about the academy's abilities, and to debase its rightful function. Fish insists that we can't make our students "into good people," and we "shouldn't try."[63]

Fish's view is closely tied to classical representatives of the liberal arts tradition, such as Cardinal Newman and John Stuart Mill, with whom he declares, "I . . . want to say that inutility is a fact about [higher education], and a defining, not a limiting, fact."[64] From this perspective we mustn't look to external goods to justify the activities of the academy. On the contrary, the university's goods are to be understood entirely in terms of the academic enterprise itself. Indeed, although Fish appeals to Newman as an authority,[65] his position is perhaps even less concerned with external goods and values than was Newman's. Newman, after all, hoped to produce "gentlemen," and when he said the liberal studies were nonutilitarian, he meant not that they didn't produce extrinsic goods, but merely that they didn't produce profes-sional or market goods.[66] Fish makes his point even more radically and po-lemically. What's the good of a liberal education, outside the experience of the thing itself? "Beats me! As far as I can tell those habits of thought and the liberal arts education that provides them don't enable you to do any-thing, and, even worse, neither do they prevent you from doing anything."[67] In a *New York Times* blog post from the same year that he published *Save the World on Your Own Time*, Fish is emphatic about this point. It is important that the academy defend itself on its own terms, that it not attempt to fash-ion its message to sell its goods beyond its own institutional walls. To do so is to invite both misunderstanding and dishonesty. A reader asks, What jus-tifies the enterprise of liberal education? Fish answers, "The demand for jus-tification . . . always come from those outside the enterprise. Those inside the enterprise should resist it, because to justify something is to diminish it by implying that its value lies elsewhere. If the question What justifies what you do? won't go away, the best answer to give is 'nothing.'"[68]

Fish's position on this point is in harmony with his reflections on literary scholarship published a decade before *Save the World on Your Own Time*. Commitment to academic life grows, or should grow, from interest in a subject, a desire to participate in a particular field of study: "We do not ordinarily choose to enter a field because it affords an opportunity to be effective in some other. . . . Rather we become *interested* in something . . . and it is usually *later*, under the pressure of anxieties created by the demand for justification, that we tell ourselves a story in which the pursuit of our interest is crucial for the improvement of the human condition."[69] We should refuse to attempt justifications for scholarly study by reference to anything extrinsic to the activity itself, since "literary interpretation, like virtue, is its own reward."[70] Why engage in this study? Fish speaks for himself: "I do it because I like the way I feel when I'm doing it. . . . That's the way it is for me. I can't stay away from the stuff. It's what I do; and that, finally, is the only justification I can offer for its practice."[71] Any other explanation for why we need literary interpretation, or any other academic study, is a form of rationalization that bypasses the truth, which is that some people do these things because they find them wonderful. Full stop. "Nice work if you can get it."[72] No other justification is possible or required. He argues in *Save the World on Your Own Time*, when asked to justify our values, that academics should "assume them and assume too your right to define and protect them. And when you are invited to explain, defend, or justify, just say no."[73] We must resist the temptation to justify our own commitments in relation to other people's concerns.

There's a lot to like in this position and in the vigor with which Fish states it. Most importantly, and attractively, it is unapologetic about scholarship and intellectual life. Fish is certainly right, to at least some degree, to suggest that all of us who think we need to justify what we do on the grounds that it will produce good workers, or, perhaps less crassly, that it will produce good citizens, or that it will make more responsible individuals in some more general sense, or that society will be "enriched" by having educated individuals, or any variation on this kind of claim, are engaged in a form of special pleading that can be thought to bespeak a lack of confidence concerning the value of what we actually do. Do we ask Itzhak Perlman to explain the value of playing the violin? There are those who recognize the extraordinary beauty of listening to him play, and that's all that needs to be said on the matter. Of course, there are those who are not drawn to this music, but we would not be honest with those individuals if we said to them: you should try to enjoy listening to Perlman because it will make you a better person, or make you more sensitive to others, or because you will learn to vote correctly in the next election. Rather, we can encourage them to empathize with the beauty of the thing, but if they do not, there is simply little left to say. Why should we think of our scholarship in the liberal arts and sciences in a different way? It may not be beauty that draws us to literature, or philosophy, or history, or language (though it might be), but the enjoyment and admiration of the scholarship and the truths at which it aims must be drawn from the goods of the activity itself. It is this practice, and the enjoyment thereof, that we as teachers are introducing our students to. To say more than this, Fish suggests, is to not sufficiently appreciate our own commitments, to suffer from an unjustified lack of professional confidence. And there's even more bad news: this lack of appreciation for our own craft is a source of corruption to it. Fish refuses to traffic in the platitudes about higher education that are so common among university marketers, administrators, and faculty themselves when they criticize the current academy or bemoan contemporary threats to the humanities and liberal education. He is a champion for the intellectual and scholarly life as a good in itself.

Fish's polemic aims at the university as a whole, or at least the full array of the arts and sciences as they would be represented in a rich and complete liberal education. But this is very misleading. It does not appear to be true that the bulk of scholars engaged with the natural sciences, for example, are motivated primarily by the intrinsic pleasures of their disciplines. This doesn't mean that it isn't common for scientists to love the beauty, order, and logic of their scientific study. But overwhelmingly this science aims not at pure research, or not just at pure research, but instead at applied goods. The goal, in fact, is often overwhelmingly utilitarian, aiming to ameliorate the human condition, "incubate" innovative economic activity, even generate wealth and fame for the most creative, lucky, and entrepreneurial of the scientists. Consider the example of molecular biologist Patrick O. Brown, formerly of Stanford University, who wanted to use a sabbatical leave to solve the biggest environmental problem he could imagine—how to dramatically reduce the amount of meat raised and consumed in our agricultural system. He invented the Impossible Burger (and now a whole line of Impossible Foods), engineering vegetarian ingredients to provide a very similar experience to eating meat in the hope that he could satisfy Americans' (and others') meat cravings without needing to raise animals in environmentally destructive numbers (as we currently do). Rather than looking at Brown as a crude pragmatist, someone only modestly committed to the academic program, many view him as a hero, as someone using his scientific training to solve profound problems facing us. It is his engagement with the utilitarian that makes him so admired, just as do those pursuing medical, engineering, and other applied technologies to help make our lives safer, healthier, and more pleasant. Fish's claims about the liberal arts seems to balkanize them within the university, to limit them not only to the colleges of arts and sciences, but even more restrictively to the humanities and fine arts.

But even here many will rebel. Why shouldn't the fine artist hope to shape the public discourse around matters, say, of justice and equity? Many won't use their art to those ends, but some will, and why shouldn't they? And if this is true of fine artists, why might it not be true of humanists? Yes, some will aim at "academizing," bringing order to our understanding of some corner of the humanities, and that is an honorable activity. But what of a political theorist such as Danielle Allen, who explores the theories of equality and the relationship between equitable citizenship and literacy? Clearly her intention is not pure philosophical observation; she hopes to participate in the creation of a "more perfect union" in the United States.[74] Or, of Melvin Rogers's commitment to a deep reading of the African American political tradition with the intention of helping to promote a democratic transformation of the polity in the United States, which he identifies as his "central preoccupation"?[75] Or, of philosopher Susan Neiman's defense of the Enlightenment as the proper soil from which to develop a morally defensible left-wing politics?[76] Fish might respond that this is all well and good for one's scholarship and publication, but not for one's teaching.[77] We might rightly ask, however, why we must patronizingly hide our scholarly work from our students. Yes, of course, those of us in the humanities and fine arts, especially, must allow our students a significant latitude to develop their own ideas and interpretations (the humanities are not sciences, in which correct answers are much more narrowly constrained). A skillful and generous teacher, however, should be able to discuss such matters honestly, at least with one's most committed and interested students. In this sense, the solution to the politicized humanities doesn't appear to be as clear as Fish suggests; it is perhaps more difficult to negotiate. It isn't that politics (or contentious issues generally) shouldn't be discussed in the classroom. Indeed, what distinguishes the humanities from, say, the natural sciences, is the degree to which they are imbued with normative concern and aim to clarify our moral arguments and sensibilities. This must be done in a way in which teachers maintain respect for their students, in which their goal is to help students to cultivate the tools for developing their own views in a manner that conforms to the standards of "philosophical" conversation—that is, conversation in which the appeal to reason, rather than rhetorical combat, is the standard. This is a high and difficult bar, and one that doesn't have the satisfying clarity of simply banishing moral issues (beyond basic intellectual virtues and commitments) from the classroom. This higher standard is not only more realistic, however, but actually more respectful of the work done by the humanities in the first place. There is no reason why we can't or shouldn't aspire to such reasonable conversation, even (or even especially) about political morality or justice, say, while also recognizing the difficulty of doing this well. Teaching, after all, is an art, and a difficult art at that, rather than a science.

The attraction of Fish's position is similar to the attraction of Max Weber's position in his famous lecture "Science as a Vocation." The "science" Weber defends has no normative content beyond the intellectual virtues, no normative meaning beyond its own internal integrity. It must be kept separate from political concerns, both in the study and the classroom. Science, by which Weber means disinterested modern scholarship, is tied to the modern project of "progress" (that is, never-ending development) even while it is divorced from "meaning" beyond its own findings. With Fish, Weber believes there is no appropriate place for the "democratic" evaluation of courses. With Fish, he believes the teacher must scrupulously avoid political commentary and advocacy: "The task of the teacher is to serve the students with his knowledge and scientific experience and not to imprint upon them his personal political views."[78] To do more is to betray the vocation of the teacher and fall into demagoguery.[79] Weber's charge is stern and austere, built around the scholarly integrity of the academic disciplines: "Science today is a 'vocation' organized in special disciplines in the service of self-clarification and knowledge of interrelated facts. It is not the gift of grace of seers and prophets dispensing sacred values and revelations, nor does it partake of the contemplation of sages and philosophers about the meaning of the universe. This, to be sure, is the inescapable condition of our historical situation."[80] The message is familiar, even if the emphasis is not quite the same as we find with Fish. There is a tragic quality to Weber's writing, a sense that we have given up on metaphysics and meaning in exchange for scientific understanding. This is a hard bargain: "The fate of our times is characterized by rationalization and intellectualization and, above all, by the 'disenchantment of the world.'"[81] In order to maintain our integrity, we must learn to "bear the fate of the times like a man."[82] This is a tall order, but a necessary one for Weber. The tragic element is missing from Fish's position. Instead of a difficult choice between, say, "science" and meaning, Fish simply sees and embraces professional integrity. The tragic commitment we find with Weber looks more like a game to Fish, one with rules that must be respected and enforced, but of no importance beyond itself. Weber defends the ethic of a vocation, but Fish looks much more like he's defending the appropriate boundaries of a career; professional recognition and ambition is unleashed, but only within the constraining rules imposed by the academic discipline. He suggests in *Professional Correctness* that his message throughout is "when there's a job to be done, and you want it done correctly, call in a professional."[83] The philosopher's love for truth is channeled, in Fish's hands, into a modern career opportunity.

One may object that neither the earlier college system nor the university system as it has emerged in the past 100 years or more has ever thought of its purposes as being as limited as Fish describes: even Newman thought of the moral consequences of an education in the "unity of knowledge" (which, we should note, Fish rejects in favor of an array of disciplinarily defined "knowledges") and the creation of "gentlemen." Both the earlier and the contemporary systems were designed to serve society by providing moral or civic education. But this appeal to historical description doesn't really answer Fish. His professional ethic reflects what he takes to be the coherent disciplinary structure of knowledge and scholarly activity in the modern university. It is true that an older character and civic education is now enthusiastically embraced by "residence life" and student affairs administrative staffs. These institutional elements of the modern university, however, are separate from academic affairs, and frequently in significant tension if not outright contradiction with them. The classroom and the study are not rightly involved with all the other student management concerns found in modern higher education. Professors are trained in disciplinary knowledge, universities exist primarily to provide a home for these academic disciplines to pursue their studies, and the rest of the institution's administrative concerns are only tangentially related to the academic mission. Some in the academy wish to break down the walls between academic and residential functions—by building, for example, residentially based learning communities—but the logic of Fish's position is to protect what he takes to be the mission and integrity of modern scholarship. The fact that vestigial elements of archaic higher education continue to be found outside the academic enclaves within institutions of higher learning is all the more reason to insulate the academic mission from the extraneous and insist on the centrality of the academic to the university. The fact that students and their parents are expecting more and different elements in a liberal education is reason, we might think, for universities to become more honest in their marketing and academic in their functioning.[84] We might observe, and rightly so, how little faith the modern university appears to have in its own professed pursuit of truth.

For our purposes, what's important in Fish's position, aside from the simple pleasure of watching him puncture many of the pieties and hypocrisies of the contemporary academy, is the degree to which he has given a modern, very American and professional twist to a more conventional desire to protect the pursuit of truth from what is taken to be the ignorance and hostility of democratic culture. For all his differences with thinkers such as Strauss and Oakeshott, and these differences are obviously significant, he appears to share a sense that liberal learning is an activity for the few. Others might claim that the reason for this has to do with capacity, the intellectual inability of the many to understand or to care to understand (recall Becker's cynical comment, quoted at the outset of this chapter), but for Fish this is more of a simple matter of personal interest. He makes no claim that his own passion for literary analysis is anything other than a personal preference, much the way other individuals can be driven by a love for woodworking, or music, or baseball, or any other human activity. Scholarship may be an excellence, but it is a "democratic" one in this sense: Fish never assumes that his personal proclivities and interests are anything other than personal desires on his part, just as other individuals in democratic and meritocratic society are free to cultivate their own pleasures (within the parameters of liberal protections of others) to the degree that they have appropriate talents and find appropriate social contexts in which to practice them. There is no Platonic hierarchy here, no claim that the intellect is the highest human power providing the highest human goods. Why study literature or anything else? Simply because we like it. Most will not, but that makes it no less wonderful for those who do.

At the end of *Save the World on Your Own Time*, Fish makes a pragmatic argument that if we stop trying to justify the academy, we will find our opponents to be quite interested in "having dinner" with us—that is, with talking with us about what we do. He holds out hope that such rubbing of shoulders, outside of the public spotlight where debates about the purposes of and the justifications for our universities encourage polemics and culture-war posturing, might allow for a greater understanding between academics and their current political foes.[85] If this were to happen, it would be a result of the growth of sympathy between the parties, much the way people exposed, by someone they find interesting, to an art form they have never liked or understood might find it more attractive than they had before. Such sympathy or appreciation will decidedly not come, however, by hearing an argument about the importance of the academy for the rest of the world. It will only come, if it is to come, by an increased awareness of the delights of the activity itself. This, of course, is something that one can only grow to understand. It is not to be learned simply by being told. In the end, like so many human goods, it will likely be appreciated only by a minority. There is no reason to think, from Fish's perspective, that higher education should be pursued as a universal good in a democratic society. Nowhere does he imply that it is anything other than an idiosyncratic individual pleasure. For Fish, scholarship is justified simply as a delight, rather than as an operation to rescue high culture from the corrupting influence (if not outright hostility) of democratic society.

━━━━━ One remarkable twist on the idea of protecting liberal learning and culture from democratic culture is found in an essay by Bertrand de Jouvenel, who argues for the democratization of liberal education, less to promote and strengthen democracy than to protect the survival of what he takes to be beauty and culture from the emerging democratic society. In a festschrift in honor of Robert Hutchins, Jouvenel argues that the commitment to cultural life was traditionally maintained by "gentlemen of leisure," but this figure "has utterly disappeared" in the mid-twentieth-century United States.[86] The efficient modern economy, however, is producing for the first time in history significant leisure for the laboring many. If we don't educate the demos to appreciate our cultural inheritance, it will be destroyed by the kind of mass culture Strauss felt such hostility toward.[87] "We live in majority societies where beautiful things will be wiped out unless the majority appreciates them . . . 'Convert or perish' must be the motto of the self-regarding man of taste."[88] Jouvenel's argument provides an oddly aristocratic bridge between those who fear the vulgarity of democratic culture and those who wish to make liberal learning democratically accessible. The good to be achieved includes a widespread opportunity to learn "to use one's powers,"[89] but this democratic opportunity is recommended less for the good of the many than for the protection of what is loved by a "man of taste."

The arguments for a philosophical and "cultural" liberal education we have looked at so far position themselves either against democratic culture or, at best (such as in Fish's case), as indifferent to the democratic implications of the position. Jouvenel's argument, perhaps, provides a link between arguments such as these and those, in contrast, that embrace this element of liberal education as a positive democratic good, even a necessity. Recall that in the *Apology*, there is an undercurrent suggesting less that philosophy stands in opposition to democratic culture than that it is a potential educator of that culture. There is nothing in Plato's telling of this story to suggest that those who pursue philosophy will secretively manipulate and administer democracy for its own good, or for the sake of protecting philosophy from democracy's hostility. Rather, Socrates's is an open teaching, taking place in the public square: Xenophon reports that "he was always visible."[90] His argument that democracy has lost its way and needs to continually reexamine its commitments and values is made in a manner aimed at persuading the many, not just an elite few.[91] This hope is reflected in my conclusions, at the end of chapter 3, that the civic consequences of liberal education themselves require philosophical reflection if we are to be fully responsible for these commitments. The dominant thrust of the *Apology* is a tragedy, a foundational story in which the first great Western democracy murders the founder of Western philosophy, but the subcurrent is optimistic, a hope that over time these two initially antagonistic forces can learn to cherish and cultivate one another (or at least learn to live together in peace).

We have noted the moment in our educational history when there was a great deal of optimism about this project. Unlike those who would protect liberal education from democratic culture, or, at best, think it has little immediate relevance to that culture at all, many educators in the postwar period believed in the democratization of liberal education. Arthur Bestor, for example, promoted liberal education in our public schools aimed, ultimately, at the "deliberate cultivation of the power to think."[92] Just as Hutchins and the Harvard Committee argued for a fundamentally philosophical education at the college level, Bestor resisted the vocationalism informing much of public schooling. "Genuine education," he argued, "is intellectual training," and he blamed "educationalists" (presumably progressive educators working in the tradition promoted by Dewey) for the corruption of our educational system.[93] The optimism informing this vision of democratic education is also captured by Mortimer Adler's later "Paideia Proposal," in which he argues that all democratic citizens require the form of education once reserved for aristocratic elites: "We are politically a classless society. Our citizenry as a whole is our ruling class. We should, therefore, be an educationally classless society. We should have a one-track system of schooling, not a system with two or more tracks, only one of which goes straight ahead while the others shunt the young off into sidetracks not headed toward the goals our society opens to all."[94]

With Dewey, Adler and others in Hutchins's orbit are optimistic about the democratization of education. Contra Dewey, their conception of "philosophical" or "intellectual" education required not just the vocational sociology and communitarianism Dewey promoted, but rather a more conventional intellectual exposure to cultural artifacts and philosophical traditions. "Popular education is designed to endow the people as a whole with precisely the kinds of intellectual power that have hitherto been monopolized by an aristocratic few,"[95] writes Bestor.

At the end of the day, however, Bestor, as we saw with Hutchins and others, is largely concerned with the civic consequences of liberal learning, with the degree to which liberal education will promote and protect contemporary society by teaching a shared philosophical tradition. The Socratic tradition gives us reason to expand this project. First, the primary good to be received is for individuals rather than the polity. The ultimate goal is the singular life, well examined. Yes, Socrates suggests that the polis would benefit if citizens took this examination seriously, but the mechanism for how this benefit would be enjoyed is remarkably underdefined in the story; the civic good appears as a secondary consequence of having individual citizens living more deliberate and examined lives, rather than a good directly cultivated. The promotion of a philosophical education as a central element of liberal learning, if not the foundational element, rests less on the consequences for others and groups than for the individual student herself. Valuable civic consequences may reasonably be anticipated, or perhaps prayed for, but are not the primary object or concern of this education.

When Jouvenel argues that the sense of beauty and culture the "man of taste" enjoys is something of such great value that it requires attempting to educate the many to value it, he is assuming that an education to these things is a good in itself, perhaps one of the highest goods available to us. Someone sympathetic to Dewey (or to Marx, for that matter) is likely to find such an appeal to be little more than a signaling of class hubris, a snobbery, a promotion of decadent culture growing from and reflecting unjust human relations. We have seen that Dewey himself frequently wrote this way, and although there are more subtle recognitions in his work about the ways in which cultural artifacts (literature, philosophy, art) may continue to speak to our current conditions and problems, the overwhelming thrust of his ideas is to see predemocratic culture as an encumbrance to be sloughed off as we build a new, democratic culture. For all the seeming aristocratic pretension of Jouvenel's ideas, however, he nonetheless points us toward a universe of human insight, expression, and achievement that appears to both delight and educate one who is taught and encouraged to observe it. In fact, despite the degree to which Jouvenel seems to express a much older and less democratic sensibility, he is opening a door to the idea that a "philosophical" or "cultural" education is not only valuable in itself but is capable of being cultivated and enjoyed by the democratic many, and that this would not only be good for "beauty and culture," but would, likewise, be good for all those who learn to become "individuals of taste." Once we slightly alter the point of view, we see a full-throated defense of the personal value of understanding, or of appreciating the most powerful examples of human reflection and creativity, as goods to be embraced without concern for instrumental consequences. Why should one value such things? Because they are wonderful, because they delight, because they move us, because they help us think about and address our own concerns, anxieties, and confusions. That is all, and it is more than enough.

This philosophical defense of liberal learning grows from the idea that philosophy itself is a "love of wisdom," it is something not just to use but to desire. This is also perhaps the least common defense offered of liberal education. Who has the time for such indulgence? Democratic citizens are not people of leisure, and they must, so it seems, focus on earning their living and performing their civic obligations. That appears to be enough for most of us, and it certainly reflects, we might say, "bourgeois culture." This brings to mind Thoreau's lament about the "incessant business" of society in the opening passages of "Life without Principle": "This world is a place of business. What an infinite bustle! I am awaked almost every night by the panting of the locomotive. It interrupts my dreams. There is no sabbath. It would be glorious to see mankind at leisure for once. It is nothing but work, work, work . . . I think that there is nothing, not even crime, more opposed to poetry, to philosophy, ay, to life itself, than this incessant business."[96]

For all his rhetorical overkill (he was self-consciously fond of exaggeration), there is power to Thoreau's claim that the industriousness of our lives is not always conducive to thoughtful reflection, to "poetry, to philosophy, ay, to life itself." We recognize the value of leisure not just as a time to recuperate from work, but for cultivating, experiencing, and, one hopes, enjoying some of the nonmarket values that life has to offer. We should want people to have the tools not only to make their living and perform their duties, but to engage seriously with questions of meaning, with living thoughtfully and not just reflexively. With Thoreau, we might wish to live "deliberately," to "put to rout all that was not life," so as to avoid discovering when it comes time to die, that we "had not lived" in the fullest, most rewarding ways.[97] This is just to say, in different words, what Plato reports Socrates to have taught 2,500 years ago, that the life worth living is an examined life.

We have seen that Danielle Allen includes "eudaemonistic" values as essential for a complete education, including values that prepare students to have rewarding relationships and experiences in spaces of intimacy and leisure,[98] but these values recede in importance in her analysis of civic and utilitarian goods. Likewise, Martha Nussbaum suggests that we need to educate people's "souls," but her emphasis on the goals of liberal education is also overwhelmingly civic. "From early on," Nussbaum approvingly observes, "leading educators connected the liberal arts to the preparation of informed, independent, and sympathetic democratic citizens," just as she continues to do in her own work.[99] Fish is a relatively lonely voice defending the pursuit of knowledge as a form of pleasure valuable in itself. Although he notes this, he also chooses not to develop this argument as a defense of a more democratically accessible liberal learning. He refuses to promote this learning as a good for all, as a justification for why the public should support liberal education, or why individuals in general should pursue such learning. He simply observes that for some people this is an intrinsically valuable activity. Aside from Fish, even though there are occasional nods in this direction, this is not an argument people commonly develop for promoting liberal education in a democratic society. Perhaps our bourgeois sensibilities really do rule out such obviously leisured goods.

It is not at all clear, however, that this should be the case. I very much hoped when my own children were being educated that they would learn to love much of what liberal learning had to offer. As a teacher, I advise my students, especially when they first arrive on campus, to be open not just to learning skills that will be professionally helpful in the future but also to studying the full complexity of their relationships and obligations to others. I also encourage them to investigate why people may love different disciplines and genres in the arts and sciences. What is it that draws the scientist to her work, or the poet to his words, or the historian to the archive? What do people enjoy in music and art? What are they drawn to in literature and sociology and chemistry? What is the love that drives people in all these different fields, and can they, the students, begin to sympathize with this love? I know that such "falling in love" is not by any means an assured outcome of a strong liberal education. I also know that I would wish it as a crowning achievement, perhaps the highest achievement, for every student. To learn to appreciate, perhaps even to love, and certainly to be able to draw upon as resources for imagining and constructing their own lives, this broad exposure to cultural artifacts from across the arts and sciences would seem to be something we would wish for our own. If so, why wouldn't we wish this for all?

The assumption of those who view liberal learning as rightly restricted to the few is that it requires something special, or at least idiosyncratic, to make one open and capable of receiving it. To hold this view, however, is to misunderstand what is studied and aimed for in a liberal education, even when it aims to think about "truth." The question isn't about the distribution of talents that would allow individuals to become professional scholars, teachers, or specialists in any of the academic disciplines. The talents for developing professional expertise in any of these fields is likely no more or less widely distributed than the talents required by any other profession. A liberal education, in contrast, exposes individuals from the broad range of talents to books and ideas, art, music, and science—the full array of cultural artifacts that illuminate a shared human condition. This point is made by Roosevelt Montás when he argues that the "greatest value of a liberal education" lies precisely in its ability to turn students' "eyes inward, into an exploration of their own humanity under the provocation of works that have proven their power to inspire just such self-reflection."[100] The democratic claim Montás makes is that we are all equally subject to certain human problems, questions, concerns, fears, and anxieties, and that liberal learning provides an opportunity to learn, first, that we are not alone in these matters, and second, some of the resources available for helping us think through, contend, and live with them.[101] Wilson Carey McWilliams and Susan Jane McWilliams suggest that liberal education provides the "grappling hooks" by which students "can consider the enduring questions of human existence— of love, of loss, of time, of death—which they know to animate their lives."[102] For them, "Democratic moral education presumes that the big questions— those matters that are as difficult as they are enduring—are universal questions, questions that undergird and animate every human life, and as such they can be addressed in terms that are universally accessible. Like democracy itself, its hypothesis is that, closely examined, the ordinary proves to be extraordinary, just as the common is the greatest of all political mysteries, the proposition that all of us are created equal."[103]

To suggest that liberal education must wrestle with significant questions is not to suggest that any of us, even the most talented and insightful, have complete or fully satisfactory answers to them. It is to suggest that all of us must and do wrestle with them, and that a liberal education provides us with materials for helping us with this most human process. To suggest that only a few are the appropriate audience for such an education is to cast doubt on the equality animating the commitment to democracy itself.

▬▬▬▬ There is a significant, even paradoxical, ambiguity in the Platonic telling of Socrates's story that complicates our understanding of the relationship between the "philosophical" and the "civic" elements of liberal learning. On the one hand, Socrates's example appears to suggest that pursuing the philosophical component of a liberal education will draw one away from public life and the concerns of both economic flourishing and civic engagement. On the other hand, we find Socrates claiming that this central element of liberal learning will bring us back to all our obligations with a more informed and responsible perspective. Concerning the first position, we have already seen that in the *Apology* Socrates claims to have led a life outside of politics, and he even suggests that his philosophical commitments would have led him to be viewed as a threat to the political world: "Do you suppose that I should have lived as long as I have if I had moved in the sphere of public life, and conducting myself in that sphere like an honorable man, had always upheld the cause of right, and conscientiously set this end above all other things?"[104] Likewise, in the *Gorgias* he praises, above all, the philosopher "who has minded his own affairs and hasn't' been meddlesome."[105] It is also true, however, that in the *Gorgias* he claims not just that he has avoided politics in order to be a good *man*, but rather that in pursuing philosophy he was actually acting as the best *citizen*: "I believe that I'm one of a few Athenians—so as not to say I'm the only one, but the only one among our contemporaries—to take up the true political craft and practice the true politics."[106] In the *Apology* he seems to make this same point by describing himself as a stinging fly who has been sent by the gods to annoy, and to awaken, the sleepy horse that is Athens: "It is my belief that no greater good has ever befallen you in this city than my service to my God."[107] His philosophical mission of encouraging people to value the most important things in life, and not merely to pursue their unreflective desires, infuriated a good many of his fellow citizens. It is clear from these comments, however, that Socrates did not feel that it was sufficient to withdraw into private life. His civic contributions are eccentric, but his philosophical investigations take place in public and have implications for public, and not merely private, affairs. In this sense, a philosophical education is both a private and a public good.

Socrates, then, not only denies that he represents a threat to Athenian society, but claims to the contrary that he represents the best civic commitments of any citizen. The implication is that philosophical knowledge is potentially an ally to democratic politics, despite the obvious tension between truth claims and common sense (or public opinion) so dramatically illustrated by the story of Socrates's trial and execution. Properly understood, we might hope, individuals will be more thoughtful, more responsible, if they receive a "philosophical" education. Simply put, we may hope that liberally educated individuals will serve democratic society well, that emphasizing not just civic but philosophical knowledge will be a clear service for democracy. Fish's deep skepticism about this is built on the claim that there is no empirical evidence for such a correlation; academic interests and skills simply don't correspond, in his view, with civic or any other virtues outside of intellectual virtues, and the world is full of wicked yet liberally educated individuals.[108] There is more to say about this, however, than Fish allows. Sergei Guriev and Daniel Treisman, for example, in their study of contemporary dictators, note that *all* individuals with a higher education are potentially threats to autocrats simply because their education, and often the career that followed this education has taught them the value of freedom of thought and the clear distinctions between what is true and untrue. This is as true for scientific and technical training as it is for liberal learning, since advanced work in all these fields requires a level of independence and creativity. Despots are right to fear not just liberal education, Guriev and Treisman think, but all higher education (even the technical training despots need to cultivate for their own political purposes).[109] We might hope that the range of human experience and perspectives to which a liberal education exposes a student will make them even more likely to be resistant to the dogmatic claims of despots and authoritarians.[110]

Elaine Scarry argues that elements of liberal learning, particularly the aesthetic recognition and appreciation of beauty, draws an individual into concern and love for the world and, beyond that, toward a respect for truth and justice: "By perpetuating beauty, institutions of education help incite the will toward continual creation." Even more, "What is beautiful is in league with what is true because truth [as does beauty] abides in the immortal sphere."[111] Beauty provokes us to care about truth, she thinks, because it gives us, "with an electric brightness shared by almost no other uninvited, freely arriving perceptual event, the experience of conviction and the experience, as well, of error."[112] Part of the value of universities, we might say, is that they preserve beautiful things (not just artworks of all types, but ideas and thought in any form) that draw us from ourselves to the true and then, she hopes, to the just.

Some will think that Scarry's argument is itself beautiful, or has a beautiful appeal, even if it is more aspirational than persuasive. We want to believe that liberally educated people will not only understand something about the truth but also respect and protect it, that they will view it as a good to be cultivated and defended. Liberally educated individuals are likely more able to understand, we hope, better and worse arguments, but beyond that, we hope they will value the better over the worse. There is, however, simply no guarantee for this. That much Fish is surely right to suggest. What is more, we live at a moment when a significant number of elites with excellent liberal educations have chosen to cast their lot with a political movement many of them had clearly and correctly identified as beyond the pale before their discovery that they would not be able to maintain a political career without submitting to its lies and undemocratic program. Even so, it is hard to believe that a more broadly educated, more liberally educated citizenry would be as subject to demagoguery as so many are today. Indeed, one wonders what would have happened if our society had maintained its commitment to liberal education from a generation ago, in schooling from secondary through higher education, as a democratic public good. Would the cynical manipulations of Donald Trump have been so successful? Too many theorists of liberal education have simply assumed that such an education will produce good citizens. There is, we willingly admit, insufficient evidence to support a direct correlation on these matters. There is reason to hope, however, that liberal education could tend more in this direction than not.[113]

Even if we are unpersuaded about this point, however, there is an even stronger argument than the civic for promoting a liberal education with a philosophical and literary bent, and that is less for the sake of the whole than for the good of the individual student. We might even say that it should be the democratic birthright of any citizen—out of simple and foundational respect for their human equality—to have the opportunity to be exposed to the delight of the true and the beautiful. Such a commitment won't guarantee a virtuous citizenry, but there are reasons to hope it may help. We also can't expect it to resolve the ancient quarrel between philosophy and democracy, but a democratic faith in liberal education aims to give both goods their due by cultivating the possibility of an "examined life" for all.

Conclusion

I have suggested that we find at least three partially plausible arguments in support of liberal education: (1) the cultivation of skills, practices, and intellectual habits that will be advantageous when students enter the workforce; (2) the development of understandings and commitments that will encourage good and responsible citizenship; (3) the promotion of opportunities for clarity of philosophical insight and aesthetic delight. No liberal education can guarantee that a student will gain any of these values, let alone all three. A comprehensive and ambitious program of liberal learning will aim, nonetheless, to achieve some level of success on all three counts.

My acceptance of the inclusion of vocational concerns within our conception of a liberal education, I need to admit, is grudging and partial. It is true, I argued in chapter 2, that in a democracy all education must be aware of the nonaristocratic character of students, of the need they will (almost) all have to earn their livings after completing their formal education.[1] It is also true, however, that the vocational demands on education imperially threaten to subsume the whole of the educational enterprise. Frank Donoghue noted, without pleasure, that "the liberal arts model of higher education, with the humanities at its core, is crumbling as college credentials become both more expensive and more explicitly tied to job preparation."[2] Under contemporary conditions students would be foolish not to respond to market incentives out of the most basic concern for their future economic independence and well-being. The danger in these trends isn't that we will include components of vocational preparation within liberal programs.[3] The danger is that we lose liberal arts sensibilities and programs altogether. In a sign of the times, the *New York Times* recently covered a report by the state auditor of Mississippi suggesting that the state invest more in vocational programs, such as engineering and business, and less in liberal arts majors simply on the grounds of expected return on investment. The auditor had himself majored in political science as an undergraduate and regretted that those with his background don't command the same professional salaries as, say, engineers and computer scientists. In answer to criticisms such as this, the author notes that Jeffrey Cohen, the dean of humanities at Arizona State University, "defends his domain as a pathway toward not just a job but a lifetime of career reinvention. 'Our students are living in a time when the career that they've trained for is not likely to be the career that they're going to be following 10 years later.' . . . Studying the humanities, he argues, will teach them how to be nimble."[4] Arizona State is one of the minority of universities with relatively healthy enrollments in the humanities, and it is clear that this success has been built on the marketing savvy with which they have tied such studies to the prospect of vocational success. How else are we to keep the humanities, arts, and social sciences alive in the social context of such attitudes as those of the Mississippi state auditor?

The dangers of moving in this direction, however, are significant. I noted at the end of chapter 2 that Stefan Collini thinks that "skills-talk represents a failure of nerve." His words are worth considering again: skills-talk "is an attempt to justify the activity [e.g., the study of the humanities] not in its own appropriate terms, but in terms derived from another set of categories altogether, categories drawn from the instrumental world of commerce and industry."[5] When we reduce the humanities, and liberal education more generally, to such utilitarian and market oriented evaluation, the battle is in danger of being lost from the start. If these are the appropriate standards, how can we even imagine activities that derive their justifications from other values? Will these other elements of human life simply atrophy? Or, will our judgments concerning them become corrupted by inappropriate market values? Collini: "One has to make, over and over again, the obvious point that a society does not educate the next generation in order for them to contribute to its economy. It educates them in order that they should extend and deepen their understanding of themselves and the world, acquiring, in the course of this form of growing up, kinds of knowledge and skill which will be useful in their eventual employment, but which will no more be the sum of their education than that employment will be the sum of their lives."[6] Instead of educating people for the full breadth a human life, vocationalism threatens to overwhelm all other educational values and purposes.

And the imperial claims of vocationalism don't end with threats to the breadth of liberal learning. They threaten the university's very conception of itself, the way it functions, the values that animate it. Mitch Daniels, the former governor of Indiana, who also served as the president of Purdue University, recently attacked the institution of academic tenure in the following terms: "Pick up any business magazine or how-to management book, and you'll run into words like 'nimble' and 'move fast' on virtually every page. The ability to change direction and shift priorities in reaction to consumer preferences or competitor actions often makes a decisive difference in marketplace success. One can't think of an enterprise less 'nimble' than the modern American university."[7] The lack of concern with anything approaching academic values is striking. Students are consumers, education is a marketplace, universities need to act like businesses, like corporations. Utilitarian efficiency in meeting consumer demand is what matters. The frankness of this position is impressive, given how frequently recent criticisms of higher education have focused on the "corporatization" of the university.[8] Daniels does nothing to camouflage the blunt market utility that he thinks would rightly guide a proper university. It is hard to see how such a university could account for either the civic or philosophical goods we discussed in chapters 3 and 4. To the degree that Daniels's voice represents the sensibilities of a significant element of the modern university, he is speaking a language in which liberal education plays, at best, a very minor "enrichment" role for what is viewed as the more serious business of job preparation. Indeed, it is not obvious that this language even can account for much of what liberal education values. Oakeshott fears that when our universities speak only the language of utility, education is replaced by apprenticeship to "domestic, industrial and commercial life."[9] Training replaces the kind of reflection liberal learning promotes and values. One is reminded of Margaret Atwood's dystopian vision of a not-too-distant future when bioengineers (the academic and commercial rock stars of the scholarly world) are educated in affluent—even luxurious—enclaves with all the best equipment, laboratories, housing, food and entertainment, while wordsmiths (among the only remaining humanists, required for the modest purpose of hawking the wares produced by the bioengineers) are educated in the "Martha Graham Academy," which can best be described as a squalid exemplar of Soviet-era dilapidated buildings with insect infestations, leaky plumbing, spoiled food, and a student body maintaining its equilibrium by cultivating irony at best and cynicism at worst. We, of course, have not reached such a point in contemporary higher education in the United States. We have flourishing history, English, and language departments in many of our universities and colleges. However, Atwood's comic/tragic vision strikes a chord for those who consider the relationship between market values and more conventional humanities and liberal arts in the academy today.[10]

Within the contemporary university there is a recognition, among those teaching in the liberal arts and sciences, that there is a significant political threat to free inquiry and debate presented by the Republican populism of recent years. Senator Marco Rubio (R-FL), in 2016, referred to liberal arts colleges as "indoctrination camps";[11] he was very clear about the degree to which Republican elites could make this a significant element of the culture war by portraying liberal education as hostile to traditional social values and mainstream beliefs about religion, sexuality, and related matters.[12] Scott Walker, former Republican governor of Wisconsin, attempted to change the mission of the state's excellent university system by removing from the "Wisconsin Idea" (that is, the system's mission statement) the words "search for truth" and "improve the human condition" and replacing them with "meet the state's workforce needs"; thus he hoped to set the stage for gutting liberal arts programs.[13] Political attacks on the humanities and liberal arts are obviously significant and unlikely to diminish anytime soon.

However, a less obvious but perhaps even more insidious threat to the humanities and liberal arts grows from a pervasive and unexamined utilitarianism found within the academy. When we consider the arguments commonly offered for explaining the decline in the humanities, we can see how little this concern has attracted the attention of observers beyond a few followers of Michael Oakeshott or Leo Strauss. One common narrative suggests, for example, that the humanities have themselves promoted programs and behaviors responsible for their own demise. The most popular form of this story is that the humanities have become irresponsibly politicized. In one form or another, the claim is that student radicals from the 1960s entered the academy as a new generation of professors who then turned their back on conventional scholarship to promote left-wing political agendas.[14] A less popular version of this argument is that in order to compete with the huge success of the natural and applied sciences in the postwar period when research universities came into their own, the humanities attempted to adopt forms of scholarship and research mimicking the scientific method. In doing so, it ended up with the worst of all worlds: both bad science and a crippled sense of what it is, traditionally and by the nature of its subject matter, the humanities can actually do and achieve.[15] Of these two narratives, I find the less popular "science envy" claim more compelling than the "politicization" claim, despite my own occasional embarrassment at the hackneyed political claims and abstruse political language displayed from time to time by some of my colleagues. Be that as it may, I don't think that either of these explanations, or any similar explanation that places the blame for the humanities' decline on the humanities themselves, can fully or even primarily account for their decline over the course of recent years. The truth is, historians, literary scholars, philosophers, and all the rest have produced remarkable, excellent scholarship during the past half century, and this is in part the result of the academy finally and significantly opening to a more diverse community of scholars participating in humanist studies than have before been welcome within our universities. Of course, the past generation has seen bad, silly, shallow, ideological, and overly politicized work produced in the humanities; this proves very little, because there's poor work in every field of human endeavor. The excellent work in history, literary studies, philosophy, and so forth is equally real, and it is this work that provides the standard we should be using to evaluate the success or failures of these disciplines.

If the humanities aren't responsible, or at least aren't largely responsible, for their own self-destruction, perhaps the very project of thinking about our values—a project at the heart of the arts and humanities, broadly conceived—is either feared or no longer widely valued in our society. Some sectors of our society reject the normative project of the humanities altogether, viewing such studies as a threat to traditional values. Within the university itself there is a powerful and increasingly unselfconscious utilitarianism at work.

The vocational and corporate orientation of the modern university threatens to make the kind of work done in the liberal arts simply irrelevant to the project of higher education. Baconian utilitarianism is so pervasive in the academy today as to be almost unchallenged and unnoticed. On the one hand, then, conservative culture-war politics threatens the humanities from without. On the other, an increasingly ascendant utilitarianism threatens the liberal arts from within. Is it any wonder that resources have moved away from the undergraduate liberal arts mission to STEM research and professional colleges?[16]

All this is not to suggest that we shouldn't include vocational concerns in our programs of liberal education. It *is*, however, to warn that such programs can easily threaten the intellectual integrity of the programs by infecting scholarly concerns with an unexamined market orientation. There are those (such as some of the thinkers I discussed in chapter 4) who think this battle is already over, that any meaningful liberal education in democratic society is hopelessly corrupted by our overwhelming commitment in these societies to comfort, pleasure, safety, longevity, and convenience. The "problems of men" that Dewey had in mind were problems related to the effective use of industry and technology to solve, democratically and justly, the material and economic challenges we face. Dewey praised these developments, but others, such as Strauss and Oakeshott, lamented them. They all recognize, however, that the demands of democratic society will minimize what have been described in this book as the conventional civic and the philosophical projects of liberal education. It is possible that in the near term liberal education will survive only in small, protected, privileged, and perhaps even partly hidden enclaves well removed from the mainstream of democratic society and uninvolved with most democratic citizens. If liberal education is to prosper, it obviously needs protection and defense from political attacks. It also, however, requires protection from the imperious claims of utility.

I noted in chapter 2 that all societies need to prepare their citizens to contribute economically. This is not itself a uniquely democratic concern. What makes a vocational focus democratic, and thereby compatible with the values of liberal education, is the degree to which vocational skills are infused with a commitment to the full range of individual freedoms, from the background knowledge and creativity that will likely allow more control over the work one does, to the moral and civic knowledge and sensitivities required if we are to pursue a vocation responsibly. China wants creative engineers and entrepreneurs to solve the increasingly complex material demands of their society, but they don't necessarily want them to also be educated to both civic and philosophical reflection.[17] A democratic society wants more broadly educated and thoughtful engineers and entrepreneurs, even if we have miles to go in achieving this goal.[18] Liberally educating people who enter all the various walks of life should ideally promote a more imaginative, engaged, and responsible workforce. These values, and not merely meeting the demands of economic and political elites, are those that should animate the vocational elements of liberal education. Although I have criticized John Dewey for not having a sufficiently expansive view of what a liberal education should look like, he seems right to me when he suggests that an educational goal is not to maximize students' future earnings or serve a corporate master so much as to maximize the degree to which careers and vocations reflect individuals' talents and considered values—that these, rather than personal wealth, are the key marks of a life lived well and freely. If it is true, as I've suggested, that the danger of including a vocational orientation within our conception of liberal education is that it can overwhelm all other, and potentially greater, values, it is also true that it is best to allow students to self-consciously prepare for careers within the context of a liberal education. For all my concerns about the potential for vocational content to corrupt liberal education, it seems to me important to resist the temptation of the position recently articulated by Zena Hitz, in which "real learning" must be radically separated from "the pressure to produce economic, social, or political outcomes."[19] Hitz contends that for "intellectual life to deliver the human benefit it provides, it must be in fact withdrawn from considerations of economic benefit or of social and political efficacy."[20] The desire to protect liberal learning from the corruptions of economics and politics, however, leads her to ignore the full range of students' needs. A free life in a democratic society requires vocational and civic capabilities and responsibilities, even for those convinced of the "dignity" and pleasures of an intellectual life, in Hitz's words, "beyond politics and social life."[21]

The economic and political challenges to liberal education have encouraged higher education administrators and marketers, especially, to emphasize the economic benefits of a broad education in the arts and sciences.

Such a development is both understandable and, to a limited degree, defensible. It is important, however, to keep these concerns in their appropriate relationship to the full array of values animating liberal learning. If we lose sight of this, we will be in danger of sacrificing the whole for the sake of a part.

▄▄▄▄▄▄ In a radio address in 1966, Theodore Adorno declares that the "premier demand upon all education is that Auschwitz will not happen again."[22] Adorno blames the "aggressive nationalism" of the late nineteenth and twentieth centuries for providing the conditions under which genocide emerged.[23] His fear is of the "blind identification with the collective" that is the hallmark of what he takes to be the Nazi personality. Education must, therefore, focus on disrupting the "brute predominance of all collectives."[24] In the context of the twentieth century's political horrors, "the only education that has any sense at all is an education in critical self-reflection."[25] Without this education, which we might rightly call liberal, it is all too easy for people to become swept up in the passions and hatreds of political grievance and chauvinism to the point that they will view all who disagree with them, or are different from them, as undeserving of any moral considerability whatsoever.[26] The danger Adorno identifies is all too present in the ethnonationalist populist movements growing within liberal democracies in the twenty-first century.[27] When Jonathan Marks writes that "the highest aim of liberal education is not a set of skills but a kind of person,"[28] he is getting at a point of the greatest political significance: that people who rationally evaluate different views and policies, who refuse to suspend discussion and reasoned judgment in favor of political passion and blind identification, are one of our only weapons against a hateful politics that can become all too common and murderous. Political scientists Steven Levitsky and Daniel Ziblatt report that in nearly every Western European nation, between 10 and 30 percent of the electorate is open to the kind of xenophobic appeals Adorno fears. In the United States, where so many of our political institutions either allow for minority rule or have been (or are being) corrupted to allow them to be captured by minorities, this minority represents a clear threat to democratic government.[29] In this political context, doing all we can to maximize the size and strength of the majority of citizens resistant to antidemocratic extremism is all the more important. Traditionally, it is thought that the educational system had a central role to play in achieving this goal, and it did so by instilling within students a basic sense of their civic duties and obligations. Among the most fundamental of these is to free oneself from the passions of the political moment, to become independent and thoughtful about the political problems we face, to be unwilling to reduce the complexity of political choices to bumper-sticker slogans and demagogic appeals.

Adorno's demand may seem like thin gruel from the perspective of those, such as Patrick Deneen, who believe the responsibility of liberal education is to reinforce and reproduce traditional communities.[30] Indeed, Adorno's demand for resistance to the claims of groups over individuals rubs very much against the communitarian grain of those who believe liberal education should strengthen moral solidarity and commitment to a shared conception of the good as a precondition for moral life. In contrast to the moral individualism Adorno promotes, this thicker conception seems a significantly more ambitious educational ideal.

Alasdair MacIntyre's thoughtful reflections on undergraduate education provide us with a less polemical understanding than Deneen's of liberal education aimed at producing a thick level of moral solidarity or consensus. MacIntyre ties his views to John Henry Newman's demand that liberal education primarily aid the student in developing a capacity for measured moral judgment: "Newman's view was that what matters about an educated individual is not primarily any set of useful skills that she or he may happen to possess, but her or his capacity for judgment, judgment both in putting these skills to work and in acts 'as a friend, as a companion, as a citizen,' in domestic life and in the pursuits of leisure."[31] This kind of judgment is distinctly different from the specialized knowledge of a discipline, such as that promoted by Stanley Fish, or a set of vocational skills, such as those promoted so commonly in the academy today. In fact, too great a focus on either of these specialized knowledges obscures the focus required for the kind of education Newman and MacIntyre have in mind. The reason for this, as I have suggested in chapter 2 and above in this conclusion, is that these more specialized forms of knowledge ask no questions about their own ends, but only about the means of pursuing them. The contemporary university, we might say, simply assumes that it is justified by its utilitarian objectives and pursues its specialized knowledge without critical self-reflection. But it is the reflection on ends that is the primary purpose of undergraduate

education, for MacIntyre. The modern university can produce brilliant engineers without the slightest understanding of their social obligations, and
clever politicians without the slightest moral sophistication. Undergraduate
education, MacIntyre suggests, is incomplete precisely to the degree that it
fails to develop responsible judgment, and this failure grows from an inappropriate emphasis on utility and specialized knowledge at the undergraduate
level. Although he is critical of Newman's elitism, he thinks the basic program
is sound and wishes to promote Newman's education for all citizens rather
than just for the few elites:[32]

> What we have to learn then from Newman is first of all that under-
> graduate education has its own distinctive ends, that it should never be
> regarded as a prologue to or a preparation for graduate or professional
> education, and that its ends must not be subordinated to the ends of the
> necessarily specialised activities of the researcher. . . . It is also that un-
> dergraduate education, when well conducted, is in key part an edu-
> cation in how to think about the ends of a variety of human activities
> and, that is to say, in how to evaluate, among others, such activities as
> those of the specialist and the researcher, the activities of those dedi-
> cated to the ends which the contemporary research university serves.
> The danger is therefore that in research universities the ability to think
> about ends, including the ends of the university, will be lost and with it
> the ability to engage in radical self-criticism, so that the leadership of
> those universities will become complacent in their wrongheadedness.[33]

The key claims here regard the need for liberal education to have its own
self-contained purposes, and that these purposes relate to the cultivation of
a disposition capable of responsible moral judgment.

MacIntyre notes early on in this piece, however, that "university teachers
are no longer members" of what he calls an "educated public, constituted by
agreement on what books every educated person needs to have read and what
skills every educated person needs to possess."[34] Here he refers back to an idea
he developed decades earlier, the ideal of an "educated public," and how this
should be the central goal of liberal education. In this earlier essay, he writes
that educators in our society have two incompatible tasks, which make their
jobs next to impossible. On the one hand, they must prepare the young for

positions in a preexisting society. On the other, they must teach them to think for themselves. He suggests that the only way that we can coherently imagine achieving both tasks is through the construction of an "educated public."[35] By this he means a large group of citizens "educated into both the habit and the opportunity of active rational debate." These citizens will agree to the standards for evaluating the strength or weakness of an argument, and "the form of rational justification from which those standards derive their authority." Finally, there will be "some large degree of shared background beliefs and attitudes, informed by the widespread reading of a common body of texts . . . which are accorded a canonical status within that particular community."[36] There are two problems we face in contemporary society, however, regarding these conditions. The first is that we are too morally and culturally fractured to agree upon the kind of canon and standards of rationality required by an educated public. The second is that this moral and cultural pluralism leads, in MacIntyre's view, to intellectual incoherence. He writes, for example, that "mass literacy in a society which lacks both canonical texts and a tradition of interpretive understanding is more likely to produce a condition of mindlessness than an educated public."[37] Liberal education, he is suggesting, is effective only under the conditions of a shared intellectual tradition: "My thesis is that the liberal arts and sciences can only be effectively appropriated and developed in the arena provided by an educated public. . . . Take away such a public with shared standards of justification, with a shared view of what the past of the society of which it is a nucleus is, with a shared ability to participate in common public debate, and you reduce the function of the liberal arts and sciences, so far as those who are not specialists are concerned, to the provision of a series of passively received consumer goods."[38]

Without an identifiable and shared intellectual tradition, and perhaps an equally agreed-upon political history, liberal education is reduced to a moral cacophony and consumer indulgence. An educated public of the sort required to achieve Adorno's goals is out of reach. MacIntyre's claim is that without a shared cultural tradition,[39] we simply have students choosing what to study in the arts and sciences the same way they would choose any consumer product that suits their fancy. Such caprice is unlikely to promote the virtues required for responsible citizenship.

MacIntyre's argument recalls the "general education" and liberal education programs of our universities in the middle decades of the twentieth century when Hutchins, the Harvard Committee, and others were promoting an education to introduce each generation of citizens to the basic cultural inheritance of what they took to be democratic society. MacIntyre is right that in rather short order, by the 1960s and 70s, higher education in the United States could not agree on the canon, the history, or the set of moral principles that would unite our own educated public of citizens. Cosmopolitan pluralism and diversity replaced the promotion of a particular tradition in the arts and humanities, leading to conservative criticisms of cultural relativism and "the closing of the American mind." Decades after MacIntyre's first defense of the idea of an educated public, and even more decades after the attack on ideologically constrained "general education" offered by higher education, one can't help but notice that those promoting a return to a narrower cultural tradition are allied with a nationalist political movement increasingly defined by the kind of xenophobic ideology that so rightly worried Adorno in the wake of the Nazi genocide. Attacks on the honest teaching of U.S. history, on the teaching of a broad array of literary and philosophical perspectives, on broadening our canons to include formerly excluded voices from within and without U.S. and European society, are justified in the name of respect for a particular tradition claimed to have (or is demanding to have) a privileged status in educating the young. The "1776 Report" has been offered as an answer to the New York Times's "1619 Project," and books discussing race or gender issues are attacked and banned on the grounds that they are "divisive" or attempting to "groom" young people for exploitation by sexual deviants. Far from promoting consensus, the current politics of solidarity is promoting intimidation, repression, and hatred of plurality. It is attempting to define the boundaries of the legitimate political community itself by narrowing who counts as a true citizen. Only in this way can a (false) consensus be imposed.

Needless to say, these politics are not what MacIntyre has in mind: he makes clear that pathological politics are to be expected in what he takes to be the moral chaos of liberal society. The boundaries on the intellectual life required to promote MacIntyre's educated public in a vast heterogeneous nation-state such as the United States can only be promoted by force—something along the lines, perhaps, of banning books and tightening control of educational curricula by the state, and perhaps even preventing significant segments of society from full and equal representation and participation in the educational project. This, of course, constitutes a violation of the principles informing both democracy and liberal education. The question raised by MacIntyre's challenge is simply this: Is there reason to think that the promotion of a form of virtue, the self-critical willingness to resist the pull of imperious group identity, is impossible in the intellectual world of a cosmopolitan and pluralist university system? The honest answer, it seems to me, is that it does make the kind of virtue envisioned by his notion of an "educated public" out of reach in heterogeneous liberal democracies, for reasons MacIntyre has in mind. There is simply too much plurality in nations such as the United States to generate the kind of ideological solidarity MacIntyre admires, and he is, of course, fully aware of this. In fact, the forms such cohesion can take in large, plural, impersonal nation-states are, Adorno warns us, likely to be pathological and dangerous.[40] Nationalist groups not only view foreign nations as threats, but unfavored groups (be they racially, ethnically, sexually, or religiously defined) within the nation as threats to national purity to be repressed and controlled to one degree or another. From the perspective of liberal education, the desire to promote an ideological consensus is a project that has failed in the United States in the past and will fail in the future as long as free intellectual inquiry is valued and protected. Liberal learning, as I have had occasion to note a number of times in this book, will always push, to one degree or another, against conventional wisdom and majority opinion.

What MacIntyre seeks, then, is more than liberal education in a society such as ours can offer, and this is perhaps even true in a more homogenous community, such as the Athenian polis (as witnessed by Socrates's fate). MacIntyre is deeply pessimistic about the possibility for significant moral lessons to be learned in the liberal education promoted within a morally pluralistic society; he contends that intellectual incoherence and a kind of intellectual consumerism is all we can expect within such large, heterogeneous liberal democracies as the United States. It seems to me, however, that we can still hope for a more modest form of virtue to be promoted by such an education. Liberal education is much more likely to promote "critical self-reflection" than civic solidarity, and this may, in fact, be virtue enough to challenge at least the very worst civic pathologies that threaten us. The basic project of the humanities and fine arts, for example, aims to expose students to a significant range of human voices and perspectives, to encourage them to reflect on both the diversity of human experience and the equality of human nature that allows significant communication and sharing across the divides of these experiences. There is no assurance that this will provoke the kind of thoughtfulness that Adorno thinks is so central to resisting pathological calls for solidarity and hatefulness toward "outsiders," but there is also little that we can imagine, from the perspective of our educational options, to be more likely to resist the allure of blind hatred and chauvinism.[41] We can imagine that a student exposed to different views, cultures, and histories might take the imperial perspective and simply view all these artifacts as illustrations of other people and groups who really have nothing to say, personally, to him or her. Thoughtfully taught, however, the richness of human experience can encourage students to sympathize with, understand, and relate to those from different times, places, and experiences. To the degree that this happens, we have reason to hope that our students will be less likely to succumb to simplistic demands for (exclusionary) solidarity. We know there are all too many examples of failures along these lines on college and university campuses. Examples of intolerance and mob-like behavior on liberal arts campuses are frequently brought to our attention as illustrative of the ideological nature of contemporary higher education.[42] I'll have more to say about this below, but for now it is enough to note that these are illustrations of the failure, rather than the character, of communities committed to liberal education. Even in these communities, the politics and passions of group solidarity can overwhelm the work of liberal learning.[43] This work is hard and uncertain in outcome.

Michael Walzer once noted that "democracy is a wager and education the means of winning it."[44] Liberal education is not a science, and no outcomes are assured. Jonathan Marks also uses the language of wagering in regard to democratic educational aspirations when he suggests that it is the "Enlightenment gamble" that the liberal polity can withstand the scrutiny of liberally educated individuals.[45] There is no certainty that these individuals will exhibit enough democratic virtue to prevent the triumph of illiberalism, or that liberal democracy will itself be virtuous (or liberal) enough to tolerate the dissension and disagreement that liberally educated people will certainly display. But it is a gamble worth taking, and the outcome worth striving for. Azar Nafisi is speaking of fiction when she writes that reading "arouses our curiosity, and it is this curiosity, this restlessness, this desire to know that makes both writing and reading so dangerous."[46] Her point applies equally well to the reading of all serious works and the danger this presents to despots and authoritarians and all who would impel individuals to conform to the dogma of a group. Her point, we might say, applies to the project of liberal education, when she suggests not that we read a "literature of resistance," but rather that we read "*literature as resistance*."[47] The freedom gained from liberal learning is unlikely to generate conformity or thoughtless dogma. This may be all the virtue we can hope for, but it is no small thing and may be virtue enough to help us resist the worst in the political world.

▬▬▬▬▬ The philosopher John Searle once commented that "one of the aims of a liberal education is to liberate our students from the contingencies of their backgrounds." Such an education, he suggests, constitutes an "invitation to transcendence."[48] This is a powerful insight for two reasons. First, it suggests that conventional criticisms of liberal education as little more than the reproduction of elite culture and power relations, such as we find from left-wing critics since Dewey and from MAGA Republicans on the right today, misses the liberatory power of the exposure to the world the humanities, the arts, the sciences, in opening new ways of thinking, and thereby new possibilities, for students. The revelation that Frederick Douglass reports in his *Narrative* about reading a dialogue between a rebellious slave and a master is to the point; literacy, for Douglass, allowed him to see his condition in a new light, to make it impossible for him to believe that the slave society into which he was born was either just or necessary.[49] This is one of the most dramatic illustrations from American letters of the point Searle is making: exposure to a world of ideas greater than our own experience is a profound aid for imagining alternatives to these experiences. This is another way of saying that such an education opens doors of possibility for the students they couldn't have imagined before this education. Liberal education, at least in principle, is an antidote to, not a cause of, unjust social relationships.

A second powerful point captured in Searle's comments is that the most profound goods of a liberal education must be viewed as goods for individual students. Emphasizing the economic benefits of liberally educated individuals along with their civic obligations and contributions can, of course, be thought of as capturing at least a modicum of concern for student's well-being; we hope to help them prosper responsibly in the economic and civic spheres as presumably something both good for them and for society at large. The emphasis in these arguments, however, is overwhelmingly on the good for society of educating the young in this way. Democracies need creative, responsible, and independent workers and citizens, and, the argument goes, that is why it is worth the cost to society to broadly provide a liberal education to the young. When we turn to the philosophical goods of a liberal education, however, the emphasis is necessarily reversed. Just as Socrates suggested that philosophical examination was a necessary component of a good life, so must we emphasize a concern for the well-being of the student at the heart of liberal learning. The perspective here is that of the teacher rather than of the society at large; we must focus on the good(s) we can bring to individual students before us. The first two concerns of liberal education imagine each new generation standing before the society as a whole and argues for an educational program from the imagined perspective and needs of that society. The philosophical concern imagines most importantly the student before the teacher. Rather than demanding, as society does, that students become a particular kind of contributor to the whole, that they freely assume what society takes to be their responsibilities, the philosophical element imagines the teacher asking, What can I do to help you live a life that is free and rewarding, that allows you to flourish in the most humane ways available to you?

Marks observes that the aim of liberal education is less to produce a set of skills than to help shape "a kind of person," by which he means simply that we hope to produce students who are well informed about the world in which they live, but even more importantly, who are also thoughtful, reasonable, nondogmatic, able to imagine the perspective of other people, and able to engage in fruitful conversation with others. These qualities of reason are central to the character of democratic citizens, Susan Neiman notes, for "the distinction between reason and violence undergirds the distinction between democracy and fascism, and any hope of resisting the slide toward fascism depends on remembering the difference."[50] But the concern in the classroom is less about the needs of democracy than aiding the student in becoming free to develop her own thoughts and commitments in a considered and coherent way. This happens not through skilled "information transfer," or the use of cutting-edge technologies, or the most scientific pedagogies. It happens through a sympathetic relationship between student and teacher. Alexander

Meiklejohn once suggested that the "relation of teacher and pupil is always a somewhat mystical one. Learning is chiefly by imitation or by contagion."[51] William Willimon and Thomas Naylor say they "dream of colleges and universities where mature adults eagerly share with those on their way to maturity the discourse of friendship."[52] Ruth Grant suggests that "we might do well to think less about how we can improve *them* [students] and more about overcoming the obstacles, personal and institutional, to conducting *ourselves* [teachers] with integrity."[53] All of these comments suggest that a critical element in liberal education is not only the scholarly expertise of the teacher, but the kind of relationship she or he builds with students. This relationship is not narrowly professional, a simple market exchange between a consumer and the provider of a service. The prevalence of market language to describe students' relationship to colleges and universities does nothing to give it dignity or to capture its full drama. Contrast such talk with Danielle Allen's claim that "laughter is education's catalyst." "Why is it so? Because laughter is a mark or source of friendship, and friendship is crucial to encountering what is novel, alien, and unsettling, and such is the business of learning."[54] The teacher must display virtues of intellect and character that inspire students, as Meiklejohn suggests, to imitate the teacher's relationship to the material being studied. There are, of course, significant professional boundaries to this relationship, but there are also very personal elements to it.[55] This gives teachers power for both good and ill, and responsible teaching in the liberal arts requires a strict ethics to channel these powers. The paradox here is that to learn to be reasonable, students must be drawn to responsible teachers. This paradox shapes the ethical environment in which liberal education takes place. The teacher must be an exemplar of scholarly investigation and discussion and must successfully invite the student to enter this world. This requires expertise, of course, but that alone is not sufficient to the craft. The teacher shows the student what it means to ask certain questions, why they are important, and the ways we can responsibly attempt to answer them.

There are three more points of significance here. The first is that exposure to the concerns raised in a liberal education are the concerns raised in the course of living a human life. One does not need to be exceptional in any way, or talented above all others, to be confronted by the problems addressed in literature, art, history, social science, and the natural sciences. The normative elements of a liberal education underscore what the McWilliamses referred to as "the greatest of all political mysteries, the proposition that all of us are created equal."[56] It is our common humanity that brings us to liberal education and allows the cultural inheritance this education addresses speak to each of us. To suggest that only a special few are interested in such questions or deserving of the leisure in which to reflect on them (with the aid of a responsible teacher) is to deny an essential sense of our equality with not just our contemporaries, but with those who have lived before (and in radically different circumstances). The skilled exposure to materials that help every student "transcend their circumstances" is owed to every young person preparing to freely assume their place in the world. Liberal education should be provided for the good of our economy and our polity, but just as much for the good of every citizen as a matter of right. Such a conclusion is required in any liberal democracy claiming to cherish and cultivate the freedom of its young and future citizens.

Second, from Dewey's time to our own, liberals and progressives have suspected that the traditional liberal arts represent a conservative educational program designed to teach a distorted view of our cultural inheritance to reinforce the power and ideology of the already powerful. The "classical education movement" today is clearly identified with Hillsdale College, conservative political theorists and historians who produced "The 1776 Report," and other fellow travelers with the new forms of Republican conservatism.[57] The liberal arts education I have defended in this work differs from these movements less in principle than in practice. The canon I propose is diverse, cosmopolitan, and always evolving, while the culture war conservatives promote a static canon to enforce a static, backward-looking worldview. I share with these conservatives the fear of overly politicized pedagogies, but I suspect such politics in their own.[58] I share the commitment to exposing students to the "best" that our cultural inheritance has to offer, but I contend that we need a vastly more expansive understanding of all that this may include than some would suggest. At the end of the day, any program of liberal education designed to promote the perspective of a specific political party or political movement is, in my view, engaged in a contradiction with the education it professes to value.

In a recent and pointed exchange in the *New York Review of Books*, Erin Maglaque criticizes the "classical education movement" defended by Harvard historian James Haskins by pointing out that Umberto Eco years ago noted one feature of fascism as "the cult of tradition" within which "there can be no advancement of learning. Truth has been already spelled out once and for all, and we can only keep interpreting its obscure message." Such an understanding of "cultural" or liberal tradition is both dangerous and a lie, and any movement today that tries to control the meaning of history and intellectual tradition in this way is equally dangerous. Maglaque suggests that only the "progressive movement" promotes a critical view of the past and is therefore the only true education.[59] In this way, she takes the bait in the culture war battles by thinking we must either defend or criticize tradition. Liberal education, however, isn't committed to either promoting or criticizing the past, but rather to the serious encounter with and reflection about it. The outcome of this reflection is not predetermined. To insist that it is, by either the right or the left, is to violate the integrity of the student we are attempting to educate to liberty.

Finally, the point must be made one more time: although a philosophical liberal education should be offered to the young as a matter of right, we may hope that such an education will promote the respect for reason that can combat a politics of brute power. The uncertainty here is great, and there is, in fact, danger in the project. The young are passionate, and often the best among them are among the most passionate. When passionate people have a growing but incomplete knowledge, and are simultaneously encouraged to significant levels of self-confidence, it is not unknown that angry, self-righteous, and highly ideological politics can take hold. Students, in times of crisis, can be among the most visionary, and the blindest, of citizens. We in the United States are still deeply divided in our understanding of the moral virtue of the student movements of the 1960s and 70s; the culture war battles that were generated at that time still find purchase in contemporary debates about the current academy.[60] For all their excesses, my sympathies are more with than against the students of that generation, but it is clear that others hold a significantly different view. I am also sensitive to the degree to which contemporary political fissures generate strains of student activism I find deeply troubling.[61] The danger of liberal education enflaming antidemocratic passions is real enough, regardless of one's own partisan politics.[62]

Recall, against these dangers, the optimistic proposal for liberal education made in Salman Rushdie's novel *Victory City*, which serves as an epigraph to this book. The founder of the city in this story, Pampa Kampana, proposes that education should no longer be controlled by religious authorities:

Instead, she set out to create a new professional class of people who would be called, simply, "teachers," who might be members of any caste, and who would possess and seek to impart the best available knowledge in a wide variety of fields—history, law, geography, health, civics, medicine, astronomy. These so-called "subjects" would be taught without any religious slant or emphasis, with a view to producing new kinds of people, broad in knowledge and mind, still well-versed in matters of faith but with a deep additional understanding of the beauty of knowledge itself, and of the responsibility of citizens to coexist with one another, and with a commitment to advancing the well-being of all.[63]

We hope, with this founder, for students who learn the "beauty of knowledge itself," and that civic responsibility and commitment to the common good will also flow from this education.

▬▬▬ To teach at all, let alone to teach the liberal arts and sciences, during dark times is to engage in an activity out of step with the moment. Crises demand engagement and action; liberal learning requires retreat and reflection. Politics aims at immediate ends; education looks to tomorrow, and to the tomorrow beyond that. Dark times require specific and detailed plans and programs, while liberal education traffics in abstractions and generalities, in experiences and ideas at least one step removed from contemporary events.

There is always a possible frustration here, a desire to turn our liberal learning into a form of politics. That, of course, would be to transform it into something else, and that something else is not something we should desire. There will be those who view the abstractions and generalities as threats to their particular and immediate programs, which, in fact, they may be; any education that makes slogans and ideological posturing the subject of skeptical scrutiny, indeed, that teaches us the dangers and falsity of such simplifications, is bound to be a threat to some who are politically engaged.

So why teach when the world is on fire? Why not turn, instead, to politics? Why continue to pursue liberal learning?

The only reason is to maintain hope for the future. We need responsible citizens to address the profound problems facing us today and threatening our tomorrow. To liberally educate the maturing generation is an act of faith that there will continue to be the potential for democratic politics and individual freedom in the future, and for the possibility of students to live meaningful, thoughtful, and richly and humanely pleasurable lives.

Success is by no means assured. To corrupt liberal education by overly politicizing it, or by simply giving up on it in favor of more immediate concerns, however, is to turn away from the possibilities of the future we profess our concern for. It is to renounce the faith owed to rising generations for whom liberty rather than submission, and reflection rather than conformity, provide their greatest hope for prospering.

▬▬ NOTES

Introduction

1. Jonathan Marks, *Let's Be Reasonable* (Princeton, NJ: Princeton University Press, 2021), 5.

2. See Katherine Brooks, "President Obama Sends Handwritten Apology to Art History Professor," *HuffPost*, February 18, 2014, https://www.huffpost.com /entry/obama-art-history_n_4809007.

3. No less an observer of higher education than Louis Menand suggests that undergraduates have "largely stopped taking humanities courses." He notes that only 8 percent of the incoming class entering Harvard University in 2021 said they intended to select majors in one of the twenty-one programs in the division of arts and humanities. See Menand, "What's So Great about Great-Books Courses?" *New Yorker*, December 20, 2021, 66.

CHAPTER 1. Liberal Education and the American Tradition

1. Plato, *The Republic*, translated by G. M. A. Grube and C. D. C. Reeve (Indianapolis: Hackett, 1992), 2; 327. I've included the standard citations for classical works after the page of the editions I cite.

2. In the *Apology*, Plato tells us that Socrates was thirty votes short of acquittal. We don't know for certain the total number of jurors, but by law it had to be at least 500. Most commonly it is thought to have been 501 in Socrates's case.

3. Aristotle, *Politics*, trans. C. D. C. Reeve (Indianapolis: Hackett, 1998), 230; 1338.

4. Aristotle, *Politics*, 235; 1340:15.

5. It also included, for Aristotle, training in the arts of music and drawing and physical training in gymnastics. See Aristotle, *Politics*, 228–31; 1337–38.

6. Historian John R. Thelin points out that Newman's book was not initially popular, but was revived and thought to be canonical for the liberal education literature in the twentieth century. See Thelin, *A History of American Higher Education*, 2nd ed. (Baltimore: Johns Hopkins University Press, 2011), 88.

7. John Henry Newman, *The Idea of a University* (New Haven, CT: Yale University Press, 1996), 45.

8. Newman, *The Idea of a University*, 77.

9. Newman, *The Idea of a University*, 25.

10. Newman, *The Idea of a University*, 83.

11. Newman, *The Idea of a University*, 81.

12. Newman, *The Idea of a University*, 78.

13. Newman, *The Idea of a University*, 109.

14. Newman, *The Idea of a University*, 85.

15. Newman, *The Idea of a University*, 89.

16. Newman, *The Idea of a University*, 90.

17. Newman, *The Idea of a University*, 125.

18. John Stuart Mill, "Inaugural Address Delivered to the University of St. Andrews, 1867," in *Collected Works of John Stuart Mill* (Toronto: University of Toronto Press, 1984), 21:218.

19. Mill, "Inaugural Address," 21:218

20. Mill, "Inaugural Address," 21:223.

21. Mill, "Inaugural Address," 21:219.

22. Mill, "Inaugural Address," 21:243.

23. Mill, "Inaugural Address," 21:249.

24. Mill, "Inaugural Address," 21:248.

25. Mill, "Inaugural Address," 21:257.

26. Mill, "Inaugural Address," 21:243–44.

27. David Foster Wallace, *This Is Water* (New York: Little, Brown, 2009), 69.

28. John Stuart Mill, *Utilitarianism* (Indianapolis: Bobbs-Merrill Co., 1957), 18.

29. Mill, *Utilitarianism*, 19.

30. George Marsden points out that "early New England had been ruled, perhaps more than any culture in history, by the educated"; Marsden, *Jonathan Edwards* (New Haven, CT: Yale University Press, 2003), 61.

31. See, for example, Orestes Brownson's attack on Horace Mann, "The Second Annual Report of the Board of Education, Together with the Second Annual Report of the Secretary of the Board," *Boston Quarterly Review* 2 (October 1839): 393–434. I discuss this in Bob Pepperman Taylor, *Horace Mann's Troubling Legacy* (Lawrence: University of Kansas Press, 2010), 68–70.

32. Carl Kastle, *Pillars of the Republic* (New York: Hill and Wang, 1983), 33.

33. Quoted in E. D. Hirsch, *The Making of Americans* (New Haven, CT: Yale University Press, 2009), 7.

34. Maris A. Vinovskis, *Education, Society, and Economic Opportunity* (New Haven, CT: Yale University Press, 1995), 77.

35. Merle Curti, *The Social Ideas of American Educators* (Totowa, NJ: Little-field, Adams, 1959), 100.

36. Ira Katznelson and Margaret Weir, *Schooling for All* (New York: Basic Books, 1985), 10.

37. Diane Ravitch, *The Troubled Crusade* (New York: Basic Books, 1983), xii.

38. Rush Welter, *Popular Education and Democratic Thought in America* (New York: Columbia University Press, 1962), 1. Lawrence Cremin suggests, "Whereas Emerson had looked forward to the day when education would supplant politics, Dewey announced that the day had already arrived"; Cremin, *Traditions of American Education* (New York: Basic Books, 1977), 94. Evidence for Cremin's claim can be found in John Dewey, "My Pedagogic Creed" (1897): "I believe that education is the fundamental method of social progress and reform." He also says, "I believe that every teacher should realize the dignity of his calling; that he is a social servant set apart for the maintenance of proper social order and the securing of the right social growth. I believe that in this way the teacher always is the prophet of the true God and the usherer in of the true kingdom of God"; see Dewey, *The Early Works* (Carbondale: Southern Illinois University Press, 1972), 5:93, 95.

39. W. E. B. DuBois, *The Souls of Black Folk* (New York: Library of America, 1990), 70.

40. Frederick Rudolph, *The American College and University* (Athens: University of Georgia Press, 1990), 47.

41. Rudolph, *The American College and University*, 48.

42. See Adam Harris, *The State Must Provide* (New York: HarperCollins, 2021).

43. Roger L. Geiger, *American Higher Education since World War II* (Princeton, NJ: Princeton University Press, 2019), xii.

44. Andrew Hacker and Claudia Dreifus, *Higher Education?* (New York: Times Books, 2010), 183.

45. The National Center for Education Statistics reports that in 2010, undergraduate enrollment was approximately 18.1 million students, and that number declined over the next decade (2021) by 15 percent to 15.4 million. See https://nces.ed.gov/programs/coe/indicator/cha.

46. Hacker and Dreifus, *Higher Education?*, 101.

47. The National Center for Education Statistics reports 837,100 full-time faculty in 2021. The total number of faculty is 1.5 million. See https://nces.ed.gov/programs/coe/indicator/csc.

48. Thomas Jefferson, *Notes on Virginia* (Chapel Hill: University of North Carolina Press, 1982), 146–49.

49. Historian James Axtell notes that because Harvard was the only college in the early colonies, it needed to "prepare a diverse cross-section of *future* leaders and professionals" (not just clergy). He also points out, however, that the "function of [college] education was less to make these young men eligible for membership in the elite than to complete and confirm their qualification, right, and obligation to govern that already existed"; Axtell, *Wisdom's Workshop: The Rise of the Modern University* (Princeton, NJ: Princeton University Press, 2016), 116; James Axtell, *The School upon a Hill: Education and Society in Colonial New England* (New Haven, CT: Yale University Press, 1974), 208.

50. Catharine Beecher, *The Duty of American Women to Their Country* (New York: Harper and Brothers, 1845), 3–4.

51. Beecher, *The Duty of American Women*, 32.

52. Derek Bok, *Our Underachieving Colleges* (Princeton, NJ: Princeton University Press, 2006), 22.

53. Roger L. Geiger, *The History of American Higher Education: Learning and Culture from the Founding to World War II* (Princeton, NJ: Princeton University Press, 2015), 524.

54. Thelin, *History of American Higher Education*, 41–42.

55. Rudolph, *The American College and University*, 47.

56. Yale Report of 1828 ("Reports on the Course of Instruction in Yale College by a Committee of the Corporation and the Academical Faculty": New Haven, 1828), https://www.yale.edu/about-yale/president-leadership/governance-historic-documents/historic-documents-reference-material, 6.

57. Yale Report of 1828, 14.

58. Yale Report of 1828, 15.

59. Yale Report of 1828, 15.

60. Yale Report of 1828, 35.

61. Yale Report of 1828, 36.

62. Yale Report of 1828, 51.

63. Yale Report of 1828, 29.

64. Yale Report of 1828, 34–35.

65. Yale Report of 1828, 38.

66. Rudolph, *The American College and University*, 12.

67. Yale Report of 1828, 30.

68. Thelin, *A History of American Higher Education*, 41.

69. See note 49, above.

70. Thelin, *A History of American Higher Education*, 90.

71. The American Association of University Professors' (AAUP) *1915 Declaration of Principles* captures nicely the scholarly sensibility of the new research university. Here it is declared that "scientific knowledge is essential to civilization," that professors are to become "scientific experts," and that the "modern university is becoming more and more the home of scientific research"; see https://aaup-ui.org/Documents/Principles/Gen_Dec_Princ.pdf.

72. John Guillory, *Professing Criticism* (Chicago: University of Chicago Press, 2022), 33.

73. Bruce Kuklick, "The Emergence of the Humanities," in *The Politics of Liberal Education*, ed. Darryl J. Gless and Barbara Hernstein Smith (Durham, NC: Duke University Press, 1992), 209.

74. Kuklick, "The Emergence of the Humanities," 209–10.

75. Irving Babbitt, *Literature and the American College* (Boston: Houghton, Mifflin and Co., 1908), 31.

76. Babbitt, *Literature and the American College*, 65.

77. Babbitt, *Literature and the American College*, 70.

78. Babbitt, *Literature and the American College*, 240.

79. Babbitt, *Literature and the American College*, 251.

80. Alexander Meiklejohn, *The Liberal College* (Boston: Marshall Jones, 1920), 50.

81. Meiklejohn, *The Liberal College*, 59.

82. Meiklejohn, *The Liberal College*, 26.

83. Meiklejohn, *The Liberal College*, 23.

84. Robert Maynard Hutchins, *The Higher Learning in America* (New Haven, CT: Yale University Press, 1936), 36.

85. Hutchins, *The Higher Learning in America*, 58.

86. Hutchins, *The Higher Learning in America*, 65.

87. Historian Julie Reuben notes that the "great books" programs, developed in the 1920s at Chicago, Columbia, and elsewhere, were offered as alternatives to social science "citizenship" courses as the "model core curriculum"; Reuben, *The Making of the Modern University* (Chicago: University of Chicago Press, 1996), 228.

88. Report of the Harvard Committee, *General Education in a Free Society* (Cambridge, MA: Harvard University Press, 1945), 53.

89. Report of the Harvard Committee, *General Education in a Free Society*, 54.

90. Report of the Harvard Committee, *General Education in a Free Society*, 70.

91. Report of the Harvard Committee, *General Education in a Free Society*, 72–74.

92. Report of the Harvard Committee, *General Education in a Free Society*, 95.

93. Report of the Harvard Committee, *General Education in a Free Society*, 43.

94. Louis Menand, *The Marketplace of Ideas* (New York: W. W. Norton, 2010), 40.

95. Report of the Harvard Committee, *General Education in a Free Society*, 4.

96. Report of the Harvard Committee, *General Education in a Free Society*, 12.

97. President's Commission on Higher Education, *Higher Education for American Democracy* (New York: Harpers and Brothers, 1947), 1:17.

98. President's Commission on Higher Education, *Higher Education for American Democracy*, 1:18.

99. President's Commission on Higher Education, *Higher Education for American Democracy*, 1:6.

100. President's Commission on Higher Education, *Higher Education for American Democracy*, 2:26.

101. President's Commission on Higher Education, *Higher Education for American Democracy*, 1:101.

102. President's Commission on Higher Education, *Higher Education for American Democracy*, 1:51.

103. Victor L. Butterfield, *The Faith of a Liberal College* (Middletown, CT: Wesleyan University Press, 1955), 3.

104. Butterfield, *The Faith of a Liberal College*, 3.

105. Butterfield, *The Faith of a Liberal College*, 28.

106. Reuben, *The Making of the Modern University*, 229.

107. Julie Reuben, "Virtue and the History of the Modern American University," in *Cultivating Virtue in the University*, ed. Jonathan Brant, Edward Brooks, and Michael Lamb (Oxford: Oxford University Press, 2022), 35.

108. Will Bunch, *After the Ivory Tower Falls* (New York: HarperCollins, 2022), 64.

109. W. B. Carnochan notes, "What is important about the years between the wars is not that they produced true consensus but that they did not"; Carnochan, *The Battleground of the Curriculum* (Stanford, CA: Stanford University Press, 1993), 87.

110. Reuben, "Virtue and the History of the Modern American University," 33.

111. Allan Bloom, *The Closing of the American Mind* (New York: Simon and Schuster, 1987); John Agresto, *The Death of Learning* (New York: Encounter Books, 2022).

112. James M. Buchanan and Nicos E. Devletoglou, *Academia in Anarchy* (New York: Basic Books, 1970).

113. Bunch, *After the Ivory Tower Falls*, 88.

114. Bunch, *After the Ivory Tower Falls*, 87.

115. Roger Geiger writes of the 1970s as a "dismal decade" for higher education: "After three decades of exertions by state and federal governments to erect the world's most comprehensive and competent system of higher education, the tide was turning toward privatization" (Geiger, *American Education since World War II*, 269).

116. See https://www.theguardian.com/us-news/2017/oct/06/donald-trump
-jr-says-college-campuses-teach-americans-to-hate-their-country-and-religion.

117. See, for example, George Will's pleasure at seeing what he calls the "leakage
of prestige from politicized universities" resulting from student demonstrations at Columbia University and elsewhere against the war in Gaza. See Will, "The Leakage of
Universities' Prestige amid Protests Is Most Welcome," *Washington Post*, April 26, 2024.

118. Andrew Delbanco, *College: What It Was, Is, and Should Be* (Princeton,
NJ: Princeton University Press, 2012), xv.

119. Contrast the values of liberal democracy with these comments by Ioannis
Metaxas, the fascist Greek dictator, in his first address to Greek university students
in the 1930s: "I forbid any of you, male or female, to have any ideas other than those
of the State. I require you not only to have the same ideas as the state, but to believe
in them and to work accordingly with enthusiasm. If any of you have different ideas
he or she had better not be educated"; see Roderick Beaton, *Greece* (Chicago: University of Chicago Press, 2019), 258.

120. Alexis de Tocqueville, *Democracy in America*, ed. and trans. Harvey C.
Mansfield and Delba Winthrop (Chicago: University of Chicago Press, 2002), 199.

121. Tocqueville, *Democracy in America*, 403.

122. Bob Pepperman Taylor, *Horace Mann's Troubling Legacy* (Lawrence: University Press of Kansas, 2010), 66–67.

123. See Karl Jaspers, *The Idea of the University* (Boston: Beacon Press, 1959), 97.

124. Jill Lepore, *These Truths: A History of the United States* (New York: W. W.
Norton, 2018), xiv. Lepore is echoing Alexander Hamilton in *Federalist*, no. 1: "It has
frequently been remarked that it seems to have been reserved to the people of this
country, by their conduct and example, to decide the important question, whether societies of men are really capable or not of establishing good government from reflection and choice, or whether they are forever destined to depend for their political con-
stitutions on accident and force"; see Alexander Hamilton, James Madison, John Jay,
The Federalist Papers, ed. Clinton Rossiter (New York: Mentor Books, 1999), 1. Thanks
to an anonymous reviewer for reminding me of Hamilton's comment.

CHAPTER 2. Action

1. Plato, *Republic*, trans. G. M. A Grube and C. D. C. Reeve (Indianapolis:
Hackett, 1992), 199; 527b.

2. Plato, *Republic*, 200; 527d.

3. Henry Adams, *The Education of Henry Adams*, in *Henry Adams* (New
York: Library of America, 1983), 768.

4. Cathy N. Davidson, *The New Education* (New York: Basic Books, 2017), 4.

5. Mark C. Taylor, *Crisis on Campus* (New York: Alfred A. Knopf, 2010), 8, 16.

6. Jason Wingard, *The College Devaluation Crisis* (Stanford, CA: Sanford University Press, 2022), 9, 39.

7. Corinee Ruff, "Computer Science, Meet Humanities: In New Majors, Opposites Attract," *Chronicle of Higher Education*, January 28, 2016, http://chronicle .com/article/Computer-Science-Meet/235075.

8. Jeffrey J. Selingo, "It's Time to End College Majors as We Know Them," *Chronicle of Higher Education*, May 20, 2018.

9. Educational Advisory Board, *Reclaiming the Value of the Liberal Arts for the 21st Century*, 2016, https://eab.com/resources/research-report/reclaiming-the -value-of-the-liberal-arts-for-the-21st-century/.

10. SimpsonScarborough, "Selling the Value: Positioning and Marketing Colleges of Arts & Sciences in a Pre-Professional-Focused World," CCAS Annual Meeting, Austin, TX, November 2014.

11. Editors of *Scientific American*, "STEM Education Is Vital—but Not at the Expense of the Humanities," *Scientific American*, October 1, 2016.

12. Davidson, *The New Education*, 100.

13. Scott Jaschik, "Study Documents Economic Gains from Liberal Arts Education," *Inside Higher Ed*, February 15, 2019.

14. Randall Stross, *A Practical Education: Why Liberal Arts Majors Make Great Employees* (Stanford, CA: Redwood Press, 2017), 240.

15. Tim Cresswell, "The Promise of the Experiential Liberal Arts," *Chronicle of Higher Education*, September 2, 2018, https://www.chronicle.com/article/the-promise -of-the-experiential-liberal-arts/.

16. Matthew Hora, *Beyond the Skills Gap* (Cambridge, MA: Harvard Education Press, 2016), 9.

17. William G. Durden, "A Practical Approach for Reinventing Liberal Arts Education," *Inside Higher Ed*, February 28, 2018.

18. American Association of Colleges and Universities (AAC&U), "Statement on Liberal Learning," October 1998, http://www.aacu.org/About/statements/liberal _learning.cfm.

19. Danielle Allen, *Education and Equality* (Chicago: University of Chicago Press, 2016), 17.

20. Fareed Zakaria, *In Defense of Liberal Education* (New York: W. W. Norton, 2016).

21. Mortimer J. Adler, *The Paideia Proposal* (New York: Macmillan, 1982).

22. Again, see Katherine Brooks, "President Obama Sends Handwritten Apology to Art History Professor," *HuffPost*, February 18, 2014, https://www.huffpost .com/entry/obama-art-history_n_4809007.

23. It is also noteworthy, an anonymous reviewer pointed out, that President Obama sent his own children to the Sidwell Friends School, a school unusually rich in opportunities to study the arts and humanities.

24. Woodrow Wilson, "What Is College For?," in *The Papers of Woodrow Wilson* (Princeton, NJ: Princeton University Press, 1975), 19:337.

25. Wilson, "What Is College For?," 19:338–39.

26. Wilson, "What Is College For?," 19:346.

27. Wilson, "What Is College For?," 19:345. It is interesting to note that Henry Seidel Canby, who graduated from Yale (which he took to be one of the last great representatives of the old college system) in 1899, had a different take on the role of the extra-curriculum during the "Gothic age" of the college (that is, the period when so many campuses were transformed with the construction of Gothic style buildings). The modern research university was utilitarian through and through, but the old colleges such as Yale understood that the students saw little or no connection between their formal studies and real work, "or, for that matter with real life." Indeed, faculty "felt, and rightly, that it might be the last chance to bring them into contact with any values not purely utilitarian." The unofficial curriculum, however, made up of the extracurricular clubs, sports teams, and organizations of various types were the locations for students' true preparation for action in the world beyond college. "In short, college life [i.e., the extra-curriculum], which was so often criticized or laughed at, did educate for adult life afterward, and specifically for American life in what was its most typical if not its most admirable aspect" (that is, the world of business, wealth, and power); see Canby, *Alma Mater: The Gothic Age of the American College* (New York: Farrar and Rinehart, 1936), 134, 74–75.

28. Quoted in Bob Pepperman Taylor, *Citizenship and Democratic Doubt* (Lawrence: University Press of Kansas, 2004), 87.

29. "After Nietzsche's devastating criticism of those 'last men' who 'invented happiness,' I may leave aside altogether the naïve optimism in which science—that is, the technique of mastering life which rests upon science—has been celebrated as the way to happiness. Who believes in this?—aside from a few big children in university chairs or editorial offices"; Max Weber, "Science as a Vocation," in *From Max Weber: Essays in Sociology* (New York: Oxford University Press, 1946), 143.

30. Yuval Noah Harari, *Homo Deus: A Brief History of Tomorrow* (New York: Harper, 2017), 202.

31. Roger Geiger, *American Higher Education since World War II* (Princeton, NJ: Princeton University Press, 2019), 355.

32. He writes, for example, that "the attempt to live in the past by way of inviting the soul of our youth to a leisurely and liberal culture merely throws the mass of them upon athletics and extra-curricular activities for their daily sustentation"; John Dewey, "The Modern Trend toward Vocational Education in Its Effect upon the

Professional and Non-Professional Studies of the University," in *The Middle Works* (Carbondale: Southern Illinois University Press, 1985), 10:156–57.

33. Dewey, "The Modern Trend toward Vocational Education," 10:157.

34. Dewey, "The Prospects of the Liberal College," in *The Middle Works* (Carbondale: Southern Illinois University Press, 1988), 15:200.

35. Dewey, *The Educational Situation*, in *The Middle Works* (Carbondale: Southern Illinois University Press, 1976), 1:302.

36. I will look in some detail at the exchanges with both Alexander Meiklejohn and Robert Hutchins in chapter 3.

37. John Dewey, "Learning to Earn: The Place of Vocational Education in a Comprehensive Scheme of Public Education," in *Middle Works*, 10:144.

38. Dewey, *The School and Society*, in *Middle Works*, 1:17.

39. Dewey, *The School and Society*, 1:18.

40. Dewey, "The Modern Trend Toward Vocational Education," 10:154.

41. Dewey, "American Education Culture," in *Middle Works*, 10:200.

42. Dewey, *Democracy and Education*, in *The Middle Works* (Carbondale: Southern Illinois University Press, 1985), 9:231.

43. Dewey, *Democracy and Education*, 9:210.

44. Dewey, *Democracy and Education*, 9:196.

45. John Dewey, "Challenge to Liberal Thought," in *The Later Works* (Carbondale: Southern Illinois University Press, 2008), 15:275.

46. Dewey, "Challenge to Liberal Thought," 15:273.

47. Dewey, *Democracy and Education*, 9:221, 222.

48. Dewey, *Democracy and Education*, 9:159.

49. Dewey, "American Education Culture," 10:198.

50. Jessica Riskin writes of this period: "This new science defined itself by its separateness from all other modes of understanding—by its reductionism, instrumentalism, utilitarianism, and pragmatism. It had no time for Greek or Latin, literature or history, speculations or interpretations, or any idea without immediate industrial and economic application. It had little time for books." She is addressing less democratic forms of the new optimism about science than Dewey's, but much of what she says nonetheless resonates with both Dewey's thought and that of eugenicists and social Darwinists. See Riskin, "A Poisonous Legacy," *The New York Review*, June 12, 2023, 35.

51. Dewey, *Democracy and Education*, 9:143.

52. Dewey, *Democracy and Education*, 9:179.

53. John Dewey, "Our Educational Ideal in Wartime," in *Middle Works*, 10:181.

54. Dewey, *Democracy and Education*, 9:310.

55. Dewey, *Democracy and Education*, 9:204.

56. Dewey, *Democracy and Education*, 9:370.

57. Dewey, *School and Society*, 1:16.

58. John Dewey, "The Problem of the Liberal Arts College," in *Later Works*, 15:279 (italics original).

59. "A truly liberal, and liberating, education would refuse today to isolate vocational training on any of its levels from a continuous education in the social, moral, and scientific contexts within which wisely administered callings and professions must function" (Dewey, "Challenge to Liberal Thought," 264).

60. Friedrich Nietzsche, "On the Future of Our Educational Institutions," https://la.utexas.edu/users/hcleaver/330T/350kPEENietzscheFutureTableCut.pdf, 2.

61. Michael Oakeshott, *The Voice of Liberal Learning* (Indianapolis: Liberty Fund, 2001), 83, 89.

62. Christopher Jencks and David Riesman, *The Academic Revolution* (Garden City, NY: Doubleday, 1968), 244.

63. Jencks and Riesman, *The Academic Revolution* 13.

64. Harry D. Gideonse, *The Higher Learning in a Democracy* (New York: Farrar and Rinehart, 1937), 14.

65. Jason Brennan and Phillip Magness, *Cracks in the Ivory Tower* (New York: Oxford University Press, 2019), 35.

66. Brennan and Magness, *Cracks in the Ivory Tower*, 81 and chap. 3 generally. Another "debunker" is Bryan Caplan, who laments that "*most* of what schools teach has no value in the labor market," and that "about 40% of graduates earn degrees in comically—or tragicomically—useless subjects"; Caplan, *The Case against Education* (Princeton, NJ: Princeton University Press, 2018), 68, 205. Caplan is focusing on primary and secondary education, but his point is the same as that of Brennan and Magness: the "liberal" elements of education are woefully irrelevant to the vocational purposes of education.

67. Upton Sinclair, *The Goose Step: A Study of American Education* (Pasadena, CA: self- published, 1922, 1923), 368.

68. Michael J. Sandel, *The Tyranny of Merit* (New York: Farrar, Straus and Giroux, 2020), 104, 169. Richard Reeves makes the same point: "Postsecondary education in particular has become an 'inequality machine'"; Reeves, *Dream Hoarders* (Washington, DC: Brookings, 2017), 11.

69. Laurence Veysey, *The Emergence of the American University* (Chicago: University of Chicago Press, 1965), 14.

70. Veysey, *The Emergence of the American University*, 16–17.

71. Nathan Heller has recently reported, for example, that in 2012, 20 percent of Harvard students majored in the humanities, but that in 2023 only 7 percent intend to; see Heller, "The End of the English Major," *New Yorker*, March 6, 2023, 31. This process has been at work for more than a generation. "Since 1963 . . . 'liberal

knowledge' has been in retreat, greatly mourned but not even slightly revived, giving way to vocational and professional studies, as well as to greater and greater specialization within the arts and sciences"; Clark Kerr, *The Uses of the University* (Cambridge, MA: Harvard University Press, 1963), 144.

72. Clearly, there is much that can be done to bring us significantly closer to Dewey's vision than we currently are. A reinvigorated labor movement, for example, would go a long way in giving workers significantly more control over working conditions than most currently enjoy. My point isn't to suggest that we can't (or, heaven forbid, shouldn't!) significantly democratize economic life. Rather, it is that Dewey's conception of economic democratization will appear to many, as it does to me, as both vague and utopian in comparison to the real constraints, both legal and ideological, on democratic participation in capitalist economies.

73. Dewey, *Democracy and Education*, 9:361.

74. Dewey, *Democracy and Education*, 9:367, 368.

75. Dewey, *Democracy and Education*, 9:370.

76. Dewey, *School and Society*, 1:20.

77. Raymond Boisvert, a sensitive and thoughtful reader of Dewey, argues that "Dewey admits the irreducibility of pluralism and sets harmony, not unity, as the appropriate human ideal." Robert Talisse, in contrast, concludes that "democracy understood as a 'way of life' in Dewey's sense is resolutely opposed to pluralism." My own reading of the material discussed above suggests to me a much more intense desire on Dewey's part for social unity than Boisvert finds. See Boisvert, *John Dewey: Rethinking Our Time* (Albany: State University of New York Press, 1998), 10; Talisse, *A Pragmatist Philosophy of Democracy* (New York: Routledge, 2007), 45, and 45–48 for the discussion leading to his conclusion.

78. John Patrick Diggins criticizes Dewey on precisely this point, suggesting that Dewey's attempt to dissolve the conflict between "virtue" and "interest" in a democratic synthesis is far from persuasive. See Diggins, "Republicanism and Progressivism," *American Quarterly* 37 (Fall 1985): 586.

79. An anonymous reviewer rightly points out that the recent COVID-19 pandemic presented us with any number of examples of morally difficult choices for physicians, ranging from being single parents with thereby heightened responsibilities to their children, to working in irresponsibly unsafe environments because of a lack of sufficient protective gear or other protective measures, to being forced to work through levels of exhaustion and grief beyond what can reasonably be expected of any human being.

80. It is remarkable to note the limited role, at best, that, Dewey, arguably the most important twentieth-century American philosopher, appears to play in the development of twentieth-century higher education when we read some of the stan-

dard historical studies. Frederick Rudolph and, more recently, John Thelin, don't mention Dewey at all, and he plays only a very minor role in Roger Geiger's study as an advocate of "life skills" and "socio-civic competence"; see Frederick Rudolph, *The American College and University: A History* (Athens: University of Georgia Press, 1990); John R. Thelin, *A History of American Higher Education*, 2nd ed. (Baltimore: Johns Hopkins University Press, 2011). Roger L. Geiger, *The History of American Higher Education* (Princeton, NJ: Princeton University Press, 2015), 434, 457.

    81. Stefan Collini, *What Are Universities For?* (London: Penguin, 2012), 144.

CHAPTER 3. Virtue

    1. Jesse Wegman, "Trump's Lawyers Should Have Known Better," *New York Times*, October 27, 2023, https://www.nytimes.com/2023/10/27/opinion/trump -lawyers.html.

    2. Adam R. Nelson, *Education and Democracy: The Meaning of Alexander Meiklejohn, 1872–1964* (Madison: University of Wisconsin Press, 2001), xiv.

    3. Alexander Meiklejohn, *Education between Two Worlds* (New York: Harper and Brothers, 1942), 67.

    4. Meiklejohn, *Education between Two Worlds*, 67.

    5. Meiklejohn, *Education between Two Worlds*, 127.

    6. Alexander Meiklejohn, *What Does America Mean?* (New York: W. W. Norton, 1972), 42.

    7. Meiklejohn, *What Does America Mean?*, 42.

    8. See John Dewey, *The Public and Its Problems*, ed. Melvin Rogers (Athens, OH: Swallow Press, 2016).

    9. Meiklejohn, *Education between Two Worlds*, 177.

    10. Meiklejohn, *Education between Two Worlds*, 180.

    11. Meiklejohn, *Education between Two Worlds*, 193.

    12. Meiklejohn, *What Does America Mean?*, 65.

    13. Meiklejohn, *What Does America Mean?*, 66.

    14. Meiklejohn, *What Does America Mean?*, 26–27. Recall Ludwig Wittgenstein's comment: "We feel that even if all possible scientific questions be answered, the problems of life have still not been touched at all"; Wittgenstein *Tractatus Logico-Philosophicus* (New York: Harcourt, Brace and Co., 1922), 89, https://www.gutenberg .org/files/5740/5740-pdf.pdf.

    15. Nelson, *Education and Democracy*, 172.

    16. Meiklejohn, *Education between Two Worlds*, 103.

    17. Meiklejohn, *What Does America Mean?*, 233.

18. Meiklejohn, *Education between Two Worlds*, 105–6.

19. Meiklejohn, *Education between Two Worlds*, 282.

20. Meiklejohn, *Education between Two Worlds*, 282.

21. These are among the "essential" writers Meiklejohn identifies in *What Does American Mean?*, 233.

22. Alexander Meiklejohn, *Freedom and the College* (New York: Century, 1923), 105.

23. Meiklejohn, *What Does America Mean?*, 194–95.

24. Meiklejohn, *Education between Two Worlds*, 277.

25. Meiklejohn, *Education between Two Worlds*, 283.

26. Meiklejohn, *Education between Two Worlds*, 286.

27. Meiklejohn, *Education between Two Worlds*, 106.

28. Meiklejohn, *Education between Two Worlds*, 200.

29. "It is chiefly natural science which is responsible for the opinion that knowledge has no unity" (Meiklejohn, *Freedom and the College*, 195).

30. Alexander Meiklejohn, *The Liberal College* (Boston: Marshall Jones, 1920), 23.

31. Meiklejohn, *The Liberal College*, 26.

32. Meiklejohn, *The Liberal College*, 89.

33. Meiklejohn, *What Does America Mean?*, 101.

34. Nelson, *Education and Democracy*, 127.

35. Meiklejohn, *Freedom and the College*, 105.

36. Meiklejohn, *The Liberal College*, 30.

37. Meiklejohn, *The Liberal College*, 50.

38. Meiklejohn, *The Liberal College*, 55.

39. Meiklejohn, *The Liberal College*, 59.

40. Meiklejohn, *The Liberal College*, 89.

41. Quoted in Nelson, *Education and Democracy*, 95.

42. Nelson, *Education and Democracy*, 86.

43. John Dewey, "Challenge to Liberal Thought," *The Later Works* (Carbondale: Southern Illinois University Press, 2008), 15:264, 265.

44. "The very heart of political democracy is adjudication of social differences by discussion and exchange of views. This method provides a rough approximation of the method of effecting change by means of experimental inquiry and test: the scientific method" (Dewey, "Challenge to Liberal Thought," 15:273).

45. Dewey, "Challenge to Liberal Thought," 15:274.

46. Dewey, "Challenge to Liberal Thought," 15:275.

47. Dewey, "Challenge to Liberal Thought," 15:275.

48. Dewey, "Challenge to Liberal Thought," 15:266.

49. Dewey, "Challenge to Liberal Thought," 15:264–65.

50. Dewey, "Challenge to Liberal Thought," 15:274.

51. Alexander Meiklejohn, "A Reply to John Dewey by Alexander Meiklejohn," in Dewey, *The Later Works*, 15:476.

52. Meiklejohn, "A Reply to John Dewey by Alexander Meiklejohn," 15:485.

53. Meiklejohn, "A Reply to John Dewey by Alexander Meiklejohn," 15:336.

54. Meiklejohn, "A Reply to John Dewey by Alexander Meiklejohn," 15:337.

55. The problem here is severe, in Hutchins's view. To justify the kind of sacrifice necessary to defeat Hitler, we need a clear understanding of the value of democracy. But this, he suggests, is precisely what we currently lack, with our overwhelming materialism and moral relativism, which makes clear commitments to principle impossible. "Precisely here lies our unpreparedness. Such principles as we have are not different enough from Hitler's to make us very rugged in defending ours in preference to his. Moreover, we are not united and clear about such principles as we have." And: "It is our duty to our country to do our part to recapture and revitalize those principles which alone make life worth living or death on the field of battle worth facing"; Robert Maynard Hutchins, *Education for Freedom* (Baton Rouge: Louisiana State University Press, 1943), 94, 96.

56. He criticizes what he calls the "cult of scientism, a cult to which, curiously enough, very few natural scientists belong" (Hutchins, *Education for Freedom*, 33). Elsewhere, he writes: "Science has trivialized other fields of learning"; Robert M. Hutchins, *The University of Utopia* (Chicago: University of Chicago Press, 1953), 16.

57. "Materialism has captured our culture. It has captured our state. It has captured education" (Hutchins, *Education for Freedom*, 42).

58. He accuses President Eliot of Harvard of being a "great criminal" who pursued the "task of robbing American youth of their cultural heritage," by replacing a required curriculum with an elective system. The curricular focus now becomes "relevance" to the immediate interests, almost inevitably material and vocational interests, of students. "Triviality, mediocrity, and vocationalism take over because we have no standard by which to judge them" (Hutchins, *Education for Freedom*, 25, 26).

59. He attacks what he calls the "cult of immediacy, or of what may be called presentism" (Hutchins, *Education for Freedom*, 32).

60. His view is that education is currently caught in a bind: it reflects the sensibilities and commitments of the society at large, but these sensibilities and commitments are not fully democratic—they are simply too corrupted by moral relativism and materialist individualism to be so; yet it also needs to cultivate moral values and ideals upon which democracy must rest. We must, therefore, "reconstruct education, directing it to virtue and intelligence" (rather than desire and emotion). To do so will be to actually act contrary to the perceived interests and views of many. See Hutchins, *Education for Freedom*, 47, and 48–63 passim.

61. He criticizes the "method of disposing of philosophy by placing it in a certain time and then saying that time is gone" (Hutchins, *Education for Freedom*, 32–33).

62. Universities must instruct students in the good life, and "a good life is a life directed to knowing the truth and doing justice" (Hutchins, *Education for Freedom*, 103).

63. Robert Maynard Hutchins, *The Conflict in Education in a Democratic Society* (New York: Harper and Brothers, 1953), 66.

64. Hutchins, *University of Utopia*, 35.

65. Hutchins, *Education for Freedom*, 15.

66. Roosevelt Montás, *Rescuing Socrates: How the Great Books Changed My Life and Why They Matter for a New Generation* (Princeton, NJ: Princeton University Press, 2021).

67. Hutchins, *The University of Utopia*, 28–29.

68. Montás, *Rescuing Socrates*, 2.

69. Thomas Ehrlich, for example, writes that Dewey believed "that most citizens, not just an elite, can have a life of the mind." But he ignores the fact that Dewey radically redefined and narrowed what "the life of the mind" could possibly mean to the democratic many. See Ehrlich, "Dewey versus Hutchins: The Next Round," in *Education and Democracy: Re-Examining Liberal Learning in America*, ed. Robert Orrill (New York College Entrance Examination Board, 1997), 259.

70. See Andrew Hacker and Claudia Dreifus, *Higher Education?* (New York: Times Books, 2010), 238.

71. Robert Maynard Hutchins, *The Higher Learning in America* (New Haven, CT: Yale University Press, 1936), 20.

72. Hutchins famously, and wrongly, opposed the G.I. Bill because he thought it would erode the integrity of college education; in truth, the returning soldiers turned out to be among the best students colleges and universities had ever enjoyed.

73. Hutchins, *The Higher Learning*, 6.

74. Hutchins, *Education for Freedom*, 67.

75. Hutchins, *The Higher Learning in America*, 32.

76. Hutchins, *The University of Utopia*, 56, 67.

77. Hutchins, *The University of Utopia*, 91.

78. Hutchins, *The University of Utopia*, 88.

79. Hutchins, *Education for Freedom*, 63.

80. Hutchins, *Education for Freedom*, 104.

81. Report of the Harvard Committee, *General Education in a Free Society* (Cambridge, MA: Harvard University Press, 1945), 4.

82. John Agresto's polemic against what he takes to be the liberal corruption of the humanities—Agresto, *The Death of Learning* (New York: Encounter Books, 2022)—noticeably avoids giving any developed argument about how he would

select the great books that should be included in a proper liberal education. See, for example, page 117, where he distinguishes between "second-rate" and "great" books, in which the former are tied to their historical moment while the latter appeal to universal themes or issues. This, of course, fails to answer why he seems to believe that Toni Morrison's work falls into the "second-rate" category; certainly, there are readers of her work who believe she profoundly probes the human condition. The fact that she sets her stories within particular times and places, and addresses particular historical problems, makes her no different from any other novelist, or even (as historians of ideas are continually reminding us) from philosophers as different as Plato, Aquinas, and Rawls. Agresto writes as if the constitution of the canon of great books is an obvious, noncontroversial matter, which, of course, it is not.

83. See chapter 1, note 22.

84. See, for example, Anthony Kronman, *Education's End* (New Haven, CT: Yale University Press, 2007).

85. See Martha Nussbaum's review of Bloom's *Closing of the American Mind*; Nussbaum, "Undemocratic Vistas," *The New York Review*, November 5, 1987. For a more expansive understanding of what to include in a proper liberal curriculum, see Nussbaum, *Cultivating Humanity* (Cambridge, MA: Harvard University Press, 1997), and Nussbaum, *Not for Profit* (Princeton, NJ: Princeton University Press, 2010).

86. Montás notes the criticism that the focus on the Western tradition in Columbia's Core Curriculum attracts. His own view, it seems to me, is judicious and defensible: "While there is no justification for an *exclusively* Western liberal arts curriculum, there is a compelling case for keeping the Western tradition at the center of general education, at least in the West. In other words, in today's world, the Western tradition is essential, but not sufficient" (Montás, *Rescuing Socrates*, 212–13).

87. Meiklejohn, *Education between Two Worlds*, 199.

88. Stanley Fish, *Save the World on Your Own Time* (New York: Oxford University Press, 2008), 11.

89. Jason Brennan and Phillip Magness, *Cracks in the Ivory Tower* (New York: Oxford University Press, 2019), 264.

90. Daniel Cottom, *Why Education Is Useless* (Philadelphia: University of Pennsylvania Press, 2003), 35.

91. Quoted in Elizabeth Kiss and J. Peter Euben, eds., *Debating Moral Education* (Durham, NC: Duke University Press, 2010), 4.

92. While campaigning, successfully, for the U.S. Senate, J. D. Vance famously suggested that "the professors are the enemy"; see Henry Reichman, "The Professors Are the Enemy," *Chronical of Higher Education*, December 14, 2021. Florida governor Ron DeSantis's takeover of New College of Florida is a more recent illustration of such views. A DeSantis spokesman defended the governor's moves by attacking

what he takes to be an elitist ideology informing much of the academy: "Like so many colleges and universities in America, New College of Florida has been completely captured by a political ideology that puts trendy, truth-relative concepts above learning"; see Nicquel Terry Ellis, "Gov. DeSantis' Conservative Takeover of a Liberal Arts College Could Silence Diversity, Critics Say," CNN.com, February 17, 2023, https://www.cnn.com/2023/02/15/us/desantis-new-college-inclusion-reaj/index.html.

93. C. Wright Mills, *Power, Politics and People* (Oxford: Oxford University Press, 1963), 368.

94. Mills, *Power, Politics and People*, 368.

95. Benjamin Rush, "A Plan for the Establishment of Public Schools and the Diffusion of Knowledge in Pennsylvania; to Which are Added, Thoughts upon the Mode of Education, Proper in a Republic," in *Essays on Education in the Early Republic*, ed. Frederick Rudolph (Cambridge, MA: Harvard University Press, 1965), 14.

96. Frederick Rudolph, *The American College and University* (Athens: University of Georgia Press, 1990), 24.

97. Rudolph, *The American College and University*, 12.

98. John Thelin, *A History of American Higher Education*, 2nd ed. (Baltimore: Johns Hopkins University Press, 2011), 24, 36.

99. Henry P. Tappan, *University Education* (New York: George P. Putnam, 1851), 18.

100. Ronald J. Daniels, *What Universities Owe Democracy* (Baltimore: Johns Hopkins University Press, 2021), 91, 130.

101. Quoted in Roger L. Geiger, *The History of American Higher Education: Learning and Culture from the Founding to World War II* (Princeton, NJ Princeton University Press, 2015), 28.

102. See chapter 2, notes 69, 70.

103. John Guillory, *Professing Criticism* (Chicago: University of Chicago Press, 2022), 29.

104. Laurence Veysey, *Emergence of the American University* (Chicago: University of Chicago Press, 1965), 63–65.

105. Veysey, *Emergence of the American University*, 72.

106. Catharine Beecher, *The Duty of American Women to Their Country* (New York: Harper and Brothers, 1845), 67.

107. For example, see Sean Wilentz, "The Paradox of the American Revolution," *New York Review of Books*, January 13, 2022.

108. Socrates makes this point poetically in the *Republic* when he speaks of education as a "turning around" of the soul. Education "isn't the craft of putting sight into the soul." That is, we shouldn't expect didactic education to be particularly effective, since it misunderstands the nature of a student's lack of understanding; it

can't be addressed by simply filling a student's mind with the right facts or ideas ("putting sight into the soul"). On the contrary, education "takes for granted that sight is there but that it isn't turned the right way or looking where it ought to look, and it tries to redirect it appropriately." True education, in Socrates's sense, is indirect. It is "the craft concerned with doing this very thing, this turning around, and with how the soul can most easily and effectively be made to do it"; Plato, *Republic*, trans. G. M. A. Grube and C. D. C. Reeve (Indianapolis: Hackett, 1992), 190; 518d.

109. See Tom Nichols, *The Death of Expertise* (New York: Oxford University Press, 2017), 28: "The death of expertise is . . . like a national bout of ill temper, a childish rejection of authority in all its forms coupled to an insistence that strongly held opinions are indistinguishable from facts."

110. Report of the Harvard Committee, *Education in a Free Society* (Cambridge, MA: Harvard University Press, 1945), 65.

111. Harvard Committee, *Education in a Free Society*, 70.

112. Harvard Committee, *Education in a Free Society*, 95.

113. Harvard Committee, *Education in a Free Society*, 72, 73.

114. Harvard Committee, *Education in a Free Society*, 43, 267.

115. For a classic study of the necessary conflict between our professed ideals and the realities of practical politic life, see Samuel P. Huntington, *American Politics: The Promise of Disharmony* (Cambridge, MA: Harvard University Press, 1983).

116. For a defense of nondidactic methods of promoting civic virtue in public schooling, see Christopher Eisgruber, "How Do Liberal Democracies Teach Values?," in *Nomos XLIII: Moral and Political Education*, ed. Stephen Macedo and Yael Tamir (New York: New York University Press, 2002), 58–86.

117. See, for example, Kronman, *Education's End*.

118. Patrick J. Deneen, "When Campuses Become Dysfunctional," *Minding the Campus, Reforming Our Universities* (blog of the Center for the University at the Manhattan Institute), May 13, 2009, https://www.mindingthecampus.org/2009/05/13/by_patrick_j_deneen_in/.

119. Deneen, "When Campuses Become Dysfunctional."

120. Patrick J. Deneen, *Why Liberalism Failed* (New Haven, CT: Yale University Press, 2018), 42.

121. Henry David Thoreau, *Walden*, in *A Week on the Concord and Merrimack Rivers; Walden, or, Life in the Woods; The Maine Woods; Cape Cod* (New York: Library of America, 1985), 350.

122. Patrick J. Deneen, *Regime Change* (New York: Sentinel, 2023), 8.

123. Deneen, *Regime Change*, 121.

124. Deneen, *Regime Change*, 47.

125. Chapter 1, note 119.

126.   One could raise doubts about this commitment, given Deneen's pilgrimage to Hungary to meet Victor Orban, whom he praised as a "model" for some U.S. conservatives. He suggested, however, that "I have not endorsed the Orban government . . . mainly because I do not know Hungarian politics well enough to praise or condemn"; see Zak Beauchamp, "The American Right's Favorite Strongman," *Vox*, August 10, 2020, https://www.vox.com/2020/5/21/21256324/viktor-orban-hungary-american-conservatives. See also Ian Ward's profile of Deneen in *Politico*, June 8, 2023, https://www.politico.com/news/magazine/2023/06/08/the-new-right-patrick-deneen-00100279.

127.   Wendell Berry, *What Are People For?* (Berkeley, CA: Counterpoint, 1990/2010), 164.

128.   Wendell Berry, *Hannah Coulter* (Berkeley, CA: Counterpoint, 2004), 151.

129.   Allan Bloom claims that students have been profoundly corrupted by an attitude like this. He writes that moral relativism has "extinguished," for most, "the real motive of education, the search for a good life"; Bloom, *The Closing of the American Mind* (New York: Simon and Schuster, 1987), 34.

130.   Wendy Brown, *Nihilistic Times: Thinking with Max Weber* (Cambridge, MA: Harvard University Press, 2023), 106.

131.   Brown, *Nihilistic Times*, 98.

132.   Agresto, *The Death of Learning*, 152.

133.   Andrew Delbanco quotes John Alexander Smith of Oxford, who addressed an incoming class: "Nothing that you learn in the course of your studies will be of the slightest possible use to you in after life—save only this—that if you work hard and intelligently you should be able to detect when a man is talking rot, and that, in my view, is the main, if not the sole, purpose of education"; Delbanco, *College: What It Was, Is, and Should Be* (Princeton, NJ: Princeton University Press, 2012), 29.

CHAPTER 4. Delight

1.   Plato, *Apology*, in *The Last Days of Socrates*, trans. Hugh Tredennick and Harold Tarrant (Baltimore: Penguin, 1975), 45; 17a–b.

2.   Plato, *Apology*, 45; 17d.

3.   He mentions that he has been guided away from politics by an inner voice (his *daimonion*) ever since he was a child (Plato, *Apology*, 64; 31d).

4.   This is why popularity on the web is almost never achieved by moderate, judicious, or subtle voices. Outrage and outrageousness provide the emotionally charged entertainment that leads to large audiences.

5. Plato, *Gorgias*, trans. Donald J. Zeyl (Indianapolis: Hackett, 1987), 65; 492e. For a modern variant of Callicles, see the character Nagasawa, a ruthless careerist in a novel by Haruki Murakami, *Norwegian Wood* (New York: Vintage, 2000). Of his ambition, he comments, "It's just the hunger I have inside me . . . I can only live with that hunger. That's the kind of man I am" (208).

6. Aristotle, *Politics*, trans. C. D. C. Reeve (Indianapolis: Hackett, 1998), 71; 1276:30.

7. We commonly find such claims in defenses of liberal education. Allan Bloom, *The Closing of the American Mind* (New York: Simon and Schuster, 1987), 108, claims that the "greatest literature addresses the permanent problems of man."

8. Carl Becker, *Detachment and the Writing of History* (Ithaca, NY: Cornell University Press, 1958), 98.

9. This argument, of course, assumes the importance of a broad understanding of the arts that can speak to broad and diverse populations.

10. "So long as there are scientists at work on a cure for cancer, the humanities will have a nearly insurmountable task in making a case in the public sphere for their great, if less obvious, social benefits"; John Guillory, *Professing Criticism* (Chicago: University of Chicago Press, 2022), 109.

11. Harry D. Gideonse, *The Higher Learning in a Democracy* (New York: Farrar and Rinehart, 1937), 19, 14.

12. Thorstein Veblen, *The Higher Learning in America* (B. W. Heubsch, 1918), 176.

13. Veblen, *The Higher Learning in America*, 275. He refers to "the palsied hands of the universities" (273).

14. Veblen, *The Higher Learning in America*, 116, 32.

15. W. E. B. DuBois was one rare contemporary of Veblen agreeing that colleges must value knowledge for its own sake, but he did not hold this to be the only good cultivated by a proper university or college, as Veblen seems to. See DuBois, "Diuturni Silenti," typescript manuscript of Fisk University Commencement Speech at his daughter's graduation in 1924, p. 6, https://credo.library.umass.edu/view/full /mums312-b196-i063.

16. Danielle Allen, *Education and Equality* (Chicago: University of Chicago Press, 2016).

17. The German philosopher Karl Jaspers was much less inhibited than his American colleagues in arguing that the university's function is simply to pursue truth. The very opening page of his *The Idea of the University* claims, "The university is a community of scholars and students engaged in the task of seeking truth." A few pages later: "The thirst for knowledge intrinsically precedes all considerations of usefulness." Finally, the contrast with the American sensibility is completed when he

suggests that "knowledge, not action, is [the university's] link with reality"; Jaspers, *The Idea of the University* (Boston: Beacon Press, 1959), 1, 14, 121.

18. Michael Oakeshott, *The Voice of Liberal Learning* (Indianapolis: Liberty Fund, 2001), 33.

19. Oakeshott, *The Voice of Liberal Learning*, 89.

20. Oakeshott, *The Voice of Liberal Learning*, 15.

21. Oakeshott, *The Voice of Liberal Learning*, 83, 21. Oakeshott's criticism of "socialization" recalls Dewey's demand that education produce, within students, "a socialized disposition"; see John Dewey, *Democracy and Education*, in *Middle Works* (Carbondale: Southern Illinois University Press, 1985), 9:204.

22. Oakeshott, *The Voice of Liberal Learning*, 152.

23. Oakeshott, *The Voice of Liberal Learning*, 104.

24. Oakeshott, *The Voice of Liberal Learning*, 116.

25. Oakeshott, *The Voice of Liberal Learning*, 8.

26. Oakeshott, *The Voice of Liberal Learning*, 15.

27. Oakeshott, *The Voice of Liberal Learning*, 16.

28. Oakeshott, *The Voice of Liberal Learning*, 115.

29. Oakeshott, *The Voice of Liberal Learning*, 113.

30. Oakeshott, *The Voice of Liberal Learning*, 117.

31. Friedrich Nietzsche, "On the Future of Our Educational Institutions" (1872), https://la.utexas.edu/users/hcleaver/330T/350kPEENietzscheFutureTableCut.pdf, 16.

32. Nietzsche, "On the Future of Our Educational Institutions," 21.

33. Nietzsche, "On the Future of Our Educational Institutions," 24.

34. Nietzsche, "On the Future of Our Educational Institutions," 30.

35. Nietzsche, "On the Future of Our Educational Institutions," 17.

36. Nietzsche, "On the Future of Our Educational Institutions," 24, 3.

37. Nietzsche, "On the Future of Our Educational Institutions," 22.

38. Nietzsche, "On the Future of Our Educational Institutions," 21.

39. Nietzsche, "On the Future of Our Educational Institutions," 21.

40. Nietzsche, "On the Future of Our Educational Institutions," 26.

41. The aristocratic commitment to inequality, for example, can appear as narrowly self-interested and vulgar to the democrat as a commitment to human equality can seem to the aristocrat. On what grounds could we convincingly claim that Dewey is less concerned with the "eternal and immutable essence of things" than was, say, Aristotle? Both democrat and aristocrat, in this case, profess a commitment to the natural moral order. Dewey's historicism in no way negates his belief in democracy as the social order in which human beings can finally achieve their true nature.

Notes to Pages 103–108   171

42. Leo Strauss, "What is Liberal Education?," http://ditext.com/strauss/liberal.html.

43. Leo Strauss, "Liberal Education and Responsibility," https://ia601004.us.archive.org/33/items/LeoStraussLiberalEducationResponsibility1960/Leo%20Strauss%20-%20%27%27Liberal%20Education%20%26%20Responsibility%27%27%20%5B~1960%5D.pdf, p. 337.

44. Strauss, "Liberal Education and Responsibility," 342.

45. Strauss, "Liberal Education and Responsibility," 343.

46. Strauss, "Liberal Education and Responsibility," 338.

47. Strauss, "Liberal Education and Responsibility," 326.

48. Strauss, "Liberal Education and Responsibility," 339.

49. All these points are from Strauss, "What Is Liberal Education?"

50. Strauss, "Liberal Education and Responsibility," 344.

51. Strauss, "Liberal Education and Responsibility," 324.

52. I should note that the gendered nature of this description is fully intentional for Strauss.

53. Strauss, "What Is Liberal Education?"

54. Strauss, "Liberal Education and Responsibility," 345.

55. Stanley Fish, "The Woe-Is-Us Books," *New York Times*, November 8, 2010.

56. "Pick up the mission statement of almost any college or university, and you will find claims and ambitions that will lead you to think that it is the job of an institution of higher learning to cure every ill the world has ever known"; Stanley Fish, *Save the World on Your Own Time* (New York: Oxford, 2008), 10.

57. Fish, *Save the World on Your Own Time*, 11.

58. Fish, *Save the World on Your Own Time*, 20.

59. It should be noted that he is primarily addressing faculty in public institutions, and his points do not apply to private colleges and universities with, for example, religious missions.

60. Fish, *Save the World on Your Own Time*, 53.

61. Fish, *Save the World on Your Own Time*, 70.

62. Fish, *Save the World on Your Own Time*, 20.

63. Fish, *Save the World on Your Own Time*, 59.

64. Fish, *Save the World on Your Own Time*, 56.

65. Fish, *Save the World on Your Own Time*, 176.

66. Recall this quote from Newman, mentioned in chapter 1 (note 15): "Liberal education makes not the Christian, not the Catholic, but the gentleman"; John Henry Newman, *The Idea of a University* (New Haven, CT: Yale University Press, 1996), 89.

67. Fish, *Save the World on Your Own Time*, 53.

68. Stanley Fish, "Think Again," *New York Times*, January 9, 2008.

69. Stanley Fish, *Professional Correctness* (Oxford: Oxford University Press, 1995), 59.

70. Fish, *Professional Correctness*, 110.

71. Fish, *Professional Correctness*, 110–11.

72. Fish, *Professional Correctness*, 114.

73. Fish, *Professional Correctness*, 166.

74. See, for example, Danielle Allen, *Our Declaration* (New York: W. W. Norton, 2015), and Allen, *Justice by Means of Democracy* (Chicago: University of Chicago Press, 2023).

75. Melvin L. Rogers, *The Darkened Light of Faith* (Princeton, NJ: Princeton University Press, 2023), 8.

76. Susan Neiman, *Left Is Not Woke* (Cambridge: Polity Press, 2023).

77. Of course, he may not concede this point at all, and suggest, say, that Allen's published work, to the degree that it advocates for a political program, is not appropriate scholarship. Such a view would appear to cast a shadow over much of Fish's own scholarly work, however, to the degree that it relates to freedom of speech and other legal issues about which he has written extensively (and influentially).

78. Max Weber, "Science as a Vocation," in *From Max Weber: Essays in Sociology* (New York: Oxford University Press, 1946), 146.

79. "He cannot do more, so long as he wishes to remain a teacher and not to become a demagogue" (Weber, "Science as a Vocation," 151).

80. Weber, "Science as a Vocation," 152.

81. Weber, "Science as a Vocation," 155.

82. Weber, "Science as a Vocation," 155.

83. Fish, *Professional Correctness*, 126.

84. Peter Levine has criticized Fish along these lines: "At no time in our history have Americans been satisfied with knowledge as the main purpose of higher education" (Levine, "Stanley Fish vs. Civic Engagement," May 25, 2004, http://www.peterlevine.ws/mt/archives/2004/05/stanley-fish-vs.html).

85. Fish, *Save the World on Your Own Time*, 166.

86. Bertrand de Jouvenel, "Toward a Political Theory of Education," in *Humanistic Education and Western Civilization*, ed. Arthur A. Cohen (New York: Holt, Rinehart and Winston, 1964), 66.

87. "The revolutions of the twentieth century, the liberation of the masses by production, created private life but gave nothing to fill it with"; Saul Bellow, *Herzog* (New York: Penguin, 1992), 137.

88. Jouvenel, "Toward a Political Theory of Education," 67.

89. Jouvenel, "Toward a Political Theory of Education," 69.

90. Xenophon, *Memorabilia*, trans. Amy L. Bonnette (Ithaca, NY: Cornell University Press, 1994), 3; 1.10.

91. Socrates was convicted by a swing difference of 30 jury votes (probably out of 501, or a vote of 280 to 221 to convict), and he suggests that if he had had more time to continue to converse with them he may very well have been acquitted.

92. Arthur Bestor, *Educational Wastelands: The Retreat from Learning in Our Public Schools* (Urbana: University of Illinois Press, 1953, 1985), 21.

93. Bestor, *Educational Wastelands*, 3, 2. Bestor suggests, for example, that "the school makes itself ridiculous whenever it undertakes to deal *directly* with 'real-life' problems, instead of *indirectly* through the development of generalized intellectual powers" (63).

94. Mortimer J. Adler, *The Paideia Proposal: An Educational Manifesto* (New York: Macmillan, 1982), 5.

95. Bestor, *Educational Wastelands*, 26.

96. Henry David Thoreau, "Life without Principle," in *Collected Essays and Poems* (New York: Library of America, 2001), 348–49.

97. Henry David Thoreau, *Walden; or, Life in the Woods*, in *A Week on the Concord and Merrimack Rivers, Walden; or, Life in the Woods, The Maine Woods, Cape Cod* (New York: Library of America, 1985), 394.

98. Allen, *Education and Equality*, 17.

99. Martha Nussbaum, *Not for Profit* (Princeton, NJ: Princeton University Press, 2010), 17–18.

100. Roosevelt Montás, *Rescuing Socrates: How the Great Books Changed My Life and Why They Matter for a New Generation* (Princeton, NJ: Princeton University Press, 2021), 18.

101. Zena Hitz makes this point by suggesting that what she calls "intellectual life" "originates in the human questions arising in and behind ordinary life." For this reason, she concludes, "Anyone seeking a good human life benefits from learning in all of its breadth and depth"; Hitz, *Lost in Thought: The Hidden Pleasures of an Intellectual Life* (Princeton, NJ: Princeton University Press, 2020), 203, 204.

102. Wilson Carey McWilliams and Susan Jane McWilliams, "Pluralism and the Education of the Spirit," in *Debating Moral Education: Rethinking the Role of the Modern University*, ed. Elizabeth Kiss and J. Peter Euben (Durham, NC: Duke University Press, 2010), 136.

103. McWilliams and McWilliams, "Pluralism and the Education of the Spirit," 137.

104. Plato, *Apology*, 65; 32e. Just before this, he had commented that "the true champion of justice, if he intends to survive even for a short time, must necessarily confine himself to private life and leave politics alone" (64; 32a).

105. Plato, *Gorgias*, 111; 526c.

106. Plato, *Gorgias*, 105; 521d.

107. Plato, *Apology*, 62; 30a.

108. Stefan Collini makes the point this way: "Almost all arguments that seem to suggest that scholarship, science, or culture turn their practitioners into 'better people' are awkwardly vulnerable to obvious counter-examples"; Collini, *What Are Universities For?* (London: Penguin, 2012), 98.

109. Sergei Guriev and Daniel Treisman, *Spin Dictators* (Princeton, NJ: Princeton University Press, 2022), 174–75.

110. The news about all forms of higher education and democratic sensibilities may not be quite as rosy as Guriev and Treisman suggest. Derek Bok reports, in data from around the turn of the present century, that engineering majors were associated with a decline in writing ability, cultural awareness, political participation, and commitment to racial understanding. Education majors were associated with a decline in problem-solving skills, critical thinking, public speaking, and general knowledge! See Bok, *Our Underachieving Colleges* (Princeton, NJ: Princeton University Press, 2006), 141.

111. Elaine Scarry, *On Beauty and Being Just* (Princeton, NJ: Princeton University Press, 1999), 8, 31.

112. Scarry, *On Beauty and Being Just*, 52.

113. Allan Bloom argues, "The regime of equality and liberty, of the rights of man, is the regime of reason. The free university exists only in liberal democracy, and liberal democracies exist only where there are free universities." He also notes, however, that "liberal education puts everything at risk and requires students who are able to risk everything." His second point is probably more exaggerated than the first, but he is right to point out both the need for a philosophical education in a democratic society and the tension this education will almost inevitably produce within that society. See Bloom, *The Closing of the American Mind*, 259, 370.

Conclusion

1. I myself completed certification as a public school teacher alongside my liberal undergraduate studies.

2. Frank Donoghue, *The Last Professors: The Corporate University and the Fate of the Humanities* (New York: Fordham University Press, 2008), xvii.

3. Matthew Hora and his colleagues write: "We conclude that the most propitious course of action for higher education in the twenty-first century is a 'new vocationalism,' or a program based on the liberal arts tradition of cultivating well-

rounded students via a multidisciplinary education, but with careful attention to students' career prospects and needs"; Matthew Hora, with Ross J. Benbow and Amanda K. Oleson, *Beyond the Skills Gap* (Cambridge, MA: Harvard Education Press, 2016), 9.

4. Anemona Hartocollis, "Can Humanities Survive the Budget Cuts?," *New York Times*, November 3, 2023, https://www.nytimes.com/2023/11/03/us/liberal-arts-college-degree-humanities.html. See the wonderful response to the state auditor's report by Beth Ann Fennelly, a former poet laureate of Mississippi and current faculty member of the University of Mississippi; Fennelly, "Stop Corporatizing My Students," *New York Times*, November 15, 2023. Fennelly writes, "It's worth noting that nowhere in the eight-page report is educational value discussed in relation to anything other than money. I wonder what value he'd ascribe to John Keats' 'Ode on a Grecian Urn.'"

5. See chapter 2, note 81.

6. Stefan Collini, *What Are Universities For?* (London: Penguin, 2012), 91.

7. Mitch Daniels, "How the Tenure Trap Paralyzes Higher Education," *Washington Post*, October 10, 2023, https://www.washingtonpost.com/opinions/2023/10/10/tenure-paralyze-higher-education/.

8. For example, see Donoghue, *The Last Professors*.

9. Michael Oakeshott, *The Voice of Liberal Learning* (Indianapolis: Liberty Fund, 2001), 89.

10. Margaret Atwood, *Oryx and Crake* (New York: Anchor Books, 2004).

11. Hora et al., *Beyond the Skills Gap*, 48.

12. Suketu Mehta, in *This Land Is Our Land* (New York: Farrar, Straus and Giroux, 2019), 138, reports that a majority of Republicans think that "universities are bad for America." The Pew Research Center reported in 2019 that 38 percent of Americans reported the belief that colleges and universities have a negative effect on society, and that this number had grown from 26 percent just seven years earlier: "The increase in negative views has come almost entirely from Republicans and independents who lean Republican. From 2015 to 2019, the share saying colleges have a negative effect on the country went from 37% to 59% among this group." In short, hostility toward higher education has been an effective element of the recent Republican culture war. See Pew Research, "The Growing Partisan Divide in Views of Higher Education," https://www.pewresearch.org/social-trends/2019/08/19/the-growing-partisan-divide-in-views-of-higher-education-2/.

13. Valerie Strauss, "How Gov. Walker Tried to Quietly Change the Mission of the University of Wisconsin," *Washington Post*, February 5, 2015.

14. The classic text here is Roger Kimball, *Tenured Radicals* (New York: Harper-Collins, 1990). A recent version is John Agresto, *The Death of Learning* (New York: Encounter Books, 2022).

15. See Anthony Kronman, *Education's End* (New Haven, CT: Yale University Press, 2007).

16. Danielle Allen reports that our educational system currently spends about $50 annually per student on STEM subjects and about 5 cents per student on civics. See Allen, *Democracy in the Time of Coronavirus* (Chicago: University of Chicago Press, 2022), 56.

17. Martha Nussbaum notes that educators focused on economic growth will not value the arts and may actually fear them. See Nussbaum, *Not for Profit* (Princeton, NJ: Princeton University Press, 2010), 23.

18. Sam Bankman-Fried, before he was convicted of an enormous crypto-currency fraud, once commented in an interview, "I would never read a book." See Jill Lepore, "Data Driven," *New Yorker*, April 3, 2023, 18.

19. Zena Hitz, *Lost in Thought: The Hidden Pleasures of an Intellectual Life* (Princeton, NJ: Princeton University Press, 2020), 23.

20. Hitz, *Lost in Thought*, 203.

21. Hitz, *Lost in Thought*, 203.

22. Theodore Adorno, "Education after Auschwitz," Radio Address, 1966, https://josswinn.org/wp-content/uploads/2014/12/AdornoEducation.pdf, p. 1.

23. Adorno, "Education after Auschwitz," 1.

24. Adorno, "Education after Auschwitz," 4.

25. Adorno, "Education after Auschwitz," 2.

26. Or, in the language of Carl Schmitt, all those who are not friends, that is, members of one's nation (however the state chooses to define this membership), are thereby enemies in fact or potential. See Schmitt, *The Concept of the Political* (Chicago: University of Chicago Press, 2007).

27. As I write these words it is being reported that Donald Trump used the occasion of Veterans Day 2023 to refer to his opponents as "vermin." There could be no better illustration of precisely the fearful group identification Adorno has in mind than this use by the former president (and current aspirant to that office) of rhetoric championed by Hitler and Mussolini to reduce their opponents to the nonhuman status of animals (Trump also used the classic dictatorial phrase of "rooting out" these domestic threats to the "true" American community). It is a short step from this kind of rhetoric, of course, to the use of any available political power for mass arrests, illegal detentions, disappearances, political thuggery, murder, and even mass killings. We might worry, in fact, that this is the ideological preparation for such crimes and disasters. See https://www.washingtonpost.com/politics/2023/11/12/trump-rally-vermin-political-opponents/.

28. Jonathan Marks, *Let's Be Reasonable* (Princeton, NJ: Princeton University Press, 2021), 62.

29. Steven Levitsky and Daniel Ziblatt, *Tyranny of the Minority* (New York: Crown, 2023), 7–9. They write: "But flaws in our Constitution now imperil our democracy" (9).

30. Or, sometimes more accurately, what are claimed to be traditional communities.

31. Alasdair MacIntyre, "The Very Idea of a University: Aristotle, Newman, and Us," *British Journal of Educational Studies* 57, no. 4 (2009): 359.

32. "So that they can begin to recognise when those who exercise power over their lives no longer know what they are doing" (MacIntyre, "The Very Idea of a University," 360).

33. MacIntyre, "The Very Idea of a University," 362.

34. MacIntyre, "The Very Idea of a University," 349.

35. Alasdair MacIntyre, "The Idea of an Educated Public," in *Education and Values*, ed. Paul H. Hirst (London: Institute of Education, University of London, 1987), 15–36.

36. MacIntyre, "The Idea of an Educated Public," 18–19.

37. MacIntyre, "The Idea of an Educated Public," 19.

38. MacIntyre, "The Idea of an Educated Public," 29.

39. The example he uses is the "common sense" philosophy of the Scottish Enlightenment (MacIntyre, "The Idea of an Educated Public," 21).

40. See Robert Kagan, *Rebellion: How Antiliberalism Is Tearing America Apart—Again* (New York: Knopf, 2024).

41. The hope, for example, is that an education in which students are exposed to a broad range of human experiences would make them more likely than individuals without such an education to recognize the grotesque inhumanity of claiming, as Donald Trump did, that some migrants aren't even human ("In some cases, they're not people, in my opinion."). See Associated Press report from March 17, 2024, https://www.npr.org/2024/03/17/1239019225/trump-says-some-migrants-are-not-people-and-warns-of-bloodbath-if-he-loses.

42. A frequently noted example is from Middlebury College in 2017. See https://www.theatlantic.com/politics/archive/2017/03/middlebury-free-speech-violence/518667/. Conservatives take these events as illustrations of the purely ideological and left-wing bias of the modern academy. See, for example, George Will, "As Enrollment Plummets, Academia Gets Schooled about Where It Went Wrong," *Washington Post*, April 19, 2023. He concludes this column by suggesting "the saturation of academia with progressive politics. Which explains this: Almost three-quarters of Democrats think colleges have a positive impact on the nation; 37 percent of Republicans do." For a conservative pushing back against the widely believed (in conservative circles) claims that the academy is hopelessly ideological, see Marks, *Let's Be Reasonable*.

43. As I write, war between Israel and Hamas is stressing the academic world's ability to appropriately respond to these passions.

44. This is Peter J. Euben's paraphrasing. See Euben, *Corrupting Youth* (Princeton, NJ: Princeton University Press, 1997), 265.

45. Marks, *Let's Be Reasonable*, 102.

46. Azar Nafisi, *Read Dangerously* (New York: HarperCollins, 2022), 5.

47. Nafisi, *Read Dangerously*, 9.

48. John Searle, "The Case for a Traditional Liberal Education," *Journal of Blacks in Higher Education*, no. 13 (Autumn 1996): 2.

49. Frederick Douglass, *Narrative of the Life of Frederick Douglass, an American Slave*, in *Autobiographies* (New York: Library of America, 1994), 42. Douglass writes, "The more I read, the more I was let to abhor and detest my enslavers. I could regard them in no other light than a band of successful robbers. . . . As I read and contemplated the subject, behold! that very discontentment which Master Hugh had predicted would follow my learning to read had already come, to torment and sting my soul to unutterable anguish" (43).

50. Susan Neiman, *Left Is Not Woke* (Cambridge: Polity Press, 2023), 70.

51. Alexander Meiklejohn, *The Liberal College* (Boston: Marshall Jones, 1920), 7–8.

52. William H. Willimon and Thomas H. Naylor, *The Abandoned Generation* (Grand Rapids, MI: William B. Eerdmans-Lightning, 1995), 96.

53. Ruth W. Grant, "Is Humanistic Education Humanizing?," in *Debating Moral Education: Rethinking the Role of the Modern University*, ed. Elizabeth Kiss and J. Peter Euben (Durham, NC: Duke University Press, 2010), 283–95.

54. Danielle Allen, "Aims of Education Address 2001," University of Chicago. https://college.uchicago.edu/student-life/aims-education-address-2001-danielle -s-allen.

55. This is where Fish's pedagogy is significantly underdeveloped. His model students look much more like graduate students than undergraduates insofar as they already have a mature sense of the beauty of scholarship rather than requiring an introduction to this beauty.

56. See chapter 4, note 103.

57. For a discussion of the influence of this movement on primary and secondary education, see Emma Green, "Old School: Have the Liberals Arts Gone Conservative?," *New Yorker*, March 18, 2024, 12–18.

58. See Danny Hakim, "How a Conservative Christian College Got Mixed Up in the 2020 Election Plot," *New York Times*, January 8, 2024. See, also, Bob Pepperman Taylor, review of *The Death of Learning* by John Agresto, *American Political Thought* 12, no. 3 (2023): 474–77.

59. Letters, "Politics in the Classroom," from James Hankins and Erin Maglaque, *New York Review of Books*, November 7, 2023, 42.

60. John Agresto, *The Death of Liberal Learning* (New York: Encounter Books, 2022), is a good illustration of the desire to fight these battles one more time.

61. My sympathies are also with attempts to make higher education more equitable and plural, despite my concerns about mistakes made in pursuing these goals and my recognition that even observers without any obvious stake in promoting culture war rhetoric are increasingly alarmed by a kind of intolerant liberalism found in some corners of the contemporary academy. Fareed Zakaria, for example, suggests that "elite universities . . . have gone from centers of excellence to institutions pushing political agendas." Political theorist John Gray is even more alarmed: "The university campus is the model for an inquisitorial regime that has extended its reach throughout our society." Danielle Allen agrees that "DEI bureaucracies have been responsible for numerous assaults on common sense," sometimes promoting a "culture" of accusation and "intimidation." She helpfully offers suggestions for thinking about building more inclusive and diverse campuses without making some of the mistakes that have alarmed even the academy's friends. If liberal education is to serve democratic citizens, it is axiomatic that they must have equitable access to the institutions providing this education. Zakaria, "Opinion: Why University Presidents Are under Fire," CNN.com, December 8, 2023; Gray, *The New Leviathans* (New York: Farrar, Straus and Giroux, 2023), 114; Allen, "We've Lost the Talent for Mutual Respect on Campus. Here's How to Get It Back," *Washington Post*, December 10, 2023.

62. David Cole, nonetheless, warns against exaggerating the level of ideological politics and hostility to free speech on campuses today. There is no reason to think that there is less political tolerance on campus than there has been in the past, and there is no reason to think that students are more guilty than other sectors of society of being unwilling to engage with views "they find disturbing, wrong, or offensive." Colleges and universities must, of course, fight against "cancel culture," but they must also recognize that we are asking students to make an effort to listen to political opponents that rising numbers of citizens in society at large seem unwilling to make. See Cole, "Who's Canceling Whom?," *New York Review of Books*, February 8, 2024, 12–13.

63. Salman Rushdie, *Victory City* (New York: Random House, 2023), 258.

▬▬▬ BIBLIOGRAPHY

Adams, Henry. *The Education of Henry Adams*. New York: Library of America, 1983.
Adler, Mortimer J. *The Paideia Proposal*. New York: Macmillan, 1982.
Adorno, Theodore. "Education after Auschwitz." Radio Address, 1966. https://joss
  winn.org/wp-content/uploads/2014/12/AdornoEducation.pdf.
Agresto, John. *The Death of Learning*. New York: Encounter Books, 2022.
Allen, Danielle. "Aims of Education Address 2001." University of Chicago. https://
  college.uchicago.edu/student-life/aims-education-address-2001-danielle
  -s-allen.
———. *Democracy in the Time of Coronavirus*. Chicago: University of Chicago
  Press, 2022.
———. *Education and Equality*. Chicago: University of Chicago Press, 2016.
———. *Justice by Means of Democracy*. Chicago: University of Chicago Press, 2023.
———. *Our Declaration*. New York: W. W. Norton, 2015.
———. "We've Lost the Talent for Mutual Respect on Campus. Here's How to Get It
  Back." *Washington Post*, December 10, 2023.
American Association of Colleges and Universities. "Statement on Liberal Learn-
  ing." October 1998. https://public.wsu.edu/~kimander/liberallearning.htm.
American Association of University Professors. *1915 Declaration of Principles*.
  https://aaup-ui.org/Documents/Principles/Gen_Dec_Princ.pdf.
Aristotle. *Politics*. Edited and translated by C. D. C. Reeve. Indianapolis: Hackett,
  1998.
Atwood, Margaret. *Oryx and Crake*. New York: Anchor Books, 2004.
Axtell, James. *The School upon a Hill: Education and Society in Colonial New En-
  gland*. New Haven, CT: Yale University Press, 1974.
———. *Wisdom's Workshop: The Rise of the Modern University*. Princeton, NJ:
  Princeton University Press, 2016.
Babbitt, Irving. *Literature and the American College*. Boston: Houghton, Mifflin and
  Co., 1908.
Beaton, Roderick. *Greece*. Chicago: University of Chicago Press, 2019.

Beauchamp, Zak. "The American Right's Favorite Strongman." *Vox*, August 10, 2020. https://www.vox.com/2020/5/21/21256324/viktor-orban-hungary-american -conservatives.

Becker, Carl. *Detachment and the Writing of History*. Ithaca, NY: Cornell University Press, 1958.

Beecher, Catharine. *The Duty of American Women to Their Country*. New York: Harper and Brothers, 1845.

Bellow, Saul. *Herzog*. New York: Penguin, 1992.

Berry, Wendell. *Hannah Coulter*. Berkeley: Counterpoint, 2004.

———. *What Are People For?* Berkeley: Counterpoint, 1990/2010.

Bestor, Arthur. *Educational Wastelands: The Retreat from Learning in Our Public Schools*. Urbana: University of Illinois Press, 1985[1953].

Bloom, Allan. *The Closing of the American Mind*. New York: Simon and Schuster, 1987.

Boisvert, Raymond. *John Dewey: Rethinking Our Time*. Albany: State University of New York Press, 1998.

Bok, Derek. *Our Underachieving Colleges*. Princeton, NJ: Princeton University Press, 2006.

Brennan, Jason, and Phillip Magness. *Cracks in the Ivory Tower*. New York: Oxford University Press, 2019.

Brooks, Katherine. "President Obama Sends Handwritten Apology to Art History Professor." *HuffPost*, February 18, 2014. https://www.huffpost.com/entry/obama -art-history_n_4809007.

Brown, Wendy. *Nihilistic Times: Thinking with Max Weber*. Cambridge, MA: Harvard University Press, 2023.

Buchanan, James M., and Nicos E. Devletoglou. *Academia in Anarchy*. New York: Basic Books, 1970.

Bunch, Will. *After the Ivory Tower Falls*. New York: HarperCollins, 2022.

Butterfield, Victor L. *The Faith of a Liberal College*. Middletown, CT: Wesleyan University Press, 1955.

Canby, Henry Seidel. *Alma Mater: The Gothic Age of the American College*. New York: Farrar and Rinehart, 1936.

Caplan, Bryan. *The Case against Education*. Princeton, NJ: Princeton University Press, 2018.

Carnochan, W. B. *The Battleground of the Curriculum*. Stanford, CA: Stanford University Press, 1993.

Cole, David. "Who's Canceling Whom?" *New York Review of Books*, February 8, 2024, 12–13.

Collini, Stefan. *What Are Universities For?* London: Penguin, 2012.

Cottom, Daniel. *Why Education Is Useless*. Philadelphia: University of Pennsylvania Press, 2003.

Cremin, Lawrence. *Traditions of American Education*. New York: Basic Books, 1977.

Cresswell, Tim. "The Promise of the Experiential Liberal Arts." *Chronicle of Higher Education*, September 2, 2018.

Curti, Merle. *The Social Ideas of American Educators*. Totowa, NJ: Littlefield, Adams, 1959.

Daniels, Mitch. "How the Tenure Trap Paralyzes Higher Education." *Washington Post*, October 10, 2023. https://www.washingtonpost.com/opinions/2023/10/10/tenure-paralyze-higher-education.

Daniels, Ronald J. *What Universities Owe Democracy*. Baltimore: John Hopkins University Press, 2021.

Davidson, Cathy N. *The New Education*. New York: Basic Books, 2017.

Delbanco, Andrew. *College: What It Was, Is, and Should Be*. Princeton, NJ: Princeton University Press, 2012.

Deneen, Patrick J. *Regime Change*. New York: Sentinel, 2023.

———. "When Campuses Become Dysfunctional." *Minding the Campus, Reforming Our Universities* (blog of the Center for the University at Manhattan Institute), May 13, 2009. https://www.mindingthecampus.org/2009/05/13/by_patrick_j_deneen_in/.

———. *Why Liberalism Failed*. New Haven, CT: Yale University Press, 2018.

Dewey, John. *The Early Works*. Vol. 5. Carbondale: Southern Illinois University Press, 1972.

———. *The Later Works*. Vol. 15. Carbondale: Southern Illinois University Press, 2008.

———. *The Middle Works*. Vol. 1. Carbondale: Southern Illinois University Press, 1976.

———. *The Middle Works*. Vol. 9. Carbondale: Southern Illinois University Press, 1985.

———. *The Middle Works*. Vol. 10. Carbondale: Southern Illinois University Press, 1985.

———. *The Middle Works*. Vol. 15. Carbondale: Southern Illinois University Press, 1988.

———. *The Public and Its Problems*. Edited by Melvin Rogers. Athens, OH: Swallow Press, 2016.

Diggins, John Patrick. "Republicanism and Progressivism." *American Quarterly* 37 (Fall 1985): 572–98.

Donoghue, Frank. *The Last Professors: The Corporate University and the Fate of the Humanities*. New York: Fordham University Press, 2008.

Douglass, Frederick. *Narrative of the Life of Frederick Douglass, an American Slave.* In *Autobiographies*, 1–102. New York: Library of America, 1994.

DuBois, W. E. B. "Diuturni Silenti." Typescript manuscript of Fisk University Commencement Speech, 1924. https://credo.library.umass.edu/view/full/mums312 -b196-i063.

———. *The Souls of Black Folk.* New York: Library of America, 1990.

Durden, William G. "A Practical Approach for Reinventing Liberal Arts Education." *Inside Higher Ed*, February 28, 2018.

Editors of *Scientific American*. "STEM Education Is Vital—but Not at the Expense of the Humanities." *Scientific American*, October 1, 2016.

Educational Advisory Board. *Reclaiming the Value of the Liberal Arts for the 21st Century.* 2016.

Ehrlich, Thomas. "Dewey versus Hutchins: The Next Round." In *Education and Democracy: Re-Examining Liberal Learning in America*, edited by Robert Orrill, 225–62. New York College Examination Board, 1997.

Eisgruber, Christopher. "How Do Liberal Democracies Teach Values?" In *Nomos XLIII: Moral and Political Education*, edited by Stephen Macedo and Yael Tamir, 58–86. New York: New York University Press, 2002.

Euben, J. Peter. *Corrupting Youth.* Princeton, NJ: Princeton University Press, 1997.

Fish, Stanley. *Professional Correctness.* Oxford: Oxford University Press, 1995.

———. *Save the World on Your Own Time.* New York: Oxford University Press, 2008.

———. "Think Again." *New York Times*, January 9, 2008.

———. "The Woe-Is-Us Books." *New York Times*, November 8, 2010.

Geiger, Roger L. *American Higher Education since World War II.* Princeton, NJ: Princeton University Press, 2019.

———. *The History of American Higher Education: Learning and Culture from the Founding to World War II.* Princeton, NJ: Princeton University Press, 2015.

Gideonse, Harry D. *The Higher Learning in a Democracy.* New York: Farrar and Rinehart, 1937.

Grant, Ruth. "Is Humanistic Education Humanizing?" In *Debating Moral Education*, edited by Elizabeth Kiss and J. Peter Euben, 283–95. Durham, NC: Duke University Press, 2010.

Gray, John. *The New Leviathans.* New York: Farrar, Straus and Giroux, 2023.

Green, Emma. "Old School: Have the Liberal Arts Gone Conservative?" *New Yorker*, March 18, 2024, 12–18.

Guillory, John. *Professing Criticism.* Chicago: University of Chicago Press, 2022.

Guriev, Sergei, and Daniel Treisman. *Spin Dictators.* Princeton, NJ: Princeton University Press, 2022.

Hacker, Andrew, and Claudia Dreifus. *Higher Education?* New York: Times Books, 2010.

Hakim, Danny. "How a Conservative Christian College Got Mixed Up in the 2020 Election Plot." *New York Times*, January 8, 2024.

Hamilton, Alexander, James Madison, and John Jay. *The Federalist Papers*. Edited by Clinton Rossiter. New York: Mentor Books, 1999.

Harari, Yuval Noah. *Homo Deus*. New York: Harper, 2017.

Harris, Adam. *The State Must Provide*. New York: HarperCollins, 2021.

Hartocollis, Anemona. "Can Humanities Survive the Budget Cuts?" *New York Times*, November 3, 2023. https://www.nytimes.com/2023/11/03/us/liberal-arts-college -degree-humanities.html.

Heller, Nathan. "The End of the English Major." *New Yorker*, March 6, 2023.

Hirsch, E. D. *The Making of Americans*. New Haven, CT: Yale University Press, 2009.

Hitz, Zena. *Lost in Thought: The Hidden Pleasures of an Intellectual Life*. Princeton, NJ: Princeton University Press, 2020.

Hora, Matthew. *Beyond the Skills Gap*. Cambridge, MA: Harvard Education Press, 2016.

Huntington, Samuel P. *American Politics: The Promise of Disharmony*. Cambridge, MA: Harvard University Press, 1983.

Hutchins, Robert Maynard. *The Conflict in Education in a Democratic Society*. New York: Harper and Brothers, 1953.

———. *Education for Freedom*. Baton Rouge: Louisiana State University Press, 1943.

———. *The Higher Learning in America*. New Haven, CT: Yale University Press, 1936.

———. *The University of Utopia*. Chicago: University of Chicago Press, 1953.

Jaschik, Scott. "Study Documents Economic Gains from Liberal Arts Education." *Inside Higher Education*, February 15, 2019.

Jaspers, Karl. *The Idea of the University*. Boston: Beacon Press, 1959.

Jefferson, Thomas. *Notes on Virginia*. Chapel Hill: University of North Carolina Press, 1982.

Jencks, Christopher, and David Riesman. *The Academic Revolution*. Garden City, NY: Doubleday, 1968.

Jourvenel, Bertrand de. "Toward a Political Theory of Education." In *Humanistic Education and Western Civilization*, edited by Arthur A. Cohen, 55–74. New York: Holt, Rinehart and Winston, 1964.

Kaestle, Carl. *Pillars of the Republic*. New York: Hill and Wang, 1983.

Kagan, Robert. *Rebellion: How Antiliberalism Is Tearing America Apart—Again*. New York: Knopf, 2024.

Katznelson, Ira, and Margaret Weir. *Schooling for All*. New York: Basic Books, 1985.

Kerr, Clark. *The Uses of the University*. Cambridge, MA: Harvard University Press, 1963.

Kimball, Roger. *Tenured Radicals*. New York: HarperCollins, 1990.

Kiss, Elizabeth, and J. Peter Euben, eds. *Debating Moral Education*. Durham, NC: Duke University Press, 2010.

Kronman, Anthony. *Education's End*. New Haven, CT: Yale University Press, 2007.

Kuklick, Bruce. "The Emergence of the Humanities." In *The Politics of Liberal Education*, edited by Darryl J. Gless and Barbara Herstein Smith, 201–12. Durham, NC: Duke University Press, 1992.

Lepore, Jill. "Data Driven." *New Yorker*, April 3, 2023.

———. *These Truths: A History of the United States*. New York: W. W. Norton, 2018.

Levine, Peter. "Stanley Fish vs. Civic Engagement." May 25, 2004. http://www.peter levine.ws/mt/archives/2004/05/stanley-fish-vs.html.

Levitsky, Steven, and Daniel Ziblatt. *Tyranny of the Minority*. New York: Crown, 2023.

MacIntyre, Alasdair. "The Idea of an Educated Public." In *Education and Values*, edited by Paul H. Hirst, 15–36. London: Institute of Education, University of London, 1987.

———. "The Very Idea of a University: Aristotle, Newman, and Us." *British Journal of Educational Studies* 57, no. 4 (2009): 347–62.

Maglaque, Erin, and James Hankins. "Politics in the Classroom" (Letters). *New York Review of Books*, November 7, 2023, 42.

Marks, Jonathan. *Let's Be Reasonable*. Princeton, NJ: Princeton University Press, 2021.

Marsden, George. *Jonathan Edwards*. New Haven, CT: Yale University Press, 2003.

McWilliams, Wilson Carey, and Susan Jane McWilliams. "Pluralism and the Education of the Spirit." In *Debating Moral Education*, edited by Elizabeth Kiss and J. Peter Euben, 125–39. Durham, NC: Duke University Press, 2010.

Mehta, Suketu. *This Land Is Our Land*. New York: Farrar, Straus and Giroux, 2019.

Meiklejohn, Alexander. *Education between Two Worlds*. New York: Harper and Brothers, 1942.

———. *Freedom and the College*. New York: Century, 1923.

———. *The Liberal College*. Boston: Marshall Jones, 1920.

———. *What Does America Mean?* New York: W. W. Norton, 1972.

Menand, Louis. *The Marketplace of Ideas*. New York: W. W. Norton, 2010.

———. "What's So Great about Great-Books Courses?" *New Yorker*, December 20, 2021, 64–68.

Mill, John Stuart. "Inaugural Address Delivered to the University of St. Andrews." In *Collected Works of John Stuart Mill*, 21:215–57. Toronto: University of Toronto Press, 1984.

———. *Utilitarianism*. Indianapolis: Bobbs-Merrill, 1957.

Mills, C. Wright. *Power, Politics and People*. Oxford: Oxford University Press, 1963.

Montás, Roosevelt. *Rescuing Socrates*. Princeton, NJ: Princeton University Press, 2021.

Murakami, Haruki. *Norwegian Wood*. New York: Vintage, 2000.

Nafisi, Azar. *Read Dangerously*. New York: HarperCollins, 2022.

National Center for Education Statistics. "Characteristics of Postsecondary Faculty." https://nces.ed.gov/programs/coe/indicator/csc.

———. "Undergraduate Enrollment." https://nces.ed.gov/programs/coe/indicator/cha.

Neiman, Susan. *Left Is Not Woke*. Cambridge: Polity Press, 2023.

Nelson, Adam R. *Education and Democracy: The Meaning of Alexander Meiklejohn, 1872–1964*. Madison: University of Wisconsin Press, 2001.

Newman, John Henry. *The Idea of a University*. New Haven, CT: Yale University Press, 1996.

Nichols, Tom. *The Death of Expertise*. New York: Oxford University Press, 2017.

Nietzsche, Friedrich. "On the Future of Our Educational Institutions." https://la.utexas.edu/users/hcleaver/330T/350kPEENietzscheFutureTableCut.pdf.

Nussbaum, Martha. *Cultivating Humanity*. Cambridge, MA: Harvard University Press, 1997.

———. *Not for Profit*. Princeton, NJ: Princeton University Press, 2010.

———. "Undemocratic Vistas." *New York Review of Books*, November 5, 1987.

Oakeshott, Michael. *The Voice of Liberal Learning*. Indianapolis: Liberty Fund, 2001.

Parker, Kim. "The Growing Partisan Divide in Views of Higher Education." Pew Research Center, August 19, 2019. https://www.pewresearch.org/social-trends/2019/08/19/the-growing-partisan-divide-in-views-of-higher-education-2/.

Plato. *Apology*. In *The Last Days of Socrates: Euthyphro; Apology; Crito; Phaedo*, translated by Hugh Tredennick and Harold Tarrant, 43–76. Baltimore: Penguin, 1975.

———. *Gorgias*. Translated by Donald J. Zeyl. Indianapolis: Hackett, 1987.

———. *The Republic*. Translated by G. M. A. Grube. Revised by C. D. C. Reve. Indianapolis: Hackett, 1992.

President's Commission on Higher Education. *Higher Education for American Democracy*. New York: Harpers and Brothers, 1947.

Ravitch, Diane. *The Troubled Crusade*. New York: Basic Books, 1983.

Reeves, Richard. *Dream Hoarders*. Washington, DC. Brookings, 2017.

Report of the Harvard Committee. *General Education in a Free Society*. Cambridge, MA: Harvard University Press, 1945.

Reuben, Julie. *The Making of the Modern University*. Chicago: University of Chicago Press, 1996.

———. "Virtue and the History of the Modern American University." In *Cultivating Virtue in the University*, edited by Jonathan Brant, Edward Brooks, and Michael Lamb, 29–43. Oxford: Oxford University Press, 2022.

Riskin, Jessica. "A Poisonous Legacy." *The New York Review*, June 12, 2023, 34–36.

Rogers, Melvin L. *The Darkened Light of Faith*. Princeton, NJ: Princeton University Press, 2023.

Rudolph, Frederick. *The American College and University*. Athens: University of Georgia Press, 1990.

Ruff, Corinee. "Computer Science, Meet Humanities: In New Majors, Opposites Attract." *Chronicle of Higher Education*, January 28, 2016. https://www.chronicle.com/article/computer-science-meet-humanities-in-new-majors-opposites-attract/.

Rush, Benjamin. "A Plan for the Establishment of Public Schools and the Diffusion of Knowledge in Pennsylvania; to Which are Added, Thoughts upon the Mode of Education, Proper in a Republic." In *Essays on Education in the Early Republic*, edited by Frederick Rudolph, 1–24. Cambridge, MA: Harvard University Press, 1965.

Rushdie, Salman. *Victory City*. New York: Random House, 2023.

Sandel, Michael. *The Tyranny of Merit*. New York: Farrar, Straus and Giroux, 2020.

Scarry, Elaine. *On Beauty and Being Just*. Princeton, NJ: Princeton University Press, 1999.

Schmitt, Carl. *The Concept of the Political*. Chicago: University of Chicago Press, 2007.

Searle, John. "The Case for a Traditional Liberal Education." *Journal of Blacks in Higher Education*, no. 13 (1996): 91–98.

Selingo, Jeffrey J. "It's Time to End College Majors as We Know Them." *Chronicle of Higher Education*, May 20, 2018.

SimpsonScarborough. "Selling the Value: Positioning and Marketing Colleges of Arts and Sciences in a Pre-Professional-Focused World." Report/presentation prepared by Elizabeth Scarborough for the CCAS Annual Meeting, Austin, TX, November 2014.

Sinclair, Upton. *The Goose Step: A Study of American Education*. Pasadena, CA: self-published, 1922/1923.

Strauss, Leo. "Liberal Education and Responsibility." https://ia801004.us.archive.org/33/items/LeoStraussLiberalEducationResponsibility1960/Leo%20Strauss%20-%20%27%27Liberal%20Education%20%26%20Responsibility%27%27%20%5B~1960%5D.pdf.

———. "What Is Liberal Education?" http://ditext.com/strauss/liberal.html.

Strauss, Valerie. "How Gov. Walker Tried to Quietly Change the Mission of the University of Wisconsin." *Washington Post*, February 5, 2015.

Stross, Randall. *A Practical Education: Why Liberal Arts Majors Make Great Employees*. Stanford, CA: Redwood Press, 2017.

Talisse, Robert B. *A Pragmatist Philosophy of Democracy*. New York: Routledge, 2007.

Tappan, Henry P. *University Education*. New York: George P. Putnam, 1851.

Taylor, Bob Pepperman. *Citizenship and Democratic Doubt*. Lawrence: University Press of Kansas, 2004.

———. *Horace Mann's Troubling Legacy*. Lawrence: University Press of Kansas, 2010.

———. Review *The Death of Learning* by John Agresto. *American Political Thought* 12, no. 3 (2023): 474–77.

Taylor, Mark C. *Crisis on Campus*. New York: Alfred A. Knopf, 2010.

Thelin, John R. *A History of American Higher Education*. 2nd ed. Baltimore: Johns Hopkins University Press, 2011.

Thoreau, Henry David. "Life without Principle." In *Collected Essays and Poems*, 348–66. New York: Library of America, 2001.

———. *Walden; or, Life in the Woods*. In *A Week on the Concord and Merrimack Rivers, Walden; or, Life in the Woods, The Maine Woods, Cape Cod*. New York: Library of America, 1985.

Tocqueville, Alexis de. *Democracy in America*. Chicago: University of Chicago Press, 2002.

Veblen, Thorstein. *The Higher Learning in America*. B. W. Heubsch, 1918.

Veysey, Laurence. *The Emergence of the American University*. Chicago: University of Chicago Press, 1965.

Vinovskis, Maris A. *Education, Society, and Economic Opportunity*. New Haven, CT: Yale University Press, 1995.

Wallace, David Foster. *This Is Water*. New York: Little Brown, 2009.

Ward, Ian. Profile of Patrick J. Deneen. *Politico*, June 8, 2023. https://www.politico.com/news/magazine/2023/06/08/the-new-right-patrick-deneen-00100279.

Weber, Max. "Science as a Vocation." In *From Max Weber: Essays in Sociology*, 129–56. New York: Oxford University Press, 1946.

Wegman, Jesse. "Trump's Lawyers Should Have Known Better." *New York Times*, October 27, 2023. https://www.nytimes.com/2023/10/27/opinion/trump-lawyers.html.

Welter, Rush. *Popular Education and Democratic Thought*. New York: Columbia University Press, 1962.

Wilentz, Sean. "The Paradox of the American Revolution." *New York Review of Books*, January 13, 2022.

Will, George. "As Enrollment Plummets, Academia Gets Schooled about Where It Went Wrong." *Washington Post*, April 19, 2023.

———. "The Leakage of Universities' Prestige Amid Protests Is Most Welcome." *Washington Post*, April 26, 2024.

Willimon, William H., and Thomas H. Naylor. *The Abandoned Generation*. Grand Rapids, MI: William B. Eerdmans-Lightning, 1995.

Wilson, Woodrow. "What Is College For?" In *The Papers of Woodrow Wilson*, 19:334–47. Princeton, NJ: Princeton University Press, 1975.

Wingard, Jason. *The College Devaluation Crisis*. Stanford, CA: Stanford University Press, 2022.

Wittgenstein, Ludwig. *Tractatus Logico-Philosophicus*. New York: Harcourt, Brace and Co., 1922. https://www.gutenberg.org/files/5740/5740-pdf.pdf.

Xenophon. *Memorabilia*. Translated by Amy L. Bonnette. Ithaca, NY: Cornell University Press, 1994.

Yale Report of 1828. https://www.yale.edu/about-yale/president-leadership/governance-historic-documents/historic-documents-reference-material.

Zakaria, Fareed. *In Defense of Liberal Education*. New York: W. W. Norton, 2016.

———. "Opinion: Why University Presidents Are under Fire." CNN.com, December 8, 2023.

■ INDEX

BOB PEPPERMAN TAYLOR

is the Elliott A. Brown Green and Gold Professor of Law, Politics, and Political Behavior at the University of Vermont. He is the author of *Lessons from "Walden": Thoreau and the Crisis of American Democracy,* which was named the winner of the American Political Science Association section award for the best book of 2020 in American political thought.

.